THE ALPHABET BOMBER

The Alphabet Bomber

A LONE WOLF TERRORIST
AHEAD OF HIS TIME

Jeffrey D. Simon

POTOMAC BOOKS   *An imprint of the University of Nebraska Press*

All rights reserved. Potomac Books is an imprint
of the University of Nebraska Press.
Manufactured in the United States of America.

∞

Library of Congress Cataloging-in-Publication Data
Names: Simon, Jeffrey D. (Jeffrey David), 1949– author.
Title: The Alphabet Bomber: a lone wolf terrorist
ahead of his time / Jeffrey D. Simon.
Description: Lincoln: Potomac Books, an imprint
of the University of Nebraska Press [2019] |
Includes bibliographical references and index.
Identifiers: LCCN 2018025504
ISBN 9781612349961 (cloth: alk. paper)
ISBN 9781640121591 (epub)
ISBN 9781640121607 (mobi)
ISBN 9781640121614 (pdf)
Subjects: LCSH: Kurbegovic, Muharem. | Bombers
(Terrorists)—United States—Case studies. | Bombing
investigation—United States—Case studies. |
Terrorism—United States—Case studies.
Classification: LCC HV6248.K795 S56 2019 |
DDC 363.325092 [B]—dc23 LC record available
at https://lccn.loc.gov/2018025504

Set in Sabon Next by E. Cuddy.
Designed by N. Putens.

CONTENTS

ILLUSTRATIONS

ACKNOWLEDGMENTS

It is a pleasure to acknowledge all the wonderful people who helped make this book possible. First and foremost, I am indebted to Dinko Bozanich, the prosecutor of the Alphabet Bomber. Dinko graciously gave of his time and shared his incredible knowledge of this case with me. His enthusiastic support for this book is greatly appreciated.

I was also fortunate to meet and interview Nancy Watson, the judge in the criminal trial, who passed away in 2004. Judge Watson was forthright in recalling her experiences dealing with the Alphabet Bomber during the long trial. Her children (Marcia Goodman, Harvey Goodman, and Brian Goodman) provided valuable insights into the life of their mother and the emotional toll the trial took on her.

Lea Purwin D'Agostino, who assisted Dinko Bozanich in prosecuting the Alphabet Bomber, was very gracious in sharing with me her recollections of this fascinating case. For their insights and information regarding the Alphabet Bomber, I also want to thank former LAPD lieutenant Max Hurlbut, who helped identify Muharem Kurbegovic as the Alphabet Bomber; FBI special agent Frederick Lanceley (retired), who worked on the case; Walt Lewis, who served as the calendar deputy district attorney in Judge

Watson's courtroom; Gerald Chaleff, who was Kurbegovic's public defender during the competency trials; and Robert Altman, who was the prosecutor during the early phases of the Alphabet Bomber case.

My colleague Bennett Ramberg provided valuable feedback and encouragement during our many discussions about this story, as did Phil Rothenberg. I am grateful to both of them. I also want to thank Terry Turchie (along with Dinko Bozanich and Bennett Ramberg) for reading the entire manuscript. Lynn McClelland from the UCLA Law Library was instrumental in advising on how to cite the many different court transcripts and other legal documents used in this book, as was Dinko Bozanich.

The staff at the California State Archives in Sacramento, where I read through more than twenty thousand pages of court transcripts, was very helpful, as were the staffs at the LA Law Library and the Charles E. Young Research Library Microfilm Room at UCLA. I am also grateful to Diane Mizrachi and Mark Quigley from UCLA for responding to my research requests.

Anthony McGinty and Ethel Pattison helped locate photos of the Los Angeles International Airport bombing from the Flight Path Museum and Learning Center, while Simon Elliott was invaluable in helping to find relevant photos for this book from the Los Angeles Times Photographic Archive, Library Special Collections, Charles E. Young Research Library, UCLA. Molly Haigh, also from the UCLA Special Collections, helped in scanning the images. Christina Rice assisted in producing photos from the Los Angeles Public Library's Herald Examiner Photo Collection, while David Houston and Garrett Green provided photos from the *Los Angeles Daily Journal*. Kelly Dyson from the Library of Congress, Bill Van Niekerken from the San Francisco Chronicle Library, and Mary Hearn and Arlene Vasquez from the Public Information Office, Los Angeles Superior Court, were also instrumental in providing relevant photos and images.

I would also like to thank the following colleagues, friends, and others who helped in many different ways: Annie Abbott, Richard Antony, Jerome Applebaum, Koki Asakura, Martin Balaban, John Barry, Theresa Hart Barry, Steve Bernard, Chere Bozanich, Richard Chasdi, Sharon Chasdi, Eddie Chan, Ken Chin, Sandy Chin, Joe Cirillo, Gary Citrenbaum, Patrick Conway,

Edwin Dagdagan, Rick Dedmon, George Galaza, Azi Gholizadeh, Kevin Grandalski, Rob Hitsous, Brian Jenkins, Steven Kafka, Eddie Kamiya, Janet Kamiya, Ken Karmiole, Scott Kernan, Ed Kobak, Ira Latto, Diane McMorris, Joe Medina, J. Reid Meloy, Sue Moran, John Mueller, James Peaco, Estella Perez, Dennis Pluchinsky, Gerald Posner, Allie Powell, Helen Purkitt, David Rapoport, Alice Richter, Albert Rivas, Mina Rome, Kenneth Ryan, Kathy Schreick-Latto, Debbie Scott-Asakura, Zareh Sevanesian, Cindy Forrestal Snell, Lorron Snell, Douglas Snyder, Shoshana Snyder, Don Steier, Gene Sunshine, Bill Teachworth, Kevin Terpstra, Diana Torres, Justin Vaughan, Donna Wald, Jessica Wolf, Carole Wood, and Ted Zwicker.

Catherine L. Hensley of CLH Editing provided superb editing skills for the manuscript and, as usual, was a joy to work with. I would also like to thank everybody at Potomac Books and the University of Nebraska Press, especially Thomas Swanson, editor, for their enthusiasm for a book about the Alphabet Bomber. This includes Elizabeth Zaleski, Jonathan Lawrence, Rosemary Sekora, Abigail Stryker, Natalie O'Neal, Nathan Putens, Jackson Adams, Tish Fobben, Andrea Shahan, and Lindsey Auten.

My amazing agent, Jill Marsal, championed this book from its very beginning, and I am indebted to her once again for her unwavering support. Nobody could ask for a better agent.

Finally, a special thanks goes to Ellen, Richard, Julie, Penya, Jack, Eric, Caleb, Oscar, Elijah, and Justine for being a very special part of my life.

THE ALPHABET BOMBER

Introduction

On the evening of August 8, 1974, Americans gathered around their television sets to witness an event that would have been unimaginable just two years earlier. President Richard Nixon, who had won reelection in a landslide over George McGovern in 1972, was about to announce his resignation from office, becoming the first U.S. president to do so. It was a shocking turn of events for the thirty-seventh president of the United States, who had seen his popularity and power erode due to the Watergate scandal.

Viewers in Los Angeles joined millions of Americans across the country in watching history unfold before their very eyes, but Angelinos also had something else on their minds. Two days earlier, a bomb had ripped through the overseas passenger terminal lobby of Pan American World Airways at Los Angeles International Airport (LAX), killing three people and injuring thirty-five others in one of the deadliest incidents of terrorism in Los Angeles history. It was also the first time an airport had been bombed anywhere in the world. The bomb, which had been placed in a locker near the check-in counter, created a ten-by-fifteen-foot hole in the wall where the lockers were located and devastated a one-hundred-foot area in the lobby, sending bodies, metal, and glass flying through the air.

One man saw his daughter "skidding past [him] on the floor."[1] Another noted that there had been an eerie silence immediately after the blast. "The whole terminal was silent," recalled Barbara Moclock. "You couldn't think of anything, anything at all. Then a few moments later, people started screaming and looking for their friends."[2]

Among those looking for their friends was Paul Kaye, a circus producer, who was distributing tickets to members of his troupe when the blast occurred. "Bodies of people were all over," he recalled. "I ran to see how many, if any, of my people had been hurt. And I found Mr. Trostl on the ground." Arturo Trostl Jr., known by his stage name, "The Great Arturo," and considered one of the best trapeze artists in the world, had been badly injured. "One side of his chest under his arm was blown away, and the upper portion of his left thigh had been blown away," said Kaye. A clown in the circus who was also a medical student attended to Trostl until the paramedics arrived. Trostl would survive his injuries and perform again, but not with the same confidence and flamboyant style he had been known for.[3]

The most seriously injured were taken on stretchers from the terminal to ambulances waiting outside. Among those was Rev. Rhett Patrick Shaughnessy, who would have to have his right leg amputated. Another injured man in the same ambulance as Shaughnessy remembered how excruciating the ride to the hospital was for the pastor. "I never heard anybody in such pain as he was in," recalled Vincent Bush. "He was yelling and screaming. He was terrified."[4]

The airport was a scene of pandemonium as first responders attended to the victims while police and federal agents sifted through the debris, looking for clues as to who might be responsible for the carnage. David Butler of the Los Angeles Police Department's Scientific Investigation Division, one of the first law enforcement officers on the scene, feared there might be a secondary explosive device at the Pan American terminal and instructed airport security personnel to evacuate people from the lobby, rope off the area, and prevent anyone from standing on the sidewalk in front of the building. He then began to search for another bomb and check for additional hazards, like ruptured natural gas mains.[5]

Then the bomb threats started pouring in. The blast had occurred at 8:10

a.m., and the news spread quickly throughout the Los Angeles area, as well as the rest of the country. People wondered whether America might now be on the verge of a wave of major terrorist attacks at airports, sporting events, restaurants, and other crowded, "soft" target areas similar to those that other countries were experiencing. By 9:30 a.m. LAX was receiving bomb threats for hangars, cargo and baggage areas, ticket counters, buildings, and aircraft. Butler handled more than fifty of these threats. "Virtually every ticket counter at L.A. Airport received a bomb threat," he said. "At one time we virtually almost had the entire airport evacuated." Explosive detection dogs were brought in to search for additional explosives.[6]

While the search at the airport did not uncover any more bombs, investigators were able to establish that the explosion had come from one of the lockers near the Pan Am ticket counter. Still, they didn't have a clue as to the person or persons responsible. That night, however, they received their first big break in the case. A man had telephoned the *Los Angeles Herald Examiner* and claimed credit for the bombing, providing the publicly undisclosed locker number where the bomb had exploded. He told the city editor, Conrad Casler, that his name was "Rasim" and that he had carried out the bombing on behalf of a group he called "Aliens of America."[7]

Casler was baffled by the caller, who spoke with a foreign accent: "I remember at one point saying: 'Now, wait a minute. What the hell is Aliens of America?' And I was ignored. And I attempted to keep him on the line a while, but I was very politely told, 'good night,' and was hung up on after this very brief conversation the first time." Casler immediately called one of his reporters who was still at the airport, and the reporter relayed the information to the bomb squad. "Within ten minutes I got a call from [the] LAPD Bomb Squad," Casler recalled, "saying that we had hit it on the head, it was correct."[8]

When people read about the phone call to Casler in the newspaper the next day, they too were baffled. Who were the "Aliens of America," and what did they want? An anxious public awaited further information about this unknown group. Then, on August 9, Angelinos received more bad news. Rasim telephoned the CBS television station in Los Angeles and told them that an audiocassette about the bombing could be found in a trash bin outside a local bank. When police recovered the tape they found with it the key to the airport locker in which the bomb had exploded. The tape included a chilling warning: "This first bomb was marked with the letter A, which stands for Airport. The second bomb will be associated with the letter L, the third with the letter I, etc., until our name has been written on the face of this nation in blood."[9] He became known in the media as the "Alphabet Bomber." And the words "Aliens of America" were stamped on the outside ring of the canister that contained the explosive.

Not until his capture would people learn that no group was behind the bombing and threats. Aliens of America existed only in the mind of the man who called himself Rasim, who was actually Muharem Kurbegovic, a Yugoslav immigrant living in Los Angeles. He'd immigrated to the United States in 1967 in search of a better life. He initially found it, thriving at engineering jobs even though he communicated at work only by writing notes. He pretended to be mute as a way of avoiding being drafted into the army during the Vietnam War. He was a loner who liked to frequent taxi dance halls in downtown Los Angeles, places where customers paid to dance with hostesses hired by the club. "I was on the verge of suicide many times before I [learned about] taxi-dance," Kurbegovic said. "And the fact there is a place I can be human no matter what is wrong with me, I can be accepted as a human being too, has saved me from actually being a drug addict or alcoholic or other kind of pervert."[10] It was at one of these dance halls, though, that Kurbegovic was arrested for lewd conduct, an arrest that would eventually trigger his turn toward violence.

Extremely bright but emotionally disturbed, Kurbegovic single-handedly brought one of America's largest cities to a standstill during the summer of 1974. Police were frustrated in their attempts to catch him. They had never before experienced such a skilled and manipulative terrorist. Kurbegovic toyed with the police and the FBI in his audiotapes and phone calls. In one tape he boasted, "FBI cannot catch us . . . because we studied the same books as FBI did, and we studied the same books as U.S. Army did."[11] In a phone call to Casler, he warned, "We have placed another one which will go off this Sunday in a crowded area. We will not say where it will be, but the bomb is 25 pounds."[12]

The public was scared and confused, not knowing what, if anything, they could do to prevent becoming a victim of the Alphabet Bomber. Many believed that their best option was to avoid going to public gatherings. A Watts Summer Festival concert at Los Angeles Memorial Coliseum that was expected to attract seventy thousand people drew only thirty-five hundred. The media added to the fear gripping Los Angeles. One banner headline that August in the *Herald Examiner* read, "LA BOMBER PLEDGES GAS ATTACK."[13] Another headline stated, "RACE AGAINST TIME TO FIND THIRD BOMB."[14] The threats and actions of the Alphabet Bomber launched one of the largest manhunts in the history of the Los Angeles Police Department.

It wasn't just Los Angeles, though, that was the target of the Alphabet Bomber's terror campaign. "We are presently building a facility to produce two tons of sarin which we hope will change the personnel of Capitol Hill," Kurbegovic said in one of his audiotapes. "Imagine what will happen if we are lucky and wind blows from [the] Supreme Court to Capitol Hill to [the] White House to [the] Pentagon."[15] For Los Angeles, he threatened to place nerve agents in the air-conditioning systems of the city's skyscrapers: "We just acquired the plans of 30 major skyscraper air conditioning systems. We visit the building, see where its air inlet is . . . and take a walk. Maybe watch a Dodgers game and enjoy ourselves."[16]

The threat of using chemical weapons wasn't just idle talk by Kurbegovic. When police searched his apartment shortly after his arrest, they were astonished at what they found. Among the items recovered were live pipe bombs, explosive materials, fuses, timing devices, two gas masks stamped "U.S. Army," a box of ten gas-mask filters and a nosepiece, catalogs for purchasing chemicals and laboratory equipment, and several books and articles on explosives, unconventional warfare, law enforcement operations and strategies, and chemical and biological weapons.[17]

One of the officers who searched the apartment stated that Kurbegovic had acquired all but one ingredient needed to build a nerve gas bomb and was about to pick up the last item, an organophosphate, at the time of his arrest.[18] Kurbegovic would stun the courtroom more than two years later when he said that the police should go back to the apartment, because more explosives and other items were hidden behind a medicine cabinet mounted on a false wall. Sure enough, when the police searched the apartment a second time, they found twenty-five pounds of sodium cyanide, a precursor for the manufacture of the nerve agent tabun.[19]

Using his ingenuity and professional experience as an engineer, Kurbegovic had built a homemade explosives and potential nerve agent factory in his Los Angeles apartment. Had he not been caught when he was, he would likely have escalated his violence to include chemical weapons "until our name has been written on the face of this nation in blood."

What, though, motivated Kurbegovic to launch his reign of terror? Like many lone wolves today, he was driven by anger and revenge, combining personal grievances (he was denied a permit to open a taxi dance hall due to his prior arrest for lewd conduct, even though he had been found not guilty of the charges by a jury) with lofty but unattainable political goals, such as his demand that all immigration, naturalization, and sex laws be declared unconstitutional.[20] There were also anticommunist and antireligious elements prevalent in his messages. "Instead of letting Soviet Communism collapse to its natural decay, the inexperienced leadership of this nation is intending to give it the free man's technology so that it can use it to enslave more people," he said in one of his audiotapes.[21] He also said, "We shall fight to the last drop of our blood [to] see this nation free of religionism, Communism, and all other pornographies of human mind."[22] How he was able to terrorize a city and toy with the authorities holds important lessons for today, as we are faced with the growing threat of lone wolf terrorism.

The Alphabet Bomber was a terrorist ahead of his time. He was among the first lone wolves to demonstrate that one does not need training, financial assistance, or logistical support from a larger organization to launch a major campaign of terror. He was also one of the first terrorists to threaten to release nerve agents in populated areas, to acquire sodium cyanide, and to use the media in a systematic way to communicate his message and to spread fear among the public.[23]

Kurbegovic also demonstrated why lone wolves can be so innovative, creative, and dangerous in their attacks. Lone wolves are not burdened by any of the group decision-making processes or intergroup dynamics that can sometimes stifle creativity in formulating plans and operations. They are free to think up any type of scenario they want and then try to act upon it, since they are accountable only to themselves.[24]

Related to this is the fact that because they are not part of a group, lone wolves don't need to be concerned, as some terrorist groups must, about alienating their supporters with a particular type of attack, such as causing too many casualties, using a weapon of mass destruction, or attacking the wrong type of target. As Kurbegovic stated in one of his tapes, "We do not ask American people to support us; in fact, we don't give a damn whether they like what we have to offer or not."[25] Also, unlike traditional terrorist organizations, lone wolves are not concerned about a potential government and law enforcement crackdown following an incident, which could lead to the virtual elimination of the group through arrests.[26]

Lone wolves are also dangerous because they are unlikely to be discovered by law enforcement or intelligence agencies prior to an attack. Since they work alone, there are no communications between members of a group to intercept, nor are there any members of a group to arrest and gain further information from. Another factor that adds to the danger of lone wolves is that they are sometimes mentally unstable (as was the case with Kurbegovic) yet highly intelligent and effective in their attacks. This was true for Theodore Kaczynski, the infamous "Unabomber," who sent package bombs to various individuals over a seventeen-year period from the late 1970s to the mid-1990s and was diagnosed as a "provisional paranoid schizophrenic" by a psychiatrist who examined him.[27] It was also true for Bruce Ivins, the U.S. Army microbiologist who was responsible for the anthrax letter attacks in 2001 and who admitted to a friend that he experienced "incredible paranoid, delusional thoughts at times."[28]

The relationship between mental illness and terrorism has long been debated among scholars, policymakers, and other observers. There have been some questionable psychological theories regarding terrorism, such as one that argues terrorists "suffer from faulty vestibular functions in the middle ear or from inconsistent mothering resulting in dysphoria."[29] These theories have now been replaced by a better understanding of the complex causes of terrorism and why certain individuals are more likely to become terrorists. Some terrorists are born in the midst of ethnic-nationalist and religious conflicts, where hatreds and desires for revenge are handed down from generation to generation. Others join terrorist movements due to a belief that violence is the only way to bring about the political or social change they desire. For the most part, individuals with mental illnesses will be screened out by a terrorist organization. Such groups do not want unpredictable and unstable members who can jeopardize their operations or cause problems within the organization.

The lone wolf, however, does not have to go through any recruitment or screening processes. Studies have identified a high percentage of individuals with mental illness among lone wolf terrorists. In a study of ninety-eight lone wolf attackers in the United States, 40 percent were found to have mental health problems, compared with 1.5 percent of the general population. In another study comparing 119 lone wolf attackers with a similar number of members of violent extremist groups in the United States and Europe, it was found that nearly 32 percent of the lone wolves had been diagnosed with a mental illness, while only 3.4 percent of terrorist group members were mentally ill.[30]

The high rate of mental illness among lone wolves raises questions regarding what role psychiatrists, psychologists, social workers, and others in the mental health community could play in trying to uncover the early warning signs of lone wolf terrorism. What are the conditions or situations that can transform a nonviolent individual who may be suffering from a mental illness into the perpetrator of a terrorist attack? What can be done to try to prevent this from occurring?

The Alphabet Bomber case gives us insight into this important issue. It can also shed light on the role that the media plays during a terrorist crisis. It has often been said that there is a symbiotic relationship between terrorists and the media. Each needs the other to achieve its objectives. For terrorists, this means gaining publicity for their cause, winning new recruits, and spreading fear beyond the immediate victims or targets of the attack. Media coverage of their attacks and threats can help achieve those goals. The media, meanwhile, uses the drama of terrorist incidents and the fear of terrorism to generate television ratings or to increase circulation of newspapers and magazines, since the public seems to be both frightened and fascinated by terrorist episodes and wants to learn more about them. As we will see, Kurbegovic skillfully used the media to keep the public on edge during his campaign of terror. What, then, should be the proper role of the media in covering terrorism? Can any realistic guidelines be utilized that both protect the freedom of the press and also avoid sensationalism in reporting on terrorism? The experience of the media during the Alphabet Bomber crisis is relevant to trying to answer these questions.

In addition to the lessons to be learned, the story of the Alphabet Bomber is also one about an extraordinary manhunt to find an elusive killer, a dogged prosecutor who was determined to bring him to justice, a pioneering female judge who endured hardships during the long criminal trial, and, of course, a cunning individual who demonstrated why lone wolf terrorism is one of the greatest threats we still face today.

1

The Making of a Terrorist

There are many different roads to becoming a terrorist. Some individuals are born into the role, such as the members of the mysterious Thuggee movement that terrorized travelers throughout India from the thirteenth to nineteenth centuries. Between five hundred thousand and one million people are believed to have died at the hands of the Thugs, who killed in the name of the Hindu goddess Kali. Membership in the group was mainly hereditary, with the Thugs trained from childhood to murder by strangulation.[1]

Terrorists can also arise from the ethnic-nationalist and religious conflicts that have long been a part of history, where hatreds and desires for revenge are handed down from one generation to the next. This will likely be the legacy of the recent wars in Iraq, Syria, Afghanistan, and other countries around the world. Political and social grievances are additional root causes for terrorism, with extremist groups exploiting various issues and using violence to achieve their objectives.

Then there is the phenomenon of the lone wolf. This is one of the most intriguing and least understood roads to becoming a terrorist. Lone wolf terrorism cuts across the entire political, religious, and social spectrum.

There have been Islamic, anti-Islamic, white supremacist, black militant, anti-abortion, pro-environment, and many other types of lone wolf terrorists. There have also been "idiosyncratic" lone wolves, individuals who espouse their own ideologies to justify their violence. Their terrorism is often based on personal grievances and the desire for revenge. They answer only to themselves as they wage a one-person war against government and society.

This was true for Muharem Kurbegovic, whose journey to becoming a terrorist took many twists and turns, beginning in a city steeped in tragedy.

The Sadness of Sarajevo

When one thinks of Sarajevo, the capital of Bosnia and Herzegovina in the former Yugoslavia, the first thing that usually comes to mind is the beginning of World War I. It was there on a sunny day—June 28, 1914, to be exact—that Archduke Franz Ferdinand, heir to the throne of Austria-Hungary, was assassinated by a member of the Black Hand, a Serbian terrorist organization. The assassination set off a flurry of events that soon culminated with several countries declaring war on each other and the world experiencing a global conflict that would eventually claim more than seventeen million military and civilian lives.[2]

Sarajevo was also the site of a forty-four-month siege that began in 1992, with Bosnian Serb forces, backed by the Serb-dominated Yugoslav Army, encircling the city and firing cannons at schools, libraries, and hospitals while snipers shot at people who were gathering water, attending funerals, or just walking the streets. More than eleven thousand people were killed and fifty thousand wounded in the longest siege of a capital city in modern history.[3]

These two catastrophes were bookends for yet another one: the invasion and occupation of Sarajevo and the rest of Yugoslavia by Nazi Germany and the Axis powers during World War II. Sarajevo, whose population at the time was divided among Muslims, Catholics, Orthodox Serbs, Jews, and Roma (Gypsies), was incorporated into the Independent State of Croatia (NDH) and placed under the control of the ultranationalist Croat Ustasha regime. Thousands of people living in Sarajevo were sent to death camps during this period, Jews being the main victims. Sarajevo's casualties during World War II, including those who were killed as Communist Partisans fighting the Axis occupiers, amounted to 10,961 people, which was 12.9 percent of the prewar population of the city.[4]

The final months of the war were among the most debilitating for the people of Sarajevo. "From September 1944 to April 1945," writes historian Emily Greble, "Sarajevo experienced its most physically and psychologically devastating chapters of the war—one characterized by bombings, police occupation, total war, terror, and the introduction of a new revolutionary government." Knowing that it was on the verge of defeat, "the Ustasha regime lashed out at Sarajevans in irrational, vengeful acts of cruelty that left the town reeling in a state of shock. Sarajevo was on the brink of a psychological collapse when the [Communist-led] Partisans arrived in April 1945."[5]

It was in this environment that Muharem Kurbegovic was born on June 1, 1943. His family, like most people in Sarajevo at the time, lived modestly. He grew up in a three-room apartment with his two sisters, one older and one younger, his parents, and his grandmother. His family usually rented out one of the rooms in the crowded apartment in order to earn extra income. While conditions under the new Yugoslav socialist regime of Marshal Josip Broz Tito were better than during the war, life was still difficult for most Sarajevans. "We grew up in poverty by American standards," Kurbegovic recalled.[6]

Growing up in postwar Sarajevo as a Muslim was also not easy for Kurbegovic, even though Muslims accounted for over one-third of the population.[7] He wondered why so few Muslims were in prestigious positions in government, industry, and other places. He believed the reason was that "there are no qualified Moslems around. We Moslems are just feeble-minded."[8] Although he did not consider himself religious, his parents sent him to an Islamic school from the ages of five to seven. He then attended a nonreligious school until he was fifteen, at which time he enrolled in the School of Engineering in Sarajevo rather than a regular high school. "I was bright," he said, "but never all the way to the top in any subject."[9] He wrote a thesis on "Elements of Machines," for which he received a grade of "very good." Upon graduation, he worked as a design engineer for about a year and a half at a railway manufacturing company where his father and older sister were also employed.[10]

Kurbegovic had a distant relationship with his father but was very close with his mother, who had a nervous breakdown when Kurbegovic was a teenager and was hospitalized for a few months. This had a strong effect on the entire family, particularly Kurbegovic. While he was close to his mother, he disliked his father, saying that he was "no good" because he was just a railroad employee with no ambition or desire to better himself. Kurbegovic also felt his father was too strict with him as a child. When his father died in 1968, Kurbegovic, who by then was in Los Angeles, chose not to attend the funeral.[11]

As a child, Kurbegovic was ill with diphtheria and had severe anemia. He also suffered from headaches and seizures. His mother sometimes sent him away for inpatient treatments in order for him to receive rest and gain weight and strength. This upset Kurbegovic, who did not like these places and would write to her to take him back home. Kurbegovic was lonely growing up and often nervous. Most of his youth was spent alone, studying or writing poems. According to his mother, he "always had big ambitions and always tried to be somebody."[12]

When he was twenty, Kurbegovic left Yugoslavia for Germany.[13] He enrolled in the Engineering University of Munich, where he earned a certificate in oil hydraulics.[14] He also worked part time for an engineering firm, where he was employed again as a design engineer.[15] He worked on hydro pumps, cylinders, valves, and accessories. In a letter of recommendation, his manager at the Munich firm wrote that Kurbegovic "produced complete, systematic, comprehensive, constructive and very good solutions, and showed himself to be a very well trained and independent designer, rich in ideas. He was honest and reliable."[16]

While Kurbegovic was living in Munich, however, his mental health deteriorated. He stated that he would hit himself repeatedly due to bothersome thoughts that he could not get rid of.[17] He claimed that he was treated in 1966 for "a severe psychosis" and for "depressions and extreme lack of concentration." He also said that he was an outpatient for two months and was given the antipsychotic drugs haloperidol and tripodal.[18]

Kurbegovic then spent a short time in Paris before immigrating to Canada in 1966 by ship. He first visited Toronto, where several of his relatives and a school friend from Yugoslavia were living, and then went to Vancouver. He traveled back and forth between Toronto and Vancouver for about eight months, working as a design engineer in both cities. On one of his train rides to Vancouver he met a student who had trouble pronouncing Kurbegovic's first name. He instead called him "Mu," which then became Kurbegovic's preferred way of being addressed.[19]

Living and working in Canada, though, was not a joyful experience for Kurbegovic. One of his employers there wrote that he was "in some cases pedantic, a fellow who knows his quality and also willing to fight for his rights if necessary. I never saw him smiling or laughing and he always gave the impression he was unhappy."[20]

Kurbegovic left Canada in January 1967 and entered the United States on a visitor's visa. He settled in Los Angeles and became a resident alien the following year.[21] It would seem that life should have been good for the Yugoslav immigrant in his new country. He was bright and had marketable skills in mechanical and design engineering for the many aerospace, defense contractor, and industrial firms located in Los Angeles. He was also a young man living in a hip, exciting city at a time when cultural, social, and political mores were changing at a dizzying pace. Life in LA, however, would ultimately prove to be frustrating and alienating for the future Alphabet Bomber.

A Fish out of Water

The late 1960s was a watershed period in U.S. political and cultural history. From the assassinations of Martin Luther King Jr. and Bobby Kennedy to the anti—Vietnam War protests sweeping college campuses, it was a time of uncertainty as to where America was heading. An incumbent U.S. president, Lyndon Johnson, shocked the nation in March 1968 when he announced that he would not run for reelection that year. Following King's assassination in April there were riots in cities across the country as well as violent clashes at the Democratic National Convention in Chicago in August. The leftist radical group the Weathermen would soon become responsible for hundreds of bombings on college campuses and other targets.[22]

Compared to other countries, however, America's experience with violence and terrorism during the late 1960s was minimal. In Europe and the Middle East, Palestinian terrorists were hijacking and blowing up planes. In Germany, the Baader-Meinhof Gang was beginning a reign of terror on capitalist and military targets that would last several decades, with the group eventually becoming known as the Red Army Faction. Their first terrorist attack occurred in 1968, when they set fire to a department store in Frankfurt, stating they intended to set a "torch against the capitalistic terror of consumerism." The group also proclaimed that their objective was "to hit the Establishment in the face, to mobilize the masses, and to maintain international solidarity."[23] In Italy, the leftist Red Brigades would soon be born and wage a terror campaign of assassinations and "kneecappings" (shooting their victims in the knees) against capitalists, government officials, military personnel, and journalists who opposed their movement. Their objective was to bring about a Marxist-Leninist revolution in Italy.[24] Meanwhile, the provisional Irish Republican Army was also emerging at this time with the goal of driving the British out of Northern Ireland and creating a united Ireland.[25]

One of the reasons the United States did not see a comparable growth of long-term extremist and terrorist movements within its borders was the absence of deep-seated ethnic-nationalist, separatist, religious, and political divisions that were the driving force for much of the terrorism around the world at the time. Extremist groups in the United States were thus not able to successfully use territorial, ethnic, religious, or political issues to build a significant following lasting beyond a few years.[26]

Even amid the turmoil in America of the late 1960s, a sense of hope permeated the country. The economy was strong, women were making major strides toward equal rights, and the United States had beaten the Russians in placing a man on the moon. Even the woeful New York Mets, the worst team in baseball for much of their existence, won the World Series in 1969, making New Yorkers believe that miracles could indeed happen.

The counterculture revolution sweeping the nation also gave hope to the youth of America. Rebellion against authority and expressions of free will in all aspects of life made for an exciting time to be young in America. As the legal analyst Jeffrey Toobin points out, "Much of the discontent in the

1960s emerged from a sense of possibility—that blacks and whites could live in harmony, that the Vietnam War could end, and that there could be a better future for all."[27]

A better future is what Muharem Kurbegovic hoped for when he arrived in Los Angeles in 1967. He was smart, ambitious, and now in the land of opportunity. But he likely knew before he came to the United States that aliens like himself (immigrants who have legally entered the United States) were required to register for the military draft after they had been in the country for six months. That was the last thing he wanted. He hadn't come all the way to America only to be shipped off to fight and perhaps die in Vietnam.[28]

How, though, would he be able to beat the draft? For the savvy and bright Kurbegovic, that meant coming up with some type of disability that would enable him to obtain a 4-F classification, which was given to a person who was not acceptable for military service due to physical, mental, or moral conditions.[29] Kurbegovic decided, therefore, that faking being mute might do the trick.[30]

He did not know, however, when he would receive the notice from the Selective Service to register for the draft. It could be in six months or some-time later. But he apparently wanted to have a track record at work of being a mute in case the draft board inquired at his place of employment. The problem, of course, was how he was going to communicate with people. He didn't know sign language, and even if he did, it was unlikely any of his coworkers or supervisors at his various engineering jobs would know it. So he came up with a solution. He would simply write notes on a pad of paper very quickly, both in response to questions, when inquiring about something, or for any other type of communication that was necessary.

That, of course, would take an incredible amount of self-control and awareness at all times. It would be very easy to forget that you're pretending to be mute and say something to someone or bang your knee against a desk or chair and exclaim, "Ouch!" Kurbegovic, however, played his part exceptionally well. He even once accidentally burned himself without uttering a sound.[31] He kept his lips sealed when he was communicating by writing notes, no matter how excited he became. Still, while faking being mute, Kurbegovic did nevertheless laugh occasionally and also grunt. He had one type of grunt for when he approved of something, and a different grunt to express disapproval. He would also throw his hands up in the air to communicate a "who knows" attitude. He had many other gestures he used when interacting with various people. When he wanted to gain someone's attention, for instance, he'd make a "che, chi" or "ch-ch" sound.[32]

But writing quick, precise notes was his main form of communication. And he was very skilled at doing it. One employer noted that Kurbegovic "had a real talent for expressing himself with a minimum of writing."[33] A coworker said that he had a "pretty good vocabulary for a guy who had not been in the U.S. very long." The coworker noted misspellings, but he attributed that to Kurbegovic's desire to write quickly as well as to not being familiar with English spelling.[34]

There are, though, some problems that can arise when you're pretending to be mute and need to call in sick to work occasionally. If you don't have many friends or relatives, as was the case for Kurbegovic, what do you do? Since no one at work had ever heard his voice, he simply called in, said his name was "Hans Steiner," and then said that his friend, Muharem Kurbegovic, could not come to work that day because he was sick. No one ever caught on that it was actually Kurbegovic calling.[35]

Kurbegovic's ruse in being a mute was successful, as he obtained a 4-F draft classification in August 1968. He had initially been classified 1-A when he reported to his local draft board in Hollywood in April. That meant he was eligible for induction into the military at any time. He had either forgotten or hadn't realized that he would need medical verification of his "disability." That spring and summer, he scurried around until he found a doctor who provided him with a certificate for the draft board attesting to his muteness.[36]

Despite putting behind him the worries about having to serve in the military, Kurbegovic continued to play mute at work. He likely didn't want to risk being discovered to have lied to the draft board, which at the time would have meant a sentence of five years in prison and a $10,000 fine.[37] He might also have worried about being deported for his crime.[38]

Being mute at work didn't seem to hurt Kurbegovic's professional career.

Joseph Durfee, who hired Kurbegovic in 1969 to work for Wintec Corporation as a design engineer for stainless steel wire-mesh filters and other products, was initially skeptical that someone who couldn't talk could perform well on the job. He was therefore prepared to turn Kurbegovic down when he arrived for the interview. However, Durfee was so impressed with Kurbegovic that contrary to his usual deliberations of about three days before hiring someone, he hired him the same day.[39]

Kurbegovic was genuinely well liked by most of the people he worked with over the years. They found him to be smart and creative. Almost everyone at his different engineering jobs addressed him as "Mu." He was a sturdily built man, at five foot eleven and 175 pounds with dark hair and blue eyes. He received positive reviews from most of his employers. Keith Nelson, president of Gier Dunkle Instruments, Inc., where Kurbegovic worked for a while in 1968 as a design engineer for radiation and vacuum instrumentation, said that he "was very bright, a very good engineer, had a good sense of humor, and could express himself very well." Nelson also noted that Kurbegovic was a very enthusiastic and ambitious young man who believed in the capitalist idea that if you worked very hard, you could make a lot of money. Ray Heller, who was the sales manager at Wintec, said that Kurbegovic was a likable person and that he would have recommended him to any other employer. According to Heller, Kurbegovic was a good employee, and he never heard anyone discount his work.[40]

Kurbegovic, however, could be quite hardheaded and opinionated. George Reed, who worked with him at his first job in Los Angeles at Rite Autotronics Corporation in 1967, said that Kurbegovic had an attitude of superiority and would argue quite vigorously (by writing notes) whenever the supervisor of engineering questioned aspects of his design. Kurbegovic, who was the designer of new products and project engineer for automotive instruments for the firm, was also resistant to change. Giacinto Tolfa, a coworker at Wintec, recalled Kurbegovic as being moody and egotistical. Tolfa said that he believed "his opinions were always right and what others had to say was dumb." According to Tolfa, Kurbegovic was also a hard person to get acquainted with because he was so opinionated.[41]

Among Kurbegovic's many different opinions was that aliens like himself who were earning their own keep and paying taxes had fewer rights than other citizens. He felt that immigrants were discriminated against in their employment opportunities. He was also upset with U.S. tax laws, which he believed were unfair because single people like himself were paying more than married couples. Kurbegovic was against all religions and vigorously defended atheism, claiming that anyone who believed in God was weak. He also once told a coworker at RPM Industries (where he worked as a design engineer for refrigeration compressors and other products from 1972 to 1974) that he was an anarchist and believed he should be able to do anything he wanted without restriction.[42]

Kurbegovic also expressed anticommunist sentiments at his many different jobs. He said (through notes) that life in Yugoslavia under the Communist leader Josip Broz Tito was very repressive. One coworker described Kurbegovic as very patriotic and desiring to become a U.S. citizen. Like many people in the country during the late 1960s and early 1970s, he was opposed to the Vietnam War. He also did not like President Richard Nixon. His dislike for the president, however, stemmed not just from the Vietnam War but also from Nixon's China policies. Kurbegovic claimed that Nixon was more liberal than he preferred and was going against traditional conservative policies by trying to improve relations between the United States and China.[43]

Some of his coworkers, though, were never sure of Kurbegovic's true beliefs and opinions, since he sometimes liked to say things for "shock value" and also to play devil's advocate in discussions. "He would challenge people to see how far he could go without being set down," said Dinko Bozanich, the prosecutor in Kurbegovic's 1974 grand jury proceedings and 1974–80 competency and criminal trials.[44] Ursula Brophy, a receptionist at RPM Industries, was particularly perturbed by Kurbegovic because he would make anti-Catholic statements knowing it would anger her because she was Catholic. He thought it was funny because he "scored a point" when she became angry. He also often walked into work and handed her a note with some cynical comment about a news story. His comments usually criticized the government. This upset Brophy, who felt that since Kurbegovic was an immigrant, if he didn't like living in America, he should just go home.[45]

But Kurbegovic was, for the most part, well liked by both supervisors and coworkers at the many different engineering jobs he held. When he was asked occasionally why he wasn't able to speak, he would come up with different explanations. He told one person that just prior to his birth, his mother had been taken in for questioning by Tito's Yugoslav secret police and that he believed this traumatic incident caused his condition at birth.[46] He told another person that the Germans had mistreated him as a child and that an incident involving boiling water caused his muteness.[47]

Kurbegovic also pretended to be a mute at his first residence in Los Angeles, where he lived for approximately three years until 1970.[48] Since he had been pretending to be a mute at work to avoid being drafted, he probably figured he should do the same at home in case the draft board ever investigated his disability claim. By the time he moved to his next apartment, however, he decided to begin talking at his residence. Perhaps he felt then that it was more likely that the draft board would investigate his workplace than his residence. Or perhaps he believed there would be little risk of someone from work discovering he could talk at home, since he lived far enough away geographically. "He was able to keep the two worlds separate," said Bozanich. "He got away with it."[49]

For a brief period of time, Kurbegovic had a girlfriend. They met in December 1969 when they were both taking a citizenship class at a local high school. Kurbegovic was pretending to be a mute at the school. Irma Mata, who was from Ecuador, felt pity for him. "When I first met Mu," she said, "he didn't speak verbally to anyone. He had informed the teacher that he was mute, but that he could hear her. I felt sorry for him and we began a relationship." When she asked him a few weeks after they began seeing each other if he had been mute from birth, Kurbegovic shocked her by answering verbally. From that point on, he communicated with her by speaking. As far as she knew, she was his only friend. "Mu was a loner," Mata said. "He had no friends and he never talked to anyone, but me and my sister."[50]

Their relationship was a rocky one. They moved in together, but Mata soon became alarmed by Kurbegovic's behavior. "He showed signs of being hostile towards other people if they made noise," she said.[51] On one occasion he threw a neighbor into the apartment building's swimming pool, and he told another neighbor that he would kill him. "These kinds of actions and Mu's impotence are what prompted me to leave." Kurbegovic, however, recalled the relationship in a more positive vein: "We concluded mutually that we don't fit together," he said. "So we simply split on friendly terms."[52]

By the end of the 1960s, Kurbegovic was not a happy camper. Socially, he didn't see himself as attractive or as fitting into his new country. Professionally, he thought he was at a dead end in his career with little chance for advancement or making a lot of money. One of his employers believed that Kurbegovic was disappointed in not having achieved the success he felt his education and intelligence should have allowed.[53] But Kurbegovic, who was relentless in coming up with ideas and then pursuing them, would soon come up with one that he hoped would change his life.

The Taxi Dance Halls

Ten cents today can't buy you much. Maybe a few minutes for your car at a parking meter. But back in the 1920s and 1930s, ten cents bought you a dance with a pretty young woman. Taxi dance halls were the rage in many cities across the United States, including Los Angeles, San Francisco, Chicago, New Orleans, and New York. The concept was simple: Just like taking a taxi and paying for the duration of the ride, at a taxi dance hall one would hire a girl for ten cents a dance. Male customers (no females except for the dancers were allowed in the clubs) would buy tickets at ten cents each and give them to the young women they wanted to dance with. A taxi dance girl would have to dance with whoever gave her a ticket. They worked on a 50 percent commission basis, earning five cents for each dance while the proprietor of the dance hall earned the other five cents. The dances lasted approximately ninety seconds each. In later years, the fixed price per dance changed to a running meter, where the customers were charged a certain amount of money for each minute they spent with a hostess, who again would earn a 50 percent commission for each customer's time.[54]

In the beginning, however, the "ten cents a dance" term was so popular that it became the title of a song written in 1930 by the famed Rodgers and Hart musical team and performed by stage and singing star Ruth Etting.

Legendary jazz singer Ella Fitzgerald, among many other recording artists in subsequent years, also performed the song, which describes the plight of a hardworking and tired taxi dance hall girl who has to deal with all sorts of men on the dance floor and is beaten down emotionally but never totally breaks. The song was viewed as symbolic of the end of the Roaring Twenties and the image of the joyful and free-spirited "flapper girls" before the beginning of the 1930s economic depression.[55]

The fascination with taxi dance halls did not escape the attention of Hollywood. In 1927, Joan Crawford appeared in a silent film, *Taxi Dancer*, while in 1931 Barbara Stanwyck starred in *Ten Cents a Dance*, a film named after the popular song. There would be several more movies made that included taxi dance halls in their plots or subplots, including *Sweet Charity* in 1969 starring Shirley MacLaine. There have also been several books written about this part of American culture.

In 1932, a young sociologist published what is still considered today the landmark study of taxi dance halls.[56] Paul Goalby Cressey was a caseworker and special investigator with the Juvenile Protective Association in Chicago when he began in 1925 a five-year study of the taxi dance halls in the city. Since the dance hall owners would not allow Cressey and his colleagues to interview the taxi dance girls and their customers, Cressey had to send in observers whom the club owners didn't know to mingle with the dancers and patrons and keep records of their findings.

Cressey and his team discovered that the taxi dancers ranged in age from fifteen to twenty-eight, with more than half coming from broken homes due to death, divorce, or the desertion of a parent. Many of them led "double lives," keeping secret from their families and others what they did at night for a living. They could make two or three times as much money as a dance hall hostess than they could working long days in a factory or store. The male customers were a diverse group, with "Chinese and Sicilians, Hawaiians and Scandinavians, Mexicans and Russians, Filipinos and Romanians, Jews and Poles, Greeks and American Indians, Hindus and Anglo-Saxon Nordics all [mingling] together." African Americans, though, were not allowed in the dance halls. The age range of the males was a wide one, from teenaged boys to men over sixty.[57]

According to Cressey, the taxi dance halls filled a void in the lives of many of its customers. This included older, unattached men who wanted to dance; men who were "socially handicapped by an unattractive personality, small stature, language difficulties, or by physical disabilities"; immigrants who did not want to socialize with others of their nationality; and young Asian men who experienced prejudices in American society at that time. "The taxi-dance hall is the only dance institution which makes a place for all these groups," Cressey wrote, "the only social opportunity afforded them in which they do not feel tinge of pity, repulsion, or social condescension."[58]

The portrait that Cressey paints of the taxi dance halls of the 1920s is one of a refuge from the hardships of urban life and temporary acceptance for those poor souls marginalized by society:

> It has arisen in response to definite trends in urban life, and it possesses the characteristics of most urban institutions. In its catering to detached and lonely people, in its deliberate fostering of stimulation and excitement, in its opportunities for pseudo-romantic attachments, it may be seen as an epitome of certain phases of urban life. On the periphery of the respectable, tolerated but not condoned by the community, it gathers to itself those who have failed to find a place in the more conventional groups and institutions of the city, and who yet need the satisfactions which inclusion in such groups affords. The taxi-dance hall, before being summarily dismissed from thought as a "den of iniquity," should be analyzed in terms of the human relationships which it fosters and in terms of the effect of these associations upon the personality and character of patrons and taxi-dancers.[59]

Nearly forty years later, a "detached and lonely" Yugoslav immigrant found Cressey's observations to ring true. For Muharem Kurbegovic, the taxi dance halls of Los Angeles provided him with the little joy he had in life and fostered the "human relationships" he did not find elsewhere. "It is more or less a very specific type of psychiatric treatment," Kurbegovic said, "a very specific form of giving a human being an encouragement to continue, to continue on living despite certain things that are bothering them."[60]

The dance halls also provided him with the idea that he was looking to change his life for the better. "Money was the most important thing in his life," said one of the taxi dancers at a club he went to frequently. He told her verbally (he did not play mute at the clubs) that "the way to get rich was to own a taxi dancer club [and that] then he would have all the money he wanted."[61] By the time Kurbegovic was frequenting the dance halls, "ten cents a dance" was long gone, replaced by a time clock system where men paid fifteen cents a minute, or nine dollars an hour, for the company of one of the hostesses working in the club. One could dance, talk, play pool, or sit at a table or booth with the woman of his choice. The dance hostesses earned half of the customers' charges for the time spent with them, or $4.50 an hour.[62]

The taxi dance halls in Los Angeles in the late 1960s and early 1970s were concentrated in a downtown area not very far from some of the residences where Kurbegovic had lived. They had names such as "Samoa," "International Ballroom," "Roseland," and "Danceland." The orchestras that had provided music for the taxi dance halls of earlier days were now replaced by jukeboxes. The women sat in rows on sofas, waiting to be chosen by the men who were separated from them by several feet of bare wood floor.[63] As with the original taxi dance halls, there was a wide range of ages and ethnicities among the male customers. They reflected the metropolitan character of Los Angeles at that time, with whites, Chicanos, Chinese, and Filipinos among the men usually found at the clubs. Blacks and Japanese, the two other major minority groups in Los Angeles during this time, were underrepresented among the clientele. Many of the nonwhites at the club were foreign-born. Most of the hostesses were young, white, from out of state, and recently divorced with young children.[64]

Kurbegovic spent most of his free time at the different taxi dance halls in Los Angeles, visiting them almost every night. He spent an average of twenty to thirty dollars each night and occasionally more than fifty dollars. For a while, he was spending even more money at the clubs, approximately four hundred dollars a week. Sometimes, he would dance just one song and then either play pool or sit and talk with the hostess he'd chosen. Other times, he preferred to dance rather than sit and talk. One taxi dancer described him as "lonely and quiet." Another recalled that he was mostly calm but at times could be "abrupt and rude." She said he seemed to purposely hurt her feelings just so he could try to make up. She believed he was the type of person who tried to "use his wits on you." Still another hostess said Kurbegovic had a "deep inferiority complex" and urged him to see a psychiatrist. And one hostess was convinced that he needed "a mother image."[65]

When he asked one of the taxi dancers out for a date, she replied, "You think I'm insane [enough] to go out with you?" He was successful, however, in getting dates with a couple of the other hostesses, but it did not turn out well. One he left stranded at Disneyland and another in Palm Springs, both times having driven with them there and then at some point suddenly disappearing. The hostess he took to Palm Springs said he got mad because she wouldn't go to bed with him. They eventually made up, and when she agreed to have sex with him, Kurbegovic could not perform due to his impotency.[66]

Kurbegovic complained to some of the hostesses that he was being discriminated against in America because he was an immigrant. He told them that immigrants were not treated fairly and that the U.S. laws regarding immigration were too strict.[67] These were the same complaints he told some of his coworkers at his different jobs in Los Angeles. And just as was the case with the people he worked with, he was genuinely liked by many of the taxi dance girls. Kurbegovic had a remarkable ability to push buttons and irritate people at times yet still come away with their admiration and even affection.

His vast experience as a customer in the taxi dance halls convinced Kurbegovic that he knew enough about the business to open one himself. This would be his ticket out of his doldrums and into a profitable career as a businessman. He also believed, or at least tried to convince others, that he would actually be providing a public service by helping lonely, unfortunate people like himself find joy and acceptance in the taxi dance halls. He had failed once before in trying to start a business when he launched a small import-export company as a joint venture with one of his bosses at work. That, however, did not deter the ambitious Kurbegovic from continuing to search for new business opportunities.[68]

In December 1971, Kurbegovic found a location not far from the other taxi dance halls in downtown Los Angeles that he figured he could turn into his own dance hall. There were two small, single-story stores that he thought could be remodeled into a single room approximately thirty-three feet wide by forty-four feet deep. Kurbegovic planned to create a 400-square-foot dance floor in the center of the premises with a waiting area and a couples' area (for a customer and a dance hall hostess) adjacent to the dance floor.[69]

Kurbegovic then began the arduous process of obtaining the permits and other documents required for operating the business. The name of his proposed dance hall was "The Taxi Dance." He first filed a business license application at city hall and then went to the building and safety department to obtain a permit. He was told there that he could only get the permit if he remodeled the building. Kurbegovic estimated that the remodeling he had in mind would cost approximately four thousand dollars. He didn't want to spend that money unless he could be assured that he would indeed be granted the permit. But there was another hitch: He also needed a permit from the police department. And Kurbegovic knew that could be a problem.[70]

The problem had to do with an incident earlier in 1971 at one of the taxi dance halls Kurbegovic frequented. On the evening of March 24 he had entered Danceland, which was located on the second floor of a building on Figueroa Street in downtown Los Angeles. He paid the admission charge and then went to the snack bar area, where he and the other customers were first directed to before being allowed to enter another area where they could pick the women they wanted to dance with.[71]

At one point in the evening, Kurbegovic went to the restroom. He would later claim that he had had a bowel movement and was in the process of pulling his pants back up when an undercover vice officer for the Los Angeles Police Department entered the restroom and arrested Kurbegovic for lewd conduct, claiming that Kurbegovic had been masturbating. Either not understanding what was happening or believing that the vice officer and his partner who assisted in escorting Kurbegovic out of the restroom in handcuffs were not really policemen, Kurbegovic began shouting, "Help.

Those are criminals. They are going to kill me. Call the police." He later calmed down when the security guard for the dance hall assured Kurbegovic that they were indeed policemen.[72]

Kurbegovic acted as his own lawyer when the lewd conduct misdemeanor trial was held in May 1971. He told the judge (verbally and not by writing notes) that he wanted the trial "to take the shame off my back and to make sure that this doesn't happen again."[73] It was a remarkable performance for someone who had no legal training. It also demonstrated how quick a learner Kurbegovic was. When the municipal court judge, Alan Campbell, asked him at the beginning of the trial if he had ever represented himself before in a trial by jury, Kurbegovic responded no but felt confident he could do a good job. "I have been studying extensively courtroom procedures," he told the judge, "and especially the 647 section of the California Penal Code [that applied to his case]. I also studied books of famous trial lawyers, and I believe that the judge, the prosecution and I can handle this case."[74]

When the district attorney's office reviewed the transcript of the lewd conduct trial years later, after Kurbegovic had been arrested for the bombing of LAX, they marveled at how quickly and on his own he had mastered the legal process. Among their handwritten notes regarding Kurbegovic were details like "easily picks up jargon and procedures," "excellent X [cross] exam," "pins down in great detail," "uses diagrams and photos," and "super good strategy."[75]

Part of Kurbegovic's strategy involved pointing out how it would have been anatomically impossible for him to have been masturbating if he was in the position the vice officer claimed he was in when he saw him.[76] The officer testified that Kurbegovic had his legs spread apart, his buttocks up off the seat, and the "heels of his shoes on the front edge of the toilet seat."[77] "It is so unbelievable," Kurbegovic told the jury. "It would be just as if I would go on a telegraph wire and walk up there and start masturbating."[78] He further stated that a person "cannot sit on the toilet bowl with his heels on the front portion of the toilet bowl and masturbate at the same time . . . and keep equilibrium."[79]

Kurbegovic wanted to use a wooden toilet seat prop that he had constructed to show the jury the implausibility of the vice officer's testimony concerning his posture on the seat. Judge Campbell would not allow it but permitted him to use a chair along with a tape measure, drawings, and photos to demonstrate his point. Kurbegovic was also allowed to drop his trousers to support his argument that they would have fallen into the toilet bowl and gotten wet if they were, as the vice officer had testified, "down around his ankles." Kurbegovic's pants were dry when he was arrested.[80]

Campbell was not pleased with Kurbegovic's behavior in the courtroom. "You are refusing to obey my directions as to the orderly procedure," the judge told Kurbegovic at one point during the trial.[81] While the jury was deliberating, the court reporter, George Kraft, who was sympathetic to Kurbegovic, spoke privately to him. Believing the jury was going to return a not guilty verdict, he warned him not to be baited by what Judge Campbell might say to him before or after the jury reached its verdict. "In the mind of the judge," Kraft told Kurbegovic, "he still believes you to be guilty. This is my feeling. And for that reason he's going to seek means to put you in jail for contempt of court." Kraft said that Campbell, in the absence of the jury, "will make statements to you to aggravate you, make you shoot off your mouth. And if you do he will find you in contempt of court and lock you up even though the jury finds you not guilty. So I would suggest to you keep your mouth shut. Don't say one word. When Judge Campbell makes certain statements to you, you keep your mouth shut."[82]

Just as Kraft had predicted, Campbell launched into a tirade against Kurbegovic before the jury returned to the courtroom with its verdict. "Have you been in court in Yugoslavia?" Campbell asked him. When Kurbegovic said no, Campbell asked him if he knew what a judge in Yugoslavia would do if an attorney or anyone else "over and over again disobeyed the judge's directions? What do you think the judge there would do?" Kurbegovic replied that there is contempt of court in Yugoslavia. He then tried to take Kraft's advice and not argue with the judge, even though he wanted "to spit in his face."[83] "I appreciate your understanding, your Honor," Kurbegovic said, "and I know I wasn't good enough [acting as my own lawyer] but I really tried. And I know you could have put me in jail for contempt of court because I disobeyed the rule but I didn't do it willfully, your Honor. I tried to follow instructions."[84]

Kurbegovic's attempt to placate the judge did not work. Campbell continued:

Well, if you appreciate what you call my understanding, you are mistaken, sir. I don't have any understanding. I don't have any excuse for you whatsoever. In my opinion, you have purposely, consistently taken advantage of every possible opportunity to turn this trial into a vehicle for your play acting and pantomiming and for your taking advantage of every possible trick in the book. You have done it in your examination of the witnesses, you have done it in your discourse with me, you have done it in your argument to the jury, you have been totally and purposely unfair, you have tried to crucify a man who is not here to defend himself [the policeman]. . . . You don't have any sympathy or understanding from me, sir. In doing things like that you have nothing but contempt from me, whether you are guilty or not guilty.[85]

Kurbegovic asked if he could respond. The judge said no. Kurbegovic then took Kraft's advice and kept quiet. Kraft would later say that Kurbegovic was not unfair to the policeman. "He [the vice officer] didn't have the evidence for such a misdemeanor accusation," Kraft said.[86] The jury agreed and found Kurbegovic not guilty. He then asked the judge if he could go home. When told he could, he left the courtroom sobbing.[87]

Kurbegovic should have felt vindicated by the jury verdict. After all, as an immigrant with no legal training and serving as his own lawyer, he had been victorious in an American court of law. But he was angry that he had been falsely arrested in the first place. He therefore sought legal advice about suing the city of Los Angeles for the arrest. Most of the lawyers he spoke to wanted him to pay a fee ranging from $600 to $4,000 before they would take the case. One lawyer, however, told him that it would be foolish and futile to try to sue the city: "There is nothing I can do for you, sir, except steal some money from you."[88] Kurbegovic nevertheless went to the Los Angeles Law Library to find cases where a plaintiff had been successful in suing the city. He couldn't find any. "I realized [then] that there is absolutely nothing that I can do within the system of law in order to redress the grievances of my false arrest against the City Hall," he said.[89]

He also soon found out that his acquittal in court was a hollow victory. In November 1971 he was laid off from his job at Wintec Corporation due to a cutback in employees. As he went about looking for another job, he learned quickly that having a prior arrest record for lewd conduct could hurt one's job prospects.[90] "When I was applying for the jobs," Kurbegovic said, "of course most jobs in my category, which was engineering, require you to have the form there where it says: 'Have you ever been arrested?' And my answer was: 'Yes.' And the question: 'What have you been arrested for?' And my answer: 'Masturbating in public restroom.' I was interviewed, and the gentleman there, or whoever interviewer was, said: 'Well, nice knowing you. Don't call us. We will call you.' So I couldn't find a job."[91] He also believed that he might be deported due to this arrest. "I go . . . [to] law library and read immigration and naturalization laws. And there it says . . . whenever an alien is sexually deviant in any way whatsoever, he's deportable."[92] As his public defender after the bombing of Los Angeles International Airport stated, "His masturbation arrest . . . became the be-all and the end-all of his life."[93]

Not finding a job during this period was also one of the motivating factors for Kurbegovic to seek to go into business for himself by owning a taxi dance hall.[94] After learning that in addition to getting a certificate of occupancy from the building and safety department he also needed a police permit, he went in January 1972 to the LAPD to fill out an application. Not long afterward, Kurbegovic received a notice of an intention to deny the permit from Captain George Milemore, who wrote that Kurbegovic "has demonstrated that he is unfit to be trusted with the privileges of a Hostess Dance Hall police permit as indicated by his conduct on March 24, 1971." The notice also stated that permits can be denied to people who have "a bad moral character, intemperate habits or a bad reputation for truth, honesty, or integrity."[95]

Even though Kurbegovic knew his prior arrest could be a problem, he was angered by the wording of the notice. "I was kind of furious as to this guy's choice of words," Kurbegovic said. "In other words, the choice of his words was so horribly offensive to me that I wanted to talk to this guy, to see him, how big he is, what kind of nerve this guy has to be a model human being and use those words towards somebody [like me]."[96] Kurbegovic had the option of requesting a hearing on the intention to deny the permit, which he did. Once again demonstrating a remarkable ability to understand the legal process and argue coherently and persuasively on his own behalf, Kurbegovic won over the police commission hearing examiner. He did not talk about the monetary motivation for opening a taxi dance hall but instead emphasized the social services he would be providing other people with such an establishment. He explained how the taxi dance hall had helped him cope with life:

> It has given me the energy to work productively in this world that has labeled certain human beings as failures due to the fact that they don't look as good as someone else; due to the fact that the God has created them differently; due to the fact that simply not everyone is fortunate enough to be attractive to everyone. And the taxi dance actually come[s] [in] there where God has failed, where God has committed the crime the taxi dance comes in and does good, and the lonely man ... [can] go in a taxi dance, have someone try to understand them, have someone to tell them that they are human beings too.[97]

Kurbegovic was sounding a lot like sociologist Paul Goalby Cressey who, as discussed earlier, wrote how the taxi dance halls of the 1920s provided detached and lonely men with "the only social opportunity afforded them in which they do not feel tinge of pity, repulsion, or social condescension."[98] The examiner recommended to the police commission board that Kurbegovic be granted the permit to open the taxi dance hall once he obtained a certificate of occupancy. His prior arrest for lewd conduct did not negatively sway the examiner. "The applicant is a fit person to be trusted with the privileges granted by a hostess dance hall permit," he concluded.[99]

When Kurbegovic received this conditional acceptance in the mail, he must have been elated. Perhaps he could finally put the arrest behind him and get on with his life. He still needed approval by the police commission board, but if the hearing officer recommended approval, wouldn't the board follow suit? When he appeared before the police commission in April 1972, though, things did not go smoothly. One of the commissioners,

Marguerite Justice, expressed concern about the lewd conduct arrest and wanted more information than was provided in the hearing examiner's report. She requested that a full transcript of that hearing be prepared and sent to the board.[100]

The next time Kurbegovic appeared before the board, in May, he was prepared for the worst. Why wouldn't they have simply accepted the hearing officer's recommendation and granted him the permit? Wanting more information about his arrest could not be a good sign. This time, therefore, he took a more assertive tone at the meeting, telling a commissioner who asked him about his arrest, "You falsely arrested me. And instead of you paying me damages, you now intend to deny my permit."[101] He also told the commissioners that there was nothing illegal or improper about the type of business he wanted to open.[102] His argument failed to sway the police board. Commissioner Emmet McGaughey made a motion to deny the permit, and Commissioner Justice seconded the motion, which was passed unanimously. The wording of the motion could not have pleased Kurbegovic: "It [is] ordered that the findings and recommendation of the Hearing Examiner not be adopted and the permit denied based upon the fact that the applicant is not a fit and proper person to have this permit as evidenced by his arrest on March 24, 1972 [sic; 1971] for violation of Section 647a P.C. (Lewd Conduct) and upon the further grounds that the issuance of the permit would not comport with the peace, health, safety, convenience and general welfare of the public."[103]

Kurbegovic would later claim that he had two Browning Hi Power pistols hidden under his shirt and was ready to assassinate the commissioners after they denied him his permit.[104] But he changed his mind. "Shortly after that denial," Kurbegovic said, "the ideas kept flashing through my mind, 'Gee, man, you just almost lost your life. For what? For killing all these [commissioners]? Why don't you kill somebody that's responsible for all of it, not just for that narrow issue. Why not kill somebody who is responsible for all of it?"[105]

He decided that it was the U.S. Supreme Court that was responsible for his possibly facing deportation and for his being in the mess he was in due to the lewd conduct arrest. "I formed the conclusion that the Supreme

Court should have destroyed the immoral elements of the immigration and naturalization laws."[106] He then stated that he traveled several times to Washington DC and actually sat in the Supreme Court ready to assassinate all the justices but couldn't pull the trigger.[107] This was likely just a fantasy of Kurbegovic's, though it can't entirely be discounted. "Back in those days," said former prosecutor Dinko Bozanich, "it would have been a lot easier to walk into the Supreme Court, and even have a firearm and perhaps do something. So, I can't exclude that he ever didn't [do what he said]. [But] I would probably say he didn't do that because he tended to plan things and then execute them. It was probably something that he had contemplated."[108]

Kurbegovic also had dreams about enacting revenge upon the Supreme Court justices. "I once was dreaming again that I am in the Supreme Court, that I just jumped the bench. And just as I drew the gun that I pulled the triggers and pointed to two extreme justices. And as I pulled both triggers gun failed to fire. Gun failing to fire woke me up. I was completely in sweat. . . . And at that time I realized: That's it. I just can't do it. I just wasn't a man. That is all there is to it. I just ain't a man. And a few months after that I applied for a job."[109]

This feeling of inadequacy would haunt Kurbegovic for some time. He was committed to seeking revenge against those he felt had wronged him but believed he wasn't yet capable of doing so. His next job, however, would give him both the confidence and skills necessary for launching a one-man campaign of terror against not only his perceived enemies but also innocent victims.

2

Until Our Name Has Been Written on the Face of This Nation in Blood

London Bridge was falling down. Or at least it was slowly sinking into the Thames River in the 1960s, due to the increased weight of modern traffic. The magnificent bridge, built in 1831 to replace its predecessor, had to be replaced again with a newer and sturdier one. What do you do, though, when you want to get rid of an old bridge, particularly a famous one that has been the subject of a nursery rhyme sung by children for centuries?[1]

One way would be to demolish it with one of those controlled explosions that usually attracts large crowds and global media. That, however, would be a sad ending for the landmark bridge. Another way would be to dismantle it and send it to its final resting place in some British junkyard. A London city council member, Ivan Luckin, came up with a better idea. Why not sell the bridge to the highest bidder? Unsure of how much interest there would be in buying a more than 130-year-old bridge, Luckin traveled to the United States in 1968 hoping to find a buyer.[2]

When he arrived in New York, Luckin touted the bridge in a press conference as "not just a bridge. It is the heir to 2,000 years of history going back to the first century A.D., to the time of the Roman Londinium."[3] The sales pitch got the attention of a wealthy and colorful American industrialist,

Robert P. McCulloch, who learned about it from a business associate who had read the story in a newspaper article.[4] McCulloch was the owner of McCulloch Corporation, which had numerous subsidiaries in many different fields, including oil, aviation, electronics, motors, chemicals, and real estate.[5] One of his real estate ventures involved purchasing land in western Arizona and developing it into a new community called Lake Havasu City. He had bought the land in 1963, but the community wasn't growing as fast as he'd hoped. A famous bridge, he thought, might be exactly what he needed to attract visitors and residents to his beloved new city. Once he won the bid, he planned to transform one of the lake's peninsulas into an island so the London Bridge would have something to span. "I had this ridiculous idea of bringing it to the Arizona desert," McCulloch would later say. "I needed the bridge, but even if I didn't, I might have bought it anyway."[6]

McCulloch bought the bridge in April 1968 for $2,460,000 and spent another $7 million over the next three years dismantling, transporting, and rebuilding it in Arizona.[7] A local newspaper gushed over news of the sale, claiming that the bridge would "be one of the most conspicuous deliveries from the Old World to the New World since the Statue of Liberty arrived from France in 1886."[8] Each of the granite bricks of the bridge was labeled in London with markers indicating its arch span, row number, and position so the bridge could be reassembled as closely as possible to the original. When it opened on October 10, 1971, with great fanfare, including skydivers, fireworks, marching bands, and hot-air balloons, a British journalist observed, "It's a supergimmick. It's all quite mad—it could only happen in America. Only an American would think of investing that much in something as crazy as this."[9]

It turned out, however, not to be as crazy a business venture as many people thought. The addition of London Bridge was exactly the tourist and residential attraction that McCulloch had envisioned for his fledgling city. The population of Lake Havasu City, which had only been a few hundred in the early 1960s when McCulloch began developing the area, grew to over ten thousand by 1974. Close to two million people also visited the London Bridge that same year. The city continued to grow, reaching fifty thousand residents by 2016, along with a flourishing tourism industry.[10]

The freethinking, big-spending McCulloch always aimed to develop products based on creative ideas. Among his successful ventures were developing the first one-person, lightweight chainsaw in the late 1940s. Some of his ideas, however, didn't pan out. During the same year that London Bridge opened, he built his first aircraft in Lake Havasu City, a J-2 gyroplane, which was a hybrid of a helicopter and an airplane. His vision was to provide "an airplane in every garage," with the gyroplanes being easy to fly and able to take off from a driveway. Although he built two hundred of the gyroplanes, the business never took off.[11]

Failure, though, didn't deter McCulloch from forging ahead. He fostered an environment of creative thinking at his company, McCulloch Corporation, and its successor, RPM Industries, and tried to attract people who, like him, were smart, bold, and somewhat eccentric. Little did he know that one of his prized employees would indeed think outside the box, but in ways that McCulloch could never have envisioned.

The Finest Job I Ever Had

Still reeling from the denial of his permit to operate a taxi dance hall, Muharem Kurbegovic was finally able to find a job in the fall of 1972, ending a year of unemployment. He was interviewed by Alan Bell, the special assistant to the president of McCulloch Corporation (i.e., Robert McCulloch). The thirty-minute interview went well. The fact that Kurbegovic only communicated by writing notes did not bother Bell or McCulloch. "I tested his knowledge of engineering," Bell said, and "I was convinced that he was a highly qualified designer and mechanical engineer and his recommendations were excellent."[12]

At first, Kurbegovic worked on a refrigeration compressor project as a design engineer. But not long after he started at McCulloch Corporation, the company and its subsidiaries were sold to Black + Decker. McCulloch kept his best people to form a new company that he named RPM Industries, after his own initials. Kurbegovic was among those he kept. McCulloch wanted his new firm to be a place of ideas and inventions, where people worked whenever they felt the inspiration. He believed that in his type of business, he couldn't just tell an employee to sit down and invent. Rather, he wanted RPM to be full of self-motivated people, and when someone got an idea, then that would be the time to work.[13]

Some of the projects at RPM were quite quirky and were essentially pet projects for McCulloch, such as a facial machine, which was a very large and expensive device. It would provide refrigerated air blasts of fifty below zero as well as hot steam to clean the pores on a person's face (McCulloch had some skin blemishes). Another project involved creating an automatic-ejecting golf cup that threw a golf ball back out of the hole after a putt was sunk.[14]

But there were also projects that reflected McCulloch's vision for the future. He believed that a major part of the transportation needs of the twenty-first century would be electric cars. He therefore developed several prototype electric cars before he died in 1977. Another idea involved developing a battery motor controller system, where a kit could be outfitted onto a conventional bicycle to power it by electric motor and also recharge the battery.[15] Whatever the project was, McCulloch encouraged his employees to not be restrained in their thinking and to not be afraid to try out new ideas.

For Kurbegovic, working at RPM Industries "was the finest job" he ever had.[16] McCulloch often worked side by side with his employees, including Kurbegovic. He viewed "Mu" as creative, analytical, and very conscientious about his work. He never saw any hostility or violent tendencies from Kurbegovic. He wanted to help him with what he thought was his disability in not being able to speak. McCulloch offered the firm's assistance in acquiring medical expertise to see whether anything could be done about Kurbegovic's muteness. But Kurbegovic told him he had already been to several doctors and that there was no hope for him.[17]

As was true with his previous jobs, Kurbegovic was well liked at RPM. He kept secret his lewd conduct arrest but not his having wanted to open a taxi dance hall. He told people that the reason he was denied a permit for the dance hall was due to his being an immigrant, as well as to the LAPD being "Mafia controlled" and freezing him out of the business.[18] While some people sensed he was angry about not obtaining the permit, no one knew he was secretly planning to take revenge on those responsible. Kurbegovic was biding his time until he felt confident he had both the knowledge and the capability to successfully hurt those who had hurt him.

That confidence came when RPM built a chemical lab in 1973 at its facility in Los Angeles. The lab was needed for projects involving high-amperage semiconductors and batteries. There was, therefore, a wide range of chemicals on the premises now. Kurbegovic experimented with the chemicals, once making a gaseous substance that appeared to be poisonous. The lab had to be evacuated until the gas cleared. He also often requested permission to work late in the shop area or laboratory. Since the inventory at RPM, including the chemicals and equipment, was loosely controlled, any employee had access to those materials.[19] Kurbegovic tried to learn everything he could about chemicals, all under the guise of trying to be a good worker. He had, of course, other plans.

The existence of the chemical lab was a godsend for Kurbegovic. So too was the presence of one of his supervisors and closest friends at work, Stephen Smith. They had an odd relationship, with constant discussions (Kurbegovic would write notes, while Smith would speak verbally) about various scenarios involving bombs, violence, threats, scams, and so forth. For Smith, this was part of the freewheeling, "think-outside-the-box" environment encouraged at RPM. He had no idea that Kurbegovic would take some of these discussions seriously for his own personal objectives. One of those discussions involved arson, and Kurbegovic asked Smith where he could buy a book on how to commit arson or how things are burned down. Smith then gave Kurbegovic his own books on various subjects, including incendiaries, booby traps, bombs, and explosives.[20]

Always the quick learner, Kurbegovic studied the book on incendiaries and made his own improvised arson devices. Investigators with the Los Angeles Fire Department (LAFD) would later say they had never seen anything like them before. Each device consisted of compressed sawdust logs and briquettes; gasoline; an amber-colored, gel-like material; paraffin wax; and a balloon with acid placed in a cardboard box. Kurbegovic was now ready to take his revenge.[21]

During the early-morning hours of November 9, 1973, Kurbegovic drove to three different residences in Los Angeles and placed a device next to each of the houses. It took less than twenty minutes to drive from one residence to the second and then to the third. Kurbegovic built the arson devices so that they would ignite approximately half an hour after he placed them at the houses, giving him plenty of time to leave the scene.[22]

Emmet McGaughey, the Los Angeles police commissioner who'd made the motion to deny Kurbegovic the permit to open a taxi dance hall, was awakened shortly after 4 a.m. by an extremely bright light. At first, he thought someone was aiming a searchlight on his house, but he soon saw that the whole front of the house was lit up with bright flames. His wife and daughter were also home at the time. He called the fire department and rushed outside to use a garden hose on the fire, which had reached an overhanging balcony on the second floor and had already burned the walls and ceiling inside. When the firemen arrived about five minutes after McGaughey called, they were able to extinguish the flames.[23]

It would end up being a busy morning for the LAFD. While they were putting out the fire at McGaughey's house, a call came in that another house was on fire. This time it was the home of Alan Campbell, the municipal judge who had presided over Kurbegovic's lewd conduct trial. Campbell and his wife were awakened by a phone call from a neighbor sometime after 4 a.m. The neighbor told them that there was a fire in front of their house and that he had already called the fire department. Campbell went outside and saw a fire burning on the front of his house and attached garage. The flames were rising over the garage door and into the eave, which projected a short distance beyond the face of the garage. He started using a garden hose to battle the flames until the firemen arrived. He and his wife then went across the street to stay at their neighbor's house until the fire was put out.[24]

Yet another call regarding a house fire was received by the fire department at 4:54 a.m. Marguerite Justice, the police commissioner who had seconded the motion by McGaughey to deny Kurbegovic the dance hall permit, was awakened along with her husband by the crackling sound of a fire. She called the fire department while her husband ran outside and used a garden hose on the fire, which had started on their porch and was now leaking into the house through the windows and doors. The fire was so hot that glass was melting and popping out of the windows and doors. After the firemen arrived, they were able to put the fire out in about thirty to forty-five minutes.[25]

The three fires baffled the police and fire investigators. They asked McGaughey, Campbell, and Justice whether they had any clues as to who might have wanted to burn down their homes. They all said they could not think of anyone who would want to do that to them. They never considered Kurbegovic a suspect, because their negative interactions with him had happened more than two years earlier in the case of Campbell and more than one year earlier in the case of McGaughey and Justice. They had forgotten all about him. The investigators could find no link among the three targets. While McGaughey and Justice knew each other from working together on the police commission, neither of them knew Campbell. "We were constantly attempting to tie a suspect or whatever suspect we were looking at in some way to all three of the victims," said LAPD officer Charles Ross. "At some point in time, another theory was developed—that Judge Campbell might have been a red herring; that it might have been someone that strictly had an ax to grind, so to speak, with McGaughey and Justice."[26]

It also might have crossed the minds of some officials that perhaps the fires were the work of a new terrorist group that had emerged in Northern California, the Symbionese Liberation Army (SLA). The leftist group wanted to incite a guerrilla war against the U.S. government and destroy the "capitalist state."[27] On November 6 they assassinated the Oakland superintendent of schools, Marcus Foster, who had recently ordered the use of private armed security guards in the city's schools in order to prevent violence there. The SLA shot him with cyanide-tipped bullets. They accused Foster of "the forming and implementation of a Political Police Force operating within the Schools of the People."[28] Was the SLA now expanding to Southern California and targeting members of the Los Angeles Police Commission? The inclusion of Judge Campbell among the targets, though, did not make sense. Why would they try to kill a municipal judge? It was the wild card in this theory, if indeed the possibility of an SLA connection to the fires was ever discussed.

Normally, an arson case would be investigated until completion by the fire department. However, since two former police commissioners were among the targets (both McGaughey and Justice were no longer on the commission), the case was turned over to the Criminal Conspiracy Section (CCS) of the LAPD. It became such a high-priority case that the CCS had to put a report every day on the desk of the chief of police, Ed Davis, regarding the status of the investigation. Little progress, however, was reported. At one point, two young men were identified as possible suspects and given polygraph tests, which they failed. Marguerite Justice, however, said that she knew them and that they were like family to her. She told the police there was no way they could have set fire to her house. Further investigation cleared the two youths.[29]

Kurbegovic must have felt pretty good in the aftermath of the arson attacks. He had finally exacted some revenge on a few of the people he was upset with and had left no clues that could point to him as the perpetrator. The judge and the two police commissioners had to have a long list of potential enemies from the numerous rulings they'd made over the years, he probably thought, so there was no reason to worry that he might become a suspect. Stephen Smith could be a problem, as Kurbegovic had asked him questions about arson before the attacks and had even borrowed a book on incendiaries from him. But Smith never said anything about the arson incidents and might very well have been unaware of them since, despite it being a high-priority investigation for the LAPD, it did not receive wide media attention.

Meanwhile, things were going well for Kurbegovic at work. Just a little over a week after the attacks, he received an excellent performance review from the person at RPM who had hired him, Alan Bell. "This man is a gifted engineer [and] has done an excellent job," Bell wrote.[30] Perhaps Kurbegovic was finally ready to move beyond his troubled past and forgo any additional thoughts of revenge. His past, however, was not going to let him go.

To Be an American

Kurbegovic always wanted to become an American citizen. By the spring of 1974 he thought he was finally going to realize his dream. He was scheduled to appear before the Immigration and Naturalization Service (INS, the predecessor to the U.S. Citizenship and Immigration Services) for his citizenship hearing on May 29 at the Federal Building in downtown Los Angeles. He asked Joseph Durfee, a former supervisor of his from Wintec Corporation, to appear at the hearing as his sponsor for citizenship. Durfee thought so much of Kurbegovic that he felt honored by this request and was more than happy to comply. Another sponsor was Keith Nelson, the president of Gier Dunkle Instruments, where Kurbegovic had been employed in 1968.[31]

On the day of the hearing, everything seemed to be going well at first. Kurbegovic was in a good mood and not nervous as he conversed (by writing notes) with Durfee and Nelson while they all waited to be interviewed by the hearing examiner. Both Durfee and Nelson signed an affidavit stating that they "have personal knowledge that the petitioner is, and during all such periods [that they have known him] has been a person of good moral character, attached to the principles of the Constitution of the United States, and well disposed to the good order and happiness of the United States, and in my opinion the petitioner is in every way qualified to be admitted a citizen of the United States." Their joint interview with the examiner lasted only five minutes and consisted of confirming their past acquaintance with Kurbegovic.[32]

Meanwhile, Kurbegovic answered correctly the basic questions on the civics exam, such as who the president of the United States is, what the three branches of government are, who the two senators from California are, and what the Fourth of July represents.[33] The major roadblock to his obtaining citizenship, however, was going to be his prior arrest for lewd conduct. If he was worried about it that day, he didn't show it. Perhaps he'd convinced himself that his acquittal in a court of law would be sufficient to make it a nonissue. "I was charged with lewd conduct when officer saw me squatting on the toilet bowl as Europeans do," Kurbegovic explained in writing to the examiner. "He never saw that before so he thought it to be lewd. . . . I was alone. I pleaded innocent. The jury trial was held. I was acquitted in 5 minutes of jury deliberation."[34]

This explanation did not sway the examiner, Margaret Jambor, who wasn't even sure Kurbegovic was telling the truth about being acquitted.

The next day, she wrote a memo to the file requesting an investigation into Kurbegovic's background and behavior:

> Petitioner, a mute, attested in writing to the record of arrest when questioned to explain what happened on 3/24/1971 in Los Angeles. The petitioner, possessing the ability to hear perfectly, but not that of oral communication, attested in writing that he was arrested for "lewd conduct" when an officer found him in a squatting position during an act of elimination, done in the European fashion, at the Danceland Ballroom.... Although he alledges [sic] that he was acquitted, and although it involved an act of human body response (i.e. elimination), it was a crime involving moral turpitude within the five year statutory period of sound moral character (i.e. May 1, 1969–May 1, 1974) and therefore should be referred to Investigations for an official disposition of the case.[35]

The five-year statutory period of "good moral character" (GMC) refers to the government's requirement that an applicant for citizenship (naturalization) exhibit GMC for five years prior to the date of filing.[36] Since Kurbegovic filed the formal application for citizenship in July 1973, his lewd conduct arrest in 1971 fell within that five-year period. Most of the criminal offenses that preclude a finding of GMC require a conviction or a plea of guilty or nolo contendere (no contest) for the crime.[37] Jambor, the hearing examiner, didn't seem to care whether Kurbegovic was telling the truth when he said he had been acquitted. She still viewed what happened at the dance hall as "a crime involving moral turpitude."[38]

When Kurbegovic learned soon after the hearing that his application for citizenship was on hold and that he was going to be investigated, he became very angry. One of the investigators "was the recipient of some hell-raising" by Kurbegovic.[39] His fears that he could be deported due to his lewd conduct arrest resurfaced. His dream of becoming a U.S. citizen was now likely doomed. For Kurbegovic, this was the last straw. The American justice system had once again failed him. An acquittal in a court of law had meant nothing in the eyes of the police commission that denied him his taxi dance hall permit. And now it seemed to mean nothing in the eyes of the INS, which would likely deny his application for citizenship. Kurbegovic wasn't going to take this lightly. Once again, he plotted his revenge.

He started off with a familiar target, Emmet McGaughey, one of the police commissioners who denied his taxi dance hall permit. Kurbegovic planned to kill McGaughey this time and not just burn his house down. On June 3, just a few days after Kurbegovic's INS hearing, McGaughey drove home from work after 5 p.m., parked his car in the carport in front of his house, and went inside to relax. He took off his jacket and tie and began reading the newspaper. Then, about five or ten minutes later, he heard an explosion. "Daddy, your car's on fire!" his daughter shouted. McGaughey called the fire department and ran outside, where he saw flames coming out of the gas tank. The fire team quickly put out the fire, and they, along with the police, eventually informed McGaughey that his car had been booby-trapped to explode.[40]

Kurbegovic had placed an improvised incendiary device inside McGaughey's gas tank, most likely while McGaughey's car was parked at his workplace. The device consisted of a small plastic pill vial filled with potassium chlorate and sugar, with a green paper towel used as a separator mechanism to hold sulfuric acid. When the acid eventually penetrated through the towel, it came in contact with the chlorate and sugar, causing the fire and small explosion inside the gas tank.[41]

However, the car did not blow up, as Kurbegovic had intended. In order for that to have happened, there would have had to be a very small quantity of gasoline in the tank and a large quantity of fuel vapors. This would cause the fumes in the gas tank to explode, thereby destroying the car. If the gas tank was too full, there would not be a large explosion, since there would be too much liquid and not enough fumes. Fortunately for McGaughey, he had filled up his tank with gas that day and only driven a short distance from work to home. Though Kurbegovic's device still caused a small explosion, it would have been much worse had there been less gasoline in the tank and more vapors, and, of course, had McGaughey been driving his car at the time of the explosion.[42]

Having dodged two bullets—the November 1973 house fire and the recent car fire—McGaughey wondered who was trying so hard to kill him and why. He couldn't come up with any answers. Then, on July 5, he received a phone call around 2:40 a.m. "E. C. McGaughey?" the voice on the other end asked. "Yes," McGaughey responded. "This is the Symbionese Liberation Army calling. The date for your execution has been set. It will take place within a month. If any of the members of your family attempt to interfere with your execution, they also will be executed."[43]

Could the SLA *really be after me?* McGaughey must have thought. Perhaps the idea that this anti-establishment, anti-police terrorist group was behind the arson attacks on his home and those of former fellow police commissioner Marguerite Justice and municipal judge Allan Campbell wasn't that farfetched after all. Whereas at the time of the November 1973 fires the group was barely known outside of Northern California, by the summer of 1974 the SLA had made a name for itself throughout the country with one of the most publicized kidnappings in American history.

When a new terrorist group is formed or a cell breaks away from an existing group, it has to do something spectacular to announce its presence to the world. If the group commits just another routine attack, it risks being ignored, as the public and governments become desensitized to the "normal" flow of terrorism. By perpetrating a violent act that either causes more casualties than previous incidents or involves new types of tactics or targets, the terrorists are guaranteed widespread publicity for their cause and reactions from various parties.

The SLA thought that the assassination of Superintendent Foster in November 1973 might do the trick. They had recently formed as a group and left a document statement with a Berkeley, California, radio station, KPFA, the day after the assassination, claiming responsibility for the attack. The document protested American foreign policy, the federal funding of Oakland school security, and several other issues. It concluded with the following chilling warning: "DEATH TO THE FASCIST INSECT THAT PREYS UPON THE LIFE OF THE PEOPLE."[44] The SLA achieved its purpose in getting extensive publicity for this attack—but not the publicity they were hoping for. Foster was a popular figure, and the assassination was widely condemned. The SLA had miscalculated the public reaction, somehow mistakenly believing that people would rally to their cause after the assassination. They now needed another plan of action.[45]

The group decided on a high-profile kidnapping as their next operation. During the evening of February 4, 1974, they snatched Patty Hearst from the apartment she shared in Berkeley with her fiancé, Steven Weed. Both were attending the university there. Hearst was the granddaughter of the late newspaper mogul William Randolph Hearst and daughter of Randolph Hearst, who was chairman of the board of the Hearst Corporation. The kidnapping of a member of a famous and very wealthy family got the SLA the attention they wanted. And the group played the drama out with a keen eye toward media publicity.

They sent a communiqué to KPFA shortly after the kidnapping, stating that Patty Hearst was a "prisoner of war" and that the Hearst Corporation was the "corporate enemy of the people." In subsequent communications to KPFA, the SLA demanded that Randolph Hearst give food away to poor people in exchange for his daughter's release. Hearst established a $2 million program to distribute the food, but it turned out to be a disaster, as there was rioting and fraud at some of the locations.[46]

On April 3, Patty Hearst shocked the nation by stating in an audiotape that she was joining the SLA. Less than two weeks later, she was seen on a bank surveillance camera taking part in an armed robbery in San Francisco. Then, in May, police surrounded a house in Los Angeles where several members of the SLA were living. A shoot-out ensued that was carried live on television and resulted in the death of six SLA members. Hearst wasn't at the house at the time of the shoot-out and remained on the run for more than a year afterward. She was finally caught, along with most of the remaining members of the SLA, in September 1975.[47]

The SLA was therefore on the minds of most Angelinos during the summer of 1974. No one knew for sure how large the group was or who its next target might be.[48] Kurbegovic exploited this fear with his threatening call to McGaughey on July 5. It was no coincidence that he chose the Fourth of July holiday period to place this call. Kurbegovic was going to use the holiday to take revenge on several targets. If America would not allow him to become a citizen, then he would not allow America to celebrate its independence day in peace.

On July 4, the day before his call to McGaughey, Kurbegovic called

KFWB, an all-news radio station in Los Angeles, also at around 2:40 a.m. He identified himself as Esak Rasim, "field commander in the Symbionese Liberation Army," and told the person answering the phone that in celebration of the Fourth of July and in recognition of the SLA members who died in the May shoot-out, there would be three bomb blasts—two in Marina del Rey and one in Santa Monica—and that one person would die in each blast.[49]

While there were no bomb blasts that day, there were three fires in the cities Kurbegovic had mentioned to the radio station. Two fires were set at apartment buildings in Marina del Rey and one at an apartment building in Santa Monica. Kurbegovic's reasons for choosing these targets were never revealed. However, he had once lived in an apartment complex not far from the Marina del Rey fires and had also worked for a short time with the engineering firm Gier Dunkle in Santa Monica. There were no injuries in the fires, but investigators once again marveled at the simplicity and ingenuity of the devices that were used—namely, sponges soaked in gasoline. "I've talked to people who have at least 100 years [collectively] of experience [investigating fires]," recalled prosecutor Dinko Bozanich, "and they never had heard of using sponges soaked in gasoline."[50] Kurbegovic had now used three different types of improvised arson devices for the fires he'd set at McGaughey's, Justice's, and Campbell's homes the previous November, in McGaughey's automobile gas tank in June, and now at the three apartment buildings.

But setting fires and making threatening phone calls weren't the only things Kurbegovic was busy with during this holiday period. On the same day he threatened McGaughey he also placed an audiocassette in a planter box just outside the lobby doors of the *Los Angeles Times* building.[51] Kurbegovic sent similar tapes to the Washington DC bureau of United Press International news service and to the British and Soviet embassies in Washington. A security guard at the *Times* building discovered the tape and notified his superior, who called the LAPD after listening to it. What the security guard's boss heard was alarming. Kurbegovic again identified himself as Esak Rasim, but now, instead of being affiliated with the SLA, he said that he was the "Chief Military Officer of Aliens of America." He claimed that his group had developed four nerve gases named AA1, AA2,

AA3, and AA4S, with the fourth having a "killing capacity exceeding that of sarin by the order of 10 to the fifth power." He claimed that his group had tested the nerve gases on animals and humans and was convinced that they had "a military weapon which not only liberates us from audacity and terror of United States Government, but places the burden on our shoulder to liberate entire humankind."[52]

Kurbegovic most likely got the idea of pretending to be part of a group from his friend and supervisor at RPM, Stephen Smith, who once told Kurbegovic about his experience trying to influence a local school board on a particular issue. Smith was not able to accomplish much as an individual, but once he wrote letters claiming to be part of a "taxpayers concerned group," he received widespread media exposure.[53] Kurbegovic probably thought that he, too, would obtain more media attention and credibility by claiming to be part of a new terrorist group, "Aliens of America," rather than acting as a lone wolf.

On this first tape (there would be several more later in the summer), Kurbegovic claimed that his group had already used a nerve gas against all nine U.S. Supreme Court justices, whom he said were "historical monuments of crime, a criminal who has repeatedly ruled that an alien is not a human being and that consequently the constitutional provisions relating to [the] term 'people' do not apply." His described method of attack was unique. "On June 15, 1974," he stated, "we have sent nine postcards to the United States Supreme Court Justices. Each postcard shows the Palm Springs home of entertainer Bob Hope and reads as follows: 'It is justices of your greatness that made this nation so great. Respectively, Bob Hope.' Underneath the 11 cents postage stamp on each postcard there is a disc of lead containing approximately .01 milligram of AA4S nerve gas together with approximately 1 milligram of camouflaging compounds and volatility inhibitors."[54]

Kurbegovic also claimed that time-release devices containing AA4S nerve gas had been placed in several cities in the United States and other countries. "We ... possess the ability to deliver an exterminating, selective, and precisely timed blow to mass population centers throughout the world." He issued an "ultimatum to surrender" to governments everywhere and called for an "end to all Nationalism, Religionism, Fascism, Racism, and Communism."[55]

Although Aliens of America was an unknown group and Kurbegovic's claims regarding placing nerve gas in cities around the world were farfetched, his threats couldn't be dismissed outright, because he had partially followed through with at least one of them. On June 16, 1974, postcards addressed to each of the Supreme Court justices were intercepted at the Palm Springs post office. Just as Kurbegovic had described, the front of each postcard was a picture of Bob Hope's Palm Springs home, and the back of each card had the greeting to the justices. "We received these postcards in the pickup from the city mail," post office foreman Arthur Smith told a grand jury in September 1974, "and they were run through the canceling machine. . . . [T]he cancellers that we have kind of ripped them up, at least tore up the stamps because . . . there was something underneath the stamps." Smith thought at first it was toy caps, but on further inspection he "could see that they were metal vials of something." He testified that when each vial went through the canceler, "whatever was in it discolored the stamps."[56]

Robert Altman, who was a deputy district attorney in Los Angeles at the time and questioned Smith at the grand jury hearing, recalled the postcard incident as being a hoax.[57] In a tape made later in the summer of 1974, Kurbegovic confirmed that there had been no nerve gas under the stamps: "The postcard hoax itself was thought out by our theoreticians who claim that a reasonable man will pause to think if someone points a gun at him, whether the gun is loaded or empty. We were pointing an empty gun, but we were not pointing it at a reasonable man. That is why it was inescapably necessary to load our gun with one bullet, to fire it, and to see what would happen. We hope that we will never have to fire another bullet."[58]

The one "bullet" that Kurbegovic referred to was not a bullet at all. It was a bomb, and it would send shock waves throughout Los Angeles and the rest of the country.

The LAX Bombing

Arturo Trostl Jr. grew up in a family where tragedy, danger, and risk were the norms of daily life. His father was known in circuses around the world as "The Great Arturo," a high-wire aerialist who always performed without a net. Arturo Sr. immigrated to the United States from Vienna in 1935. He was from a performing family that had toured Europe for several generations. He carried on the tradition in the United States, with his entire family part of the circus act. A year before Arturo Jr. and his twin sister, Hedy, were born in 1952, his seventeen-year-old sister, Evy, who, in a few days, was going to quit the circus and reenter high school, fell sixty feet from a high wire while her father and thousands of spectators in Baltimore watched in horror. Trostl, who was on the high platform when his daughter fell, quickly slid down a rope and rushed to her aid. "I can't breathe daddy," she kept moaning. "Help me. It hurts." Evy was taken to a hospital, where she died with her father collapsing at her bedside. She was buried a few days later in Tampa, Florida, in her circus ring costume. When asked if this meant the end of "The Great Arturo," a circus manager replied, "I don't know. It's hard to tell. This is about all Arturo knows. . . . Perhaps after the shock is gone [he'll perform again]."[59]

Not only did the elder Trostl perform again, but the death of his daughter did not even make him think twice about using a net for his family's high-wire act. Less than a year later, he took out an advertisement in *Billboard*, the amusement industry's leading newsweekly at that time, mocking a New York safety law that required life nets and other safety precautions for trapeze artists, tightrope walkers, and other aerial performers. He used the name of another son, Nicky, who was performing with him, to attract booking agents for state fairs. "Attention, Southern Fair Secretaries!!" the ad began. "Due to the new safety laws for all high acts, all my New York State Fairs have been canceled. Here is your chance to book a real grandstand attraction, 'The Great Arturo & Nicky' on the high wire."[60]

The younger Arturo, also known as "Cookie," eventually became part of the act along with Hedy, with both doing the flying trapeze when they were children. He would also do a headstand on a platform carried on the high wire by his father and Nicky. Arturo Jr. became famous in his own right, being featured in the national magazine *Look* when he was only eleven years old in an article titled "Cookie! the Wonder Boy." "I want to be one of the great aerialists," he told the magazine.[61]

By the time he was in his twenties, he was married and performing around the world as an independent contractor with various circus troupes. It was with one of those troupes, the International Three-Ring Circus, that he was scheduled to travel to Hawaii on August 6, 1974. Trostl, who, like his father, was known as "The Great Arturo," was considered the finest male "heel and toe" trapeze artist in the world, performing barefooted and suspended from his heels and toes thirty to thirty-five feet above the ground without a safety net.[62]

Trostl arrived at LAX around 8 a.m. for the 9 a.m. flight on Pan American World Airways. He was with his wife and baby boy and had already placed most of his luggage in three lockers near the Pan American ticket counter the night before. A skycap helped him take his remaining baggage out of his van that morning and bring it to the ticket counter, where he obtained his boarding pass. They then went to the lockers to retrieve the rest of the luggage. A man who wanted to put his luggage in a locker but was not familiar with how the coin-operated lockers worked asked Trostl for his assistance. Trostl explained that he should put two quarters in the machine, put his luggage in a locker, close the door, and then turn and remove the key.[63]

Trostl started to walk back to the ticket counter when the man approached him again. "What are quarters?" asked George Moncur. He was flying from his home country of New Zealand to Scotland and was unfamiliar with American currency. He'd had a layover in Los Angeles and decided to spend the day visiting Disneyland. Trostl showed Moncur what a quarter was and watched as he successfully operated the machine. Just as Moncur was removing the key from the door, Trostl heard a loud pop and then an explosion. He saw a tremendous amount of orange-red flames come out from the lockers.[64]

It was 8:10 a.m. Trostl described what happened next, as only an aerialist who had spent so much time during his professional life suspended in the air could do in such great detail:

> I felt the impact, like a heavy 200 mile-an-hour wind. And it just started to lift me in the air. And I started moving up towards the ceiling and

back. I turned over. And I watched—the lockers themselves started to come apart. It was really strange. It seemed like it was in slow motion. Everything started, stopped, slowed down. I watched myself turn and float.... The ceiling was coming apart—started to fall. And pieces started flying. Big pieces of locker started flying all over the place. And I saw [Moncur] come up into the air with his head between his legs [and] he was just completely bent over. And then I saw a whole wall of lockers ... just head directly at the skycap himself and just mow him down like a steamroller. And then ... it blew me quite a ways. I landed on the floor. And then everything started happening real fast.[65]

Trostl lay wounded on the ground, moaning and in great pain. He suffered severe burns and injuries to his left thigh and chest.[66] A large piece of shrapnel tore up his thigh muscle and hit his rib cage. He also had shrapnel in his face, neck, and bladder. A medical student who performed as a clown just as a hobby and was traveling with the circus troupe tried to relieve some of Trostl's pain until the paramedics arrived. Trostl spent two weeks in a hospital and worked hard to rehabilitate himself so he could return to what he loved, the circus.[67] He was performing again by early 1975. But "The Great Arturo" would never be the same. "[He was] not as good or as reckless as he had performed in the past," his former manager and circus producer, Paul Kaye, said. "He would swing on the trapeze and catch himself by his heels. And some of that confidence that he had, that flamboyant style seemed to be gone."[68]

Also lying on the floor in great pain was Rev. Rhett Patrick Shaughnessy. He was pastor of the Northwest Missionary Church in Phoenix, Arizona, and had a five-minute weekday radio program titled *The Old Time Religion*. Before becoming a pastor, Shaughnessy, who was a high school dropout and ex-marine, had led a rough life, being described by one friend as "a boozer and a loser." He was flying from LAX to South Korea to preach at a monthlong series of interdenominational evangelistic meetings. He was standing at the Pan Am ticket counter when the blast occurred and was blown almost thirty feet into the air. "I felt like I was falling down a well and everything was black," he recalled. "I couldn't tell what altitude my body was in. But I felt the sensation of moving." Once he landed on the floor, he began to feel the pain. His right leg had been practically blown off, with the tissues greatly distorted and shredded and the muscles stripped off the bone. He was bleeding from his head and asked a nearby friend's wife, who was a nurse, to hold his head. She did so, but was screaming and crying. "She's a nurse," Shaughnessy said, "and she was panic-stricken. So I knew I was really badly injured without being able to see everything."[69]

Shaughnessy, thirty-four years old, was taken to a hospital where a doctor told him that they would have to amputate his right leg at the hip. "I remember saying to the doctor, 'Don't amputate at the hip because I got a lot of work to do yet. I don't want to lose it all.'" Doctors were able to save a small portion from the hip halfway down to his thigh. He took solace in the thought that he didn't need his leg to continue to be a pastor. Shaughnessy testified several years later how he came to terms with what happened to him: "I don't believe there are any accidents with God. Therefore, God allowed this to happen. He could have stopped it if he wanted to, but he didn't. I believe he's in control of my life. And that things he allows to come into my life he allows. Therefore, he allowed it. So there must have been a good purpose."[70]

No one, though, could yet see any purpose in what had just occurred at the Pan American terminal. The public and law enforcement agencies could only wonder if it was a terrorist attack. If it was, then there could be a multitude of suspects. Among these would be radical leftist groups such as the Weather Underground and the SLA, both of which had been active in Los Angeles in 1974. The Weather Underground had recently bombed the Los Angeles office of the California attorney general, Evelle Younger, claiming it was done in solidarity with "our sisters and brothers" in the SLA.[71] But the Weather Underground was not known for killing innocent civilians, so a bombing at an airport would not be part of their repertoire. They had also telephoned authorities in advance of the bombing at Younger's office, and the device had exploded when no one was in the building.[72] An airport bombing would also not fit the profile of SLA activity, which focused on specific targets, avoiding mass casualties.[73] Furthermore, the SLA was greatly weakened by the death of several of their members, including their leader, Donald DeFreeze, in the May shoot-out with Los Angeles police.

A terrorist bombing at LAX would also add a new dimension to the terrorist threat in the United States. Americans had become used to the numerous domestic hijackings that had occurred since the early 1960s, but those hijackings usually did not result in loss of life. Even those Americans who were victims of hijackings overseas tended to survive the ordeal. Just a few years earlier, on September 6, 1970, the Popular Front for the Liberation of Palestine (PFLP), a splinter group from the Palestine Liberation Organization, hijacked four planes (El Al, Pan American World Airways, Trans World Airlines, and Swissair) bound for New York from Europe and the Middle East. El Al security personnel shot one of the hijackers onboard and captured another as the plane landed in London. The PFLP then hijacked another plane, a British Overseas Airlines Corporation airliner, so they could have British hostages with which to bargain for their comrade's release. It worked, as Leila Khaled, one of the most famous female terrorists in the world at that time, was released in exchange for the British hostages. Hundreds of other hostages from many different countries, including the United States, were also eventually released from the other planes.[74]

But a bombing at an airport or on a plane would heighten Americans' fears of terrorism. It would mean you could now be killed when flying across the country or just waiting at an airport ticket counter.[75] And if the LAX bombing was the work of an international terrorist group, such as the Popular Front for the Liberation of Palestine–General Command, which was responsible for two midair plane bombings in Europe in 1970, or any of the multitude of terrorist groups operating around the world, then it would mean international terrorists had now come to America to wreck havoc. Americans could now only wait until there was an answer as to who was responsible for this first bombing at an airport anywhere in the world and what, if anything, was the reason.

There was speculation that the perpetrator may have wanted to bring the bomb onboard the Pan Am flight to Hawaii. "At this point in the terminal [the lobby] you are not required to go through security yet," William Sullivan, the assistant director in charge of the FBI's Los Angeles office, explained. "[The perpetrator] probably placed it here because he couldn't go out to the airplane area with it."[76] The general manager of the Los Angeles Department of Airports, Clifton Moore, tried to defend airport security from any blame for the attack: "It's impossible to guard against something like this. There was no warning."[77]

Meanwhile, the scene at the Pan Am terminal was utter chaos. Sergeant Rodney Holcomb was the LAPD's watch commander at the airport when the blast occurred. He was at the police substation in the middle of the airport when he saw gray smoke coming out of the top of the building where the Pan Am terminal was located. He ran over with three of his men, becoming the first officers to arrive at the scene. "When I entered the building," he said, "people were running in different directions, screaming and yelling. Some of the people were injured and holding different portions of their bodies. They were running from the building, holding their arms and limping." Holcomb also saw people lying on the floor, two of whom were dead. One was the skycap, Harper Glass, who had helped Trostl retrieve his luggage from the locker, and the other was Leonard Hsu, a passenger service representative for Pan Am. They were lying near where the lockers had been before the explosion. Holcomb could see that the lockers had been blown apart and the ceiling damaged.[78]

Not long after Holcomb entered the terminal, an army of law enforcement personnel descended onto LAX. This included David Butler of the LAPD's Scientific Investigation Division, who ordered an evacuation of people from the lobby and began to search for another bomb and additional hazards such as ruptured gas mains. There were about one hundred LAPD officers, ninety FBI agents, and ten bomb experts from the U.S. Treasury Department's Bureau of Alcohol, Tobacco and Firearms (ATF). Although the LAPD had primary jurisdiction, since a homicide (the death of the two people) had been committed on city territory, both the FBI and the ATF maintained "investigative liaisons" with the police. Their jurisdiction stemmed from a law that makes it a federal crime to destroy or damage any airport facility in the United States.[79]

While investigators searched for possible additional bombs and sifted through the rubble, collecting evidence and interviewing witnesses, paramedics treated the wounded. A priest gave last rites to the two dead victims. Four emergency medical teams from Los Angeles County–USC Medical Center were there. Ambulances from the LAFD and private companies transported victims to two hospitals, while four other hospitals were on standby.[80] Emergency room personnel at one of those hospitals, Centinela Community Valley Hospital near the airport, lined up behind wheelchairs and gurney carts outside the entrance to await the arrival of the victims.[81] The three most seriously wounded from the bombing were George Moncur, Rev. Shaughnessy, and Arturo Trostl Jr. Moncur died a few days later, bringing the final casualty total to three killed and thirty-five wounded.

Not surprisingly, police and most of the airlines at LAX received numerous bomb threats in the hours after the blast. One caller claimed that the entire Pan American building was going to be blown up. Another said that an explosive device had been planted at the Continental Airlines satellite. At 10 a.m., a person called Western Airlines and said, "Western's next. I've killed one or two people already, I'm going to kill more. The bomb is already in Western's Ticketing Building. You're going to be next." At around 11 a.m., police were told that there was a "ticking device" at United Air Lines. That, however, turned out to be a radio clock. Checking out all of the threats and searching for possible additional explosives took a whole day. At one point in the afternoon, an LAPD captain notified his commander that they needed to use explosive detection dogs from other agencies, since "our dogs are worn out." By 4:30 p.m. the LAPD crime lab and bomb squad, along with the FBI and ATF investigators, had completed examining and collecting evidence from the front lobby of the terminal. They next started the laborious process of examining the actual explosion area.[82]

This was the first time investigators in the United States had to deal with an explosion at an airport. Debris was scattered throughout the terminal building. They decided to use a grid system to collect and mark the items, beginning with the furthest point from the explosion and working inward toward the point of origin. The LAPD, FBI, and others worked throughout the day and night, putting various items from the debris into barrels and taking them to a police warehouse where everything could be examined more carefully. More than twelve hundred items were collected. All of the debris had radiated out from an area along a wall near the ticket counter where there had been a bank of lockers, indicating that that was where the explosion took place.[83] Investigators also planned to reconstruct the lockers, a painstaking process that would take a few days but which they hoped might reveal the specific locker where the bomb had been placed. That, in turn, might provide some clues as to who may have been responsible.[84]

Witnesses interviewed by the FBI and LAPD at the airport gave varying accounts of what they saw before and after the explosion. Several stated they saw people they believed were suspicious. These included a man in his thirties, approximately six feet tall, who left the terminal "in a great hurry" after the blast; a woman, roughly five foot four and under thirty years old, who was rushing through the parking lot moments after the bombing; a man, five foot nine to six feet tall, who placed a cardboard box in the lockers prior to the explosion; and a man in his thirties and about five foot five who took a taxi to the airport, arriving at 7:55 a.m., took a blue flight bag into the terminal, and then ran out of the terminal without the bag and with a smile on his face immediately after the blast.[85]

None of this information, however, resulted in the identification of a possible suspect. Another taxi driver reported seeing a man acting strangely before the explosion. A composite drawing was made, and an FBI agent in Hawaii was able to identify and interview the man. He turned out to be one of the members of the circus troupe (he worked with monkeys) that Arturo Trostl Jr. was traveling with and was cleared as a suspect.[86]

The Los Angeles Fire Department also could not provide any clues as to who may have been responsible for the carnage at the airport. Fire personnel are trained to observe the behavior of spectators at fires and other emergencies, since perpetrators sometimes like to admire the aftermath of their work. No one with the fire department, however, noticed any unusual behavior on the part of the victims or spectators either inside or outside the Pan Am terminal.[87]

While the investigation into the biggest bombing in LA history since the 1910 bombing of the *Los Angeles Times* building continued,[88] Conrad Casler knew that this was going to be a long night for him too. He had been the night city editor for the *Los Angeles Herald Examiner* for seven years but had just recently given notice to his superiors that he was resigning effective the middle of the month to take a job at a local newspaper closer to his home in Claremont, California. As night city editor for the *Herald Examiner*, his duties included supervising and assigning reporters and photographers to cover all local news.[89] He was the man in charge of making sure the newspaper was on top of anything that was happening at night in the sprawling metropolis of Los Angeles and its surrounding communities. The bombing of the airport earlier that day was, of course, the top news story in Los Angeles, and he expected to be quite busy that night. Little did he know, however, how significant a role both he and his newspaper would play in the coming weeks.

The *Herald Examiner* was known as a "flashy, scrappy paper" that competed for readers and advertisers with the more staid *Los Angeles Times*. William Randolph Hearst founded the paper in 1903, naming it the *Los Angeles Examiner*, and even maintained an apartment in the *Examiner* building during the 1920s and 1930s. He had built a nationwide empire of newspapers that "appealed to a mass readership with colorful, frequently sensationalistic headlines and reporting and a bluntly bellicose, 'yellow journalism'–type editorial policy."[90] In 1962 the *Examiner*, which was a morning newspaper, merged with the afternoon *Herald-Express* to form the *Herald Examiner*. The merged paper was then published as an afternoon daily. In 1967 it was the largest-circulation afternoon newspaper in the country, with a readership of about 700,000. However, a labor strike that began that year and lasted for a decade greatly hurt the newspaper. Picketers marched in front of businesses that advertised in the *Herald Examiner*. Its circulation dropped to less than 400,000 in 1968 and continued to decline annually.[91]

But a terrorism story is always good for the media. For the *Herald Examiner*, it was particularly welcome, despite the tragedy of the event and the loss of life, since it fit the newspaper's style of aggressive reporting. As one former editor of the paper noted, "Things were always done on the cheap and we were hugely outgunned by the resources of the *Los Angeles Times*, but we held our own by covering stories in guerrilla fashion—we would seize on a good story and milk it to death, with a lot of personality and chutzpah.[92]

As Casler settled into the large editorial office on the second floor of the

Herald Examiner building that night to begin his 10 p.m. to 6 a.m. shift, surrounded by many telephones and typewriters, he figured he'd be getting a lot of crackpot calls claiming responsibility for the attack or threatening another bombing. He was used to that, since his newspaper received, on average, a couple of prank bomb threats a day "until the night before a full moon, the night of the full moon, [and] the night after the full moon [when] it triples and quadruples."[93] The full moon had already appeared on August 2, so any crank calls this night would undoubtedly be related to the bombing at the airport.

But one of the first calls he received that night at about 10:20 p.m. did not sound like a prankster. The caller provided specific information regarding the bombing. Speaking with what Casler described as an Eastern Mediterranean accent, the caller said his name was Isak Rasim and that the group Aliens of America was responsible for the airport bombing.[94] Rasim also said that aliens were being mistreated by law enforcement people within the United States. He told Casler to write down the number T-225, because that was the number of the locker in which the explosive device had been placed. He described the device as an eleven-pound AN-DNB (ammonium nitrate, dinitrobenzene) bomb and gave the dimensions of the device as eighteen inches long and five inches in diameter. He also gave Casler the number of the key for the locker, 7G585.[95]

Casler immediately called a *Herald Examiner* reporter at the airport and told him to convey that information to investigators, who were still there collecting evidence. He also called the LAPD. Even though the police had not yet reconstructed the bank of lockers where the explosion took place, investigators were able to examine the floor and wall where the lockers had been and determine that the explosion occurred near lockers T-223 to T-226. Subsequent analysis after the lockers were reconstructed over the next few days confirmed that the bomb had indeed been placed in locker T-225, that the key number was 7G585, and that it was an AN-DNB bomb.[96]

The reporter at the airport called Casler back to let him know that the police "were pretty excited" about the information he had provided. Casler then got another call, this time from an LAPD officer, saying that they were coming right over to his office. The FBI also came over a short time later. Casler was asked not to print in his newspaper the locker number, key number, or the type of explosive and its dimensions. Casler agreed, well aware that if that information were made public, more people might be encouraged to call in claiming they'd done the bombing.[97]

The LAPD and the FBI made arrangements for what to do if and when Rasim called the *Herald Examiner* again. With Casler's and the newspaper's permission, they hooked up a tape recorder to one of the six incoming telephone lines at the city desk. The switchboard operator was told that any suspicious calls that might be the person calling back should be put on the first of these six lines. And no calls were to be put on that line except calls of a suspicious nature that might be the person calling back.[98]

Casler broke the news of the phone call from the mysterious man in the next edition of the newspaper. Meanwhile, he waited each night, hoping Rasim (who was in fact Kurbegovic) would call again. Kurbegovic, however, decided that his next move would be to make another cassette recording as he had done in early July. He telephoned the CBS television station in Los Angeles on August 9, telling them they could find a tape related to the bombing in a trash bin outside a local bank, along with the key to the airport locker where the bomb had been placed. On the tape he issued a dire warning to the country: "This is the voice of Aliens of America, Esak Rasim, Chief Military Officer, speaking. On Tuesday, August 6, 1974, we have opened your ears with an 11-pound AN-DNB bomb placed in a locker number T-225 at Los Angeles International Airport.... This first bomb was marked with the letter A, which stands for Airport. The second bomb will be associated with the letter L, the third with the letter I, etc., until our name has been written on the face of this nation in blood." When police reconstructed the canister that contained the explosive, the words "Aliens of America" were stamped on the outside ring.[99]

Kurbegovic, who became known in the media as the Alphabet Bomber, issued additional threats on this tape, including using sarin gas "to destroy the entire U.S. Capitol personnel."[100] He also expanded upon his antigovernment beliefs:

> As we have indicated earlier, we can step down from this insanity any time U.S. Government indicates it wants us to do so. All it needs to do

is to declare the entire body of immigration and naturalization laws unconstitutional, and to follow with a repeal of such laws. The principle of citizenship implies that there are citizens and slaves, and the Aliens of America being the slaves. As part of such change, all sex laws must disappear and Congress must more specifically separate church and state, as well as prohibit itself from ever passing any law relating to human sexual behavior.[101]

Kurbegovic also taunted one of his victims. "It is perhaps the God's will that Mr. Rit [sic] Shaughnessy of Phoenix, Arizona, has lost his leg. If he was an alien, he would be deported according to the immigration and naturalization law. We have earned death penalty many times over and we intend to go as far as is necessary, or as far as we can, to not only eliminate such laws, but to punish those who tolerate its existence."[102]

Police played portions of this August 9 tape at a press conference a week later, hoping someone might recognize the voice of the man calling himself Rasim. The LAPD and other law enforcement agencies didn't know if they were dealing with a lone wolf or the leader of a new terrorist group. The public was also anxious and scared. Where and when would the next bombing take place? If the terrorist or terrorists were going to actually spell out the name "Aliens of America" with a series of bombings, then anyplace in Los Angeles associated with the letter "L" could be the next target. Was it going to be the La Brea Tar Pits and Museum, a popular attraction in midtown Los Angeles? Or Larchmont Village, a quaint little neighborhood of shops and restaurants in the central part of the city? It could even be a place that doesn't have the letter "L" in its name, but if it's located in Los Angeles, then that could still be considered an "L" target.

It was going to be a tense rest of the summer in Los Angeles. On the very day that Rasim pledged more attacks, President Gerald Ford addressed the nation regarding the end of the Watergate scandal. "My fellow Americans," the new president said, "our long national nightmare is over."[103] Angelinos, however, could be forgiven if they didn't find those words very comforting. For them, the nightmare was just beginning.

3

A City in Fear

The day after the bombing, Los Angeles officials tried to reassure a jittery public that enhanced security measures would be taken to prevent a recurrence of the events of August 6. Clifton Moore outlined at a press conference a $100,000-a-year plan to boost airport security. This included the removal of all public lockers located outside security-checked areas; the relocation of all security-check areas to street entrances, which would make ticket counters accessible only to passengers and visitors who pass through electronic detection devices and have their packages searched; and an increase in the number of uniformed and plainclothes security guards at the airport. "I guess it's a sign of the times," he said.[1]

Los Angeles now joined cities around the world in adjusting to the realities of the threat of terrorism. Just one day before the bombing, President Richard Nixon, in one of his last acts as president before he resigned the office, signed into law the Anti-Hijacking Act of 1974, which, among other things, required the airport screening before boarding of all passengers and property by weapons-detecting technology, mandated a law enforcement presence at commercial service airports, and authorized the death penalty for hijackings that resulted in an individual's death.[2] Even though the airport attack was not a hijacking, the author of the bill, Rep. John Murphy (D-NY), urged that its death provision be applied to the person found guilty for the LAX bombing.[3]

The Los Angeles City Council announced on August 7 a $25,000 reward "for information resulting in apprehension of the person or persons who committed, attempted to commit or who conspired to commit such an act (the bombing)." A few days later, the airport matched that sum, with rewards eventually totaling $100,000.[4]

Meanwhile, investigators reconstructed the Pan Am lockers at a police warehouse. They had transported what was left of the lockers, along with the approximately 1,200 pieces of other debris from the explosion, and laid them out in an area the size of a basketball court. This allowed them to reconstruct the lockers as they had been positioned prior to the detonation. There were approximately 120 large pieces of metal lockers, numerous small pieces and fragments of lockers, and pieces of luggage. They were able to confirm that the explosion was centered in locker T-225. They examined what was remaining of the interior of that locker in order to determine blast and fragmentation patterns and to test for explosive residues. Those tests eventually indicated the presence of ammonium nitrates and dinitro-benzene. The former is a salt of ammonia and nitric acid, while the latter is a powder. Investigators also determined that the damage at LAX caused by the explosion was consistent with an eleven-pound AN-DNB bomb, just as Rasim had said. They were able, as noted earlier, to reconstruct the canister that contained the explosive and found the words "Aliens of America" stamped on the outside of it.[5]

Investigators, however, could not find any fragments of mechanical or electrical timing devices, such as watches or clocks (other than those that were inside someone's luggage or other belongings) that would have served as the trigger of the bomb.[6] Arleigh McCree, a member of the LAPD's Criminal Conspiracy Section, who specialized in bombing investigations and would later become head of the bomb squad, surmised that the bomb had been set off by a hypergolic initiator, a chemical-type delay mechanism in which detonation is caused by the mixing of two chemicals. "I believe it was sulfuric acid and potassium chlorate," said McCree. "Probably the separator mechanism was a balloon. When the acid eats through the balloon, it contacts the chemical and causes fire. That fire, in turn, lit a fuse, which was probably a green hobby fuse. That hobby fuse burned down to an improvised detonator, which . . . would [have] been about the diameter of a pencil and probably approximately eight inches in length. The homemade detonator was probably made of . . . a mixture of picric acid and litharge. When the detonator exploded, it initiated the ammonium nitrate and dinitrobenzene, causing . . . a tremendous explosion."[7]

Kurbegovic had once again demonstrated an impressive creativity in making a destructive device, just as he had previously done with the arson devices used in the attacks on the homes of Emmet McGaughey, Marguerite Justice, and Alan Campbell and on McGaughey's automobile. He had read several publications about the methodology of constructing hypergolic initiators and built a number of them in his Los Angeles apartment.[8]

Being creative was never a problem for Kurbegovic, who was always thinking outside the box. His insatiable curiosity and persistence in asking questions served him well for his evil intentions. He had "the ability to concentrate in a way that most normal people don't because he doesn't get distracted by anything," said Gerald Chaleff, Kurbegovic's public defender during his competency trial after his arrest. "And so he would focus on something and he could accomplish it. He could be incredibility intelligent when he focused on anything."[9]

Kurbegovic had learned from Stephen Smith, one of his supervisors and friend at RPM Industries, that any chemicals he wanted that were not available at RPM's lab could easily be purchased from chemical supply shops. Smith told him that Erb and Gray Scientific, Inc., in Culver City was a good one to use and that their catalog was available at RPM. "You just submit a purchase order [over the phone] and pick the items up," Smith said. He also told Kurbegovic that there were hardly any restrictions, such as special permits required, on the availability of hazardous chemicals, and that he would not even be asked for identification when calling in the order or picking it up.[10]

This was perfect for Kurbegovic, since he could pose as whomever he wanted to in order to not to have his purchases traced back to RPM. He told the people at Erb and Gray that he was purchasing the chemicals for the Culver City branch of Hughes Aircraft Company. Kurbegovic made several purchases in the period leading up to the LAX bombing and even had one of the salespeople help him put the chemicals into his car.[11]

Then, two days after the LAX bombing, an explosion and fire occurred at Erb and Gray at 11:15 p.m. The blast, which was caused by a pipe bomb, resulted in approximately $50,000 in damages to the Erb and Gray building and $10,000 in damages to twelve homes in the neighborhood. One neighbor was injured when struck by falling plaster from the ceiling of her front porch. All members of the Culver City Fire Department who battled the blaze suffered from the inhalation of chemical fumes. No one was ever arrested for the bombing, but prosecutor Dinko Bozanich and LAPD bomb expert Arleigh McCree both believed that Kurbegovic was responsible. "He bought many of his chemicals from [Erb and Gray]," said McCree, "but they finally became suspicious and refused to sell him any more," so he "blew up the supply house."[12]

At the same time, police were baffled by references Rasim made in his phone calls and taped messages about California senator Alan Cranston. On the night of the LAX bombing when he called Conrad Casler at the *Herald Examiner* to claim credit for the attack in the name of Aliens of America, Rasim told Casler, "Sen. Alan Cranston knows all about it." Investigators checked with Cranston's office but were unable to decipher the message. An aide to Cranston said that the senator had not received any threatening mail or phone calls.[13]

Then, on the August 9 tape in which Rasim pledged a bombing campaign "until our name has been written on the face of this nation in blood," he again mentioned Cranston, implying that the LAX bombing was carried out because Cranston had ignored a previous message from Aliens of America: "The bomb is our temporary response to the reaction that Senator Alan Cranston displayed to the taped message we have delivered to KPFK radio station a few weeks earlier."[14]

Later, it was discovered that Kurbegovic had placed a cassette tape near the radio station and called them to let them know where to find it. But before anyone from the station could retrieve the tape, Glenn Evans, who

worked at his father's scavenger and antique business located near the
KPFK studio and often drove around and picked up miscellaneous items
from the street, found the tape. Sometime between late July and early
August, he saw an item wrapped in a green paper towel lying alongside the
curb near the station. He unwrapped the towel, saw a cassette tape inside,
and put it on the front seat of his truck. He didn't bother to listen to it
and forgot all about it until August 12, when he decided to play it. To his
surprise, he heard the voice of Rasim pledging more bombings. He then
gave the tape to the FBI.[15]

On this tape, which was made before the LAX bombing, Kurbegovic
appealed to Senator Cranston to address several issues that were part of
Kurbegovic's personal agenda:

> We believe Mr. Cranston, that because you do not appeal to emotions,
> but reason, that because you are an informed man who knows how
> dangerous it is to keep church and state under the same roof, and who
> knows how dangerous it is to rape a man of his dignity without killing
> him at the same time, that you will forget the beating of empty drums
> of Watergate and other rain dancing, and get down to business of saving
> this nation from its two most acute ills, sex laws and immigration and
> naturalization laws. . . . I hope, Mr. Cranston, you will not underestimate
> our strength and determination to be treated with dignity and respect in
> accordance to our contribution to the greatness of this nation. I deeply
> believe you will succeed.[16]

Cranston was a liberal Democrat with a reputation, among other things, for
supporting immigrant and alien rights. For example, in 1971 he sponsored
a bill to prevent the deportation of any alien who had been convicted of
the possession of marijuana without the approval of the attorney general.[17]
He had also worked for an organization before World War II known as the
Common Council for American Unity, which tried to help immigrants
adjust to life in America and help Americans adjust to having immigrants in
the country.[18] He was perceived as a friend of immigrants, and Kurbegovic
believed he would be receptive to his message.

Upon learning that the LAX bomber had previously appealed to him for help, Cranston tried to explain to Rasim what had happened regarding the cassette tape. "It's only just been found and given to me," Cranston said on August 16. "That's why I haven't responded until now." He urged Rasim to "call me right now before you do anything else."[19] The *Herald Examiner* put the plea on its front page: "To Aliens of America: Senator Alan Cranston's office in the Federal Building at 1100 Wilshire Blvd., will have office personnel manning the phone today and all next week awaiting a call from members of Aliens of America." The newspaper published Cranston's office phone number, but Rasim never called.[20] He was having too much fun dealing with newspapers and radio stations.

Manipulating the Media

Kurbegovic learned from the Symbionese Liberation Army the value of utilizing the media to one's advantage. The SLA pioneered the practice of manipulating the media following its kidnapping of Patty Hearst in February 1974. The leftist revolutionary group had actually issued its first communiqué months earlier, following the assassination of Marcus Foster, Oakland's superintendent of schools. But it was in the period following the Hearst kidnapping that it flooded the media with a barrage of messages. They sent written statements to newspapers and tape recordings to radio stations.[21] Everyone awaited the next message from this mysterious group. There were demands, such as a free food program for the poor in exchange for Hearst's release, surprises such as Patty stating she had joined the SLA, and other information. While the FBI and various law enforcement agencies desperately tried to find the groups' members, the use of the media by the SLA made it appear that they had the upper hand. They were calling the shots, and law enforcement was only reacting to each new development.

But the SLA was more of a curiosity for the public than a real threat. The group did not threaten innocent civilians, nor did they instill the fear that many terrorist groups do. The same could not be said for the Alphabet Bomber. Kurbegovic had proven he could kill at random and was going to use the media to fan the flames of fear as best he could. And the media was a willing partner.

The *Herald Examiner* took the lead in reporting on the story during the summer of 1974. Part of this was due to the fact that Conrad Casler, the paper's nighttime city desk editor, had been the first person to receive a phone call from Kurbegovic after the LAX bombing, and he and others at the city desk continued to received calls from him throughout the crisis. This gave them a head start and more detailed reporting on the story than the other newspapers, including the *Los Angeles Times*. True to form, the *Herald Examiner* also covered the Alphabet Bomber story as they covered other stories, "in guerrilla fashion," and had no qualms about exploiting it "with a lot of personality and chutzpah."[22]

On the evening of August 14, Casler received another phone call from Rasim, directing him to an address on Olive Street in downtown Los Angeles, where he was told there was a cassette tape. Rasim began the conversation, as he did all his phone calls, with a code word, "T-225." That would confirm his was not a hoax call, since the locker number where the bomb exploded at LAX had not been publicly disclosed. He told Casler the new tape was under a large trash container and that he should not bring the police with him to pick it up.[23]

Not knowing whether he was retrieving a cassette tape or Rasim was tricking him with a bomb or something else, Casler drove by the address slowly. He saw the trash container in a small parking lot between two buildings. He kept driving for another block, made a U-turn, and drove back and parked directly across the street from the trash bin. He then carefully approached it. But when he smelled something burning, he immediately ran to the corner. He waited a while until the smoke odor dissipated and then walked back to the trash bin. He noticed then a green towel wrapped around an object under the dumpster. He picked it up and felt something hard inside. He went back to his office and unwrapped it in the presence of law enforcement personnel. He played the tape and had two of his reporters transcribe it, and then he turned the tape over to the LAPD and the FBI.[24]

On this tape, Kurbegovic again threatened to unleash nerve gas over populated areas:

We, the Aliens of America, indeed intend to make this nation an alternative to life elsewhere, and the only way we can do that is by fighting.

We, however, do not intend to fight a long, agonizing battle. . . . Our goal is three months from now as we shall have at latest within three months from now, two tons of sarin nerve gas which we shall deliver in one-quarter ton shells to the Capitol Hill by the use of eight single-shot cannon barrels. With it we shall destroy the entire personnel of Capitol Hill. Of course, if your Supreme Court comes into existence and if it suddenly finds that the immigration and naturalization laws are indeed un-Constitutional, and if it finds that Bible is not the supreme law of this land, and if it finds that this is the nation of free men and every restriction on freedom borders on treason, then we will not have to go through [with this].[25]

Kurbegovic also offered praise to Casler's newspaper: "This tape is being delivered to Los Angeles Herald-Examiner in our deepest admiration for their heroic and historic battle against Communism."[26] Seizing on this latest threat, the *Herald Examiner* had a banner headline the next day that read, "L.A. BOMBER PLEDGES GAS ATTACK."[27] They printed the entire transcript of the tape so that anyone who read the entire story would see that this latest threat concerned Washington DC and not Los Angeles. But still, it added to the fear gripping the city. In other tapes, Rasim singled out Los Angeles for a nerve gas attack. He stated that he was researching different ways to disperse chemical warfare agents in order to kill as many people as possible. "We just acquired the plans of thirty major skyscrapers' air conditioning systems," he said. "We visit the building, see where its air inlet is . . . and take a walk. Maybe watch a Dodgers' game and enjoy ourselves."[28]

The prospect of chemical warfare agents being put into the air-conditioning systems of Los Angeles skyscrapers greatly worried prosecutor Dinko Bozanich. "How many high-rise buildings are there in just down-town Los Angeles, in a very small confined area?" he wondered. "How many people are in one of these high-rise buildings? And if you do put something into the ventilation system [it] could cripple or kill hundreds, thousands. And yet this guy, he clearly had the brains to be able to read and understand [how to do it]."[29]

Although Rasim was threatening to utilize chemical warfare agents in his taped messages, the police and the FBI were more concerned at the time with where the next bombing might take place. They knew, if Rasim was to be believed, that the target would be associated with the letter "L," the second letter in "Aliens of America." But with countless potential "L" targets, it became a guessing game for law enforcement. Nevertheless, they prepared a list of possible sites. These included, among others, the Lincoln Heights Jail, the L.A. Rams, El Al Airlines (the "L" in "El"), and Los Alamitos (a racetrack).[30]

They also wanted to stay one step ahead of Rasim and be ready in case he didn't follow the spelling of his group's name in order, so they prepared a list of possible targets with names beginning with "I," the third letter in "Aliens of America." These included the Immigration and Naturalization Service building in downtown Los Angeles; Reverend "Ike," who was scheduled to appear at the Inglewood Forum; the Humanist Association, which was next door to IBM on Wilshire Boulevard; the Immanuel Episcopal Church; the Israeli Consulate; the Induction Center; the Department of the Interior; the IRS; Griffith Park Observatory ("Eye in the Sky"); Terminal Island; intensive care units (in all hospitals); the Mr. International weightlifters contest; the Ice Follies; and the American Independent Party.[31]

This list of some of the potential "L" and "I" targets illustrates the difficult task law enforcement faced trying to protect Los Angeles and the surrounding areas from Rasim's next bomb. Rasim also continually threw the police off his trail by dropping clues that led nowhere. For example, in a phone call to the *Herald Examiner* on August 13, he told Casler, "We have placed another one which will go off . . . this Sunday [August 18] in a crowded area." Casler tried to get more information from Rasim. "At the airport?" he asked. "No sir," Rasim replied. "We will not say where it will be . . . but . . . the bomb is 25 pounds, and we will tell you where it is if the charges for murder have been brought against former Los Angeles Police Commissioner Emmet C. McGaughey." This baffled Casler. "Who?" he asked. Rasim repeated the name and also added another one. "And the charges for murder are [also] brought against present Police Captain George Reynolds Millmore [*sic*]," Rasim stated, "They have murdered two Mexican Nationals in skid row apartments in Los Angeles and covered it up as a . . . just mistake shooting. We have the evidence which we will bring forward that they have murdered—" Casler cut him off and asked, "Where can we get the evidence?" Rasim simply replied, "We have it, good night."[32]

The phone call alarmed officials. The LAX bomber was now threatening to detonate a bomb more than twice as large as the eleven-pound bomb used at the airport. The mention of a shooting on Skid Row also baffled police. Two Mexican nationals were killed by police gunfire in an apartment on Skid Row in Los Angeles on July 16, 1970. Police had gone to the apartment looking for an armed murder suspect they believed was hiding there. They instead found six illegal immigrants who did not speak or understand English. Four of the LAPD officers involved in the shooting faced criminal charges, but these were dismissed by the court before any trial. McGaughey and Milemore had nothing to do with the incident. Police knew from a taped message they received on August 12 (the day before the phone call with Casler) that Rasim claimed credit for firebombing the homes of former police commissioners McGaughey and Justice. And now he mentioned Milemore, who was an LAPD captain and the commanding officer of the Police Commission Investigation Division, a key player in denying Kurbegovic the permit to open a taxi dance hall. They therefore now had additional information that Rasim had a gripe against the police commission. But the mention of the Skid Row shooting meant they would have to now look at all possible clues from that incident to see if any led to the identity of Rasim.

The police asked Casler not to mention the names of McGaughey and Milemore in the story he wrote about Rasim's phone call. Casler complied with this request. The *Los Angeles Times* also ran a story about the phone call, suggesting that the authorities now had a motive for the airport bombing. "The 'mistake' shooting deaths of two Mexican nationals by police four years ago surfaced Wednesday as a possible motive in the bombing at Los Angeles International Airport on Aug. 6 that took three lives," the *Times* story read. The *Times* also bought in to Rasim's ploy that he was part of a group: "The caller also reportedly used the term 'we,' raising the possibility that others might be involved."[33]

Rasim called the *Herald Examiner* again on August 16 at approximately

8:45 p.m. Casler had momentarily stepped out of the office (he sometimes arrived at work early in case Rasim called), so FBI special agent Frederick Lanceley, who was at the newspaper at the time, answered the phone. Lanceley had just recently joined the FBI. "I was very nervous," he recalled, when he realized he was talking to the Alphabet Bomber. He tried to keep him on the phone as long as he could so that the call could be traced. The FBI and the LAPD were maintaining a stakeout in a relatively small area in downtown Los Angeles where the first three numbers of the prefix of the public telephones from which Rasim was calling were located. They were hoping that when notified that Rasim was calling the *Herald Examiner*, they might be able to see someone on a public phone in that area and question him. The stakeout, though, never produced any results.[34]

As Lanceley tried to prolong the conversation over the phone, he also wanted to obtain more information from Rasim about why he wanted charges brought against McGaughey and Milemore. "What is the evidence against McGaughey and Milmore [*sic*]?" he asked. "Do you still have that?" Rasim simply replied, "Later on," and gave Lanceley the address of a Texaco station on Los Angeles Street, where he said he had put another cassette tape inside a trash bin. He said that the tape would reveal "much, much bigger things" that would happen.[35]

That night, Lanceley and an LAPD officer retrieved the tape. On it, Rasim had a surprise for everyone:

> This is the voice of Aliens of America, Esak Rasim, Chief Military officer, speaking. The letter "L" in our name stands for "locker" and it also stands for "life." We have planted an extremely sensitive, delinquent, and unpredictable bomb in a locker number 625 at L.A. Greyhound Bus Depot downtown. We believe that whoever would have attempted to remove that bomb would cause it to explode. The bomb contains no evidence whatsoever that could lead to us and consequently we can disclose its location before it blows up on its own due to the presence of amonium [*sic*] chlorate in it.
>
> Thus, we have decided that because our cause is getting publicity that it is momentarily not necessary to continue to horrify the population

of this land, and we can afford the luxury of revealing the location of such bomb and let it stand for the word, "life"! Nothing, could make us happier than if we could conclude that we can reveal the location of bomb 'I,' which is already planted.[36]

With this taped message, Rasim revealed that he was closely following his own exploits in the media and was pleased so far with how the story was playing out. Since he had credibility and had already killed people with a bomb, the police had to take the threat of a bomb at the Greyhound terminal very seriously. Rasim's description of the Greyhound bomb as containing ammonium chlorate worried bomb expert Arleigh McCree. "I sure didn't like the name of it," McCree recalled. Although he was not familiar with ammonium chlorate causing a bomb to detonate, "there are other substances that I am personally aware of that could cause that effect," he said. "And it appeared to me that this individual may have come up with an innovative idea that would work and would cause such an explosion of that bomb. So my concern was greatly increased by that person's statements about delinquent ammonium chlorate."[37]

The Greyhound Bomb

It was a Friday night, and the Greyhound terminal, located in the Skid Row section of Los Angeles, was packed with approximately a thousand travelers. Members of the bomb squad rushed to the scene, red lights flashing and sirens blaring. The terminal was evacuated, with hundreds of people now lining the adjacent streets away from the building. The sight of the bomb squad entering the bus station scared a lot of people. "I saw the bomb squad," said one traveler. "I've seen [them before] on [the] television news. I turned white."[38]

Meanwhile, Assistant Police Chief Daryl Gates had laid down guidelines for how to handle the situation inside the terminal. Officer David Butler, who was assigned to the Scientific Investigation Division due to a specialty in firearms identification and explosives and had been one of the first on the scene after the LAX bombing, recalled that Gates was concerned for the safety of his men. "I do not want you people hurt," Gates told them. "Under no circumstances are you to jeopardize your own lives for this particular call. If the bomb goes off and the building is destroyed, you are not to get injured in the process. Walk away from it."[39]

Gates and many LAPD officers were concerned that they could, in fact, be the target of the bomb inside locker 625, if there was an explosive device there. They were worried that the bomb was built so it could not be disarmed safely and that it would explode upon being handled. "As much of a problem [that Kurbegovic] created from a police standpoint and a public safety standpoint by the LAX bomb . . . and [the] tapes that are now popping up," said Dinko Bozanich, "what about if the LAPD's bomb squad had been knocked out? Now you've really got them by the huevos."[40]

After evacuating people from the bus depot, two explosive detection dogs were used to confirm that there were explosives in locker 625. Detectives Loren Wells and Dwayne Schuby worked each dog, named King and Hans, independently. Both dogs caught an airborne scent originating from locker 625 and sat down in front of the locker. When explosive detection dogs sit down in front of an object, it signals to their handlers that there are explosives at the site.[41]

Following Gates's guidelines, Butler decided to open the door to the locker remotely to reduce the risk of injury or death to him and other members of the squad. First, he and his colleagues removed the locking mechanism without opening the door. Then they attached a line to the door and pulled on the line from a safe distance. The goal was to not be in a direct line from a potential blast. Butler and three other members of the bomb squad placed themselves behind a concrete-reinforced wall around a corner east of the locker. It wasn't an ideal place, but it was the best they could find under the circumstances. Butler expected an explosion upon opening the door: "Realizing what had happened at the LAX and the amount of destruction there," he said, "and [that] we had a similar situation here in [the] lockers . . . I realized that if that bomb had gone off anywhere near the magnitude as the one at LAX, that we may not get out of that building without sustaining injuries even though we had secreted ourselves behind a one foot thick . . . of a re-enforced concrete wall." Due to the configuration of the bus depot, which was more like a long corridor than one big room, Butler and his colleagues were no more than fifteen or twenty feet away from the locker at any given time.[42]

After asking if everyone was ready, Butler said, "Let's do it." With great trepidation, he gently pulled on the line and then waited a couple of minutes. Because he was around a wall from the locker, he could not see if the door had opened. But he'd felt the tension on the end of the line and then felt the release of that tension as he'd let go. He then looked around the corner and saw that the locker door was open. He noticed a brown satchel inside. Along with the other officers, he walked to within inches of the bag, which had a flat bottom and curved top with two handles. Butler took two photographs of the satchel in order to document what it looked like prior to a possible explosion that would have destroyed the bag.[43]

Butler was now ready to open the bag and attempt to render safe any potential bomb that might be there. However, another officer, DeWayne Wolfer, the LAPD's chief forensic chemist and head of the bomb squad (and one of its first members when it was formed in 1950), argued that would be too dangerous, since they could only see one side of the bag given its position in the locker and that trying to open the bag from that position might trigger the device. Butler, therefore, hooked up a pulley system in order to extend a rope over the locker and tie it to the two handles of the satchel. This would allow him to raise the package, swing it out of the locker, and then gently bring it down to the floor. They placed a backpack they'd found in the bus depot on the floor to serve as cushioning material for the satchel.[44]

The idea was to then pull the satchel out of the bus depot and into the bomb trailer that was waiting outside the building. But as soon as Butler began pulling on the line, it broke. The package was still in the locker. He went out to the trailer and retrieved a heavier line. After attaching it to the satchel he began pulling, but once again the weight of the bag was too much, and the line was almost pulled from Butler's hands. He had managed, however, to pull the satchel from the locker, and it was now lying on the floor on its side.[45]

Things were not going as planned. And they didn't have time on their side. They weren't sure of the type of trigger and timing mechanism of the device or how it might be actuated. "We were under time restraints to work . . . as fast as we could," Butler recalled. "We couldn't take two or three hours."[46] He also knew what would occur if the device detonated inside the building:

> As you look at the Greyhound Bus Station there's a lot of window space and all the doors are glass. When you have a detonation inside a building, the first thing that's going to leave is that glass because it's not as strong as walls. Hence, if you have a very high detonation what you are doing is you are driving the broken glass away from the building and if you have people standing in front of the building there are going to be some horrible injuries from flying glass. Now, we had several hundred citizens outside. We had mothers with babies, children. And the officers out in the street were hard pressed to control the situation out there because this is basically the skid row section of Los Angeles Street. There's a lot of derelicts in the area who come wandering in and out and they can't control them all. You have people from the lower economic strata of our society, Mexican-Americans [and others] . . . utilizing that facility of the Greyhound Bus Station that don't know English. They can't comprehend what's going on.
>
> It was a no win situation out there for the patrol officers. . . . What are you going to do with 500 people? What are you going to do when you have buses coming in? Where are the Greyhound people going to put their buses? We had all these circumstances to take into factor. The circumstances where the device was located in that locker was really not that conducive to taking it apart there even if the people had been removed from the general area because if the bomb is big enough you're going to shatter windows in adjoining buildings. So where were you going to take all these people? 10 blocks? 20 blocks? We don't know.[47]

With the satchel on the ground near the locker, Butler manually pulled the bag along the floor and out of the building. He then hooked it up to another pulley system that was on the bomb trailer. The idea was to pull the satchel off the ground and into the trailer. But again, things went wrong. The line slipped out of the pulley system, and the satchel fell between the trailer and a curb.[48]

At this point, Detective Wells ran over, picked the satchel up by hand, and placed it inside the bomb tube that was in the trailer. No one knew whether the bag falling from the pulley system might have actuated a timing mechanism or something else in the device. Wolfer, the forensic chemist, then got into the truck attached to the bomb trailer and quickly drove away. He was going to take the bomb to a vacant lot between the police academy and Dodger Stadium, where they would then decide what to do with the device.[49]

If the LAPD officers present at the scene thought the immediate danger was over with the trailer moving away from the bus depot, they were mistaken. First, Wolfer had to make a U-turn after a short distance because the direction he was driving was blocked by people in the streets. Then, with sirens blaring from police cars and motorcycles escorting the trailer, a large cloud of smoke billowed out from it. That was enough to convince the motorcycle officers to peel away quickly. "There was two . . . officers in front of me," Butler said, "and all of a sudden they were gone, and they made a left turn someplace and disappeared into the evening, realizing what had happened." Butler, who was driving one of the police cars next to the trailer, tried to radio Wolfer about the smoke but learned later that Wolfer never heard the transmissions. Wolfer continued driving, unaware of the new development.[50]

Butler and the other officers driving the police cars put their vehicles between the crowd and the trailer, hoping to shield people from a possible blast effect and fragmentation. Although the device did not detonate after it started smoking, Butler knew it could do so at any second. He thought the smoke could be what was known as a "hang fire." "It [may have] started to actuate," Butler said, "but for some reason didn't complete the process and it was just hanging there. And anything could set it off. So that heightened our anxiety to get to the location as soon as possible."[51]

The police escort shut down the Hollywood and Pasadena Freeways as the bomb truck sped along to its destination. After arriving at the vacant lot, Butler stayed to keep an eye on the trailer while the other officers returned to the bus depot. The bomb squad felt they had accomplished their mission in saving lives by moving the bomb to a safe area and that there was now no urgency to dismantle or detonate the bomb. The more pressing issue was the possibility that there were additional bombs in other lockers at the bus station. When they arrived back at the bus station, however, they learned that Arleigh McCree had already, with assistance from other officers, opened every locker and examined its contents. No additional devices were found.[52]

When the bomb squad returned to the vacant lot where Butler was keeping an eye on the device, they decided to take the satchel out of the bomb tube in the trailer. Butler carried the bag to a hard blacktop area adjacent to the lot and carefully set it on the ground. Then, after photographs were taken of the device still inside the satchel, Butler physically lifted a cylinder tank from the satchel and set it down on the blacktop. The explosive detection dogs were again used and alerted the squad to the presence of explosives inside the cylinder.[53]

It was now two o'clock in the morning. Everyone was exhausted, but there was still work to be done. There was still the possibility it might explode, so they couldn't just leave the bomb at the vacant lot and come back the next day. The decision was thus made to dismantle it at the site. After everyone moved away from the immediate area, Butler began working on the device.[54] In these situations, he always imagined that he and the bomber were alone, locked in a battle of wits. He didn't like the thought that a bomber might know explosives better than he did. But he always visualized that the bomber was somehow watching him: "I know the guy watches me," he said. "If he's not in the crowd he'll watch me on television."[55]

Butler sat down and put his legs around the device. This was to prevent his bumping or knocking it over, which could happen if he was kneeling over the device. That might cause the bomb to detonate. He then began to pull the plug out of the cylinder tank using a large crescent wrench and applied even pressure to try and open it. He did this very gingerly to avoid any jerking motions that might set the bomb off. But shortly after he started to pull the plug off, he heard a hissing sound coming from inside the tank. Not knowing what caused that, he quickly moved far away from the device. Once the hissing stopped, he returned to the device. He finished removing the plug but couldn't see what was inside through the small opening where the plug had been. He therefore used a wooden rod to probe the tank's contents and extract some type of residue that could be analyzed. When he pulled the wooden rod out of the tank, he noticed that something had adhered to the probe. It looked to him like ammonium nitrate prills. Wolfer, the bomb squad leader at the site with Butler, preserved the sample.[56]

The bomb squad decided there was no reason to work on the device any further, since they weren't sure of all the chemicals and other materials that comprised the bomb and the danger it posed to them. They transported it to a police explosive locker, which was a concrete structure with a steel door and locks located in a safe area. It would be stored there until a final decision, based on the results of a chemical analysis, could be made regarding what to do with the device.[57]

A few days later, the LAPD decided not to take any more risks in trying to dismantle the bomb. They took it out to an explosives range in Chino, California, and detonated it. The residue was analyzed, and it was determined that the bomb contained ammonium nitrate, picric acid, nitrobenzene, and other chemicals and materials. The device was intended to detonate through a hypergolic initiator, like the LAX bomb, that would start a first fire from a mixture of chlorate and sugar, which would then ignite a green hobby fuse. That, in turn, would burn the adapter plug to the detonators and set them off. McCree said that the Greyhound bus bomb did not explode because "the material in the . . . cylinder had too rich a mixture of the nitrobenzene. Had there been less nitrobenzene present . . . the device would have been more susceptible to detonation, because you can get too rich a mixture."[58]

The city of Los Angeles dodged a bullet that Friday night. The bomb had been placed in a locker located in the busiest part of the depot, where most of the people there had to pass. The twenty-five-pound bomb was, at the time, one of the largest bombs in the history of Los Angeles. Police estimated that had it gone off, one hundred people would have been killed.[59] Rasim, in just over one week, had made a bomb twice as large as the one he used at LAX. The Alphabet Bomber was learning quickly how to make deadly devices, and there was no telling what kind of bomb, or even nerve gas, he was planning for his next attack.

Closing In

With the Greyhound bus terminal bomb scare over, the authorities now focused on the next letter of Rasim's alphabet scheme, the letter "I." He had said that the "I" bomb was already planted when he revealed the locker number for the Greyhound bus bomb. As noted, the police had compiled a list of potential "I" targets. But the fact that the "L" bomb was at a bus station confused a lot of people, including the police. "We're going to look everywhere [for the bomb]," said LAPD spokesman Commander Peter Hagan, "and won't disregard a place just because it begins with an 'M' and not an 'I.' We learned from the Greyhound experience that we don't have his alphabet formula down yet. Who would think of the Greyhound site as an 'L' place? It was a throw-off."[60]

Many people, though, thought that the Alphabet Bomber was indeed going in order through the alphabet, since the first bomb was at an airport, for the letter "A," and the next one was at a bus terminal, for the letter "B." The third bomb, therefore, could be at a place with the letter "C," such as the Los Angeles Coliseum. The public was confused and scared.

The *Herald Examiner* added to the public's anxiety with a banner headline on August 17: "RACE AGAINST TIME TO FIND THIRD BOMB."[61] But as usual, Rasim continued to toy with the authorities and the media. He called the *Herald Examiner* on August 17, saying he had decided to postpone his next bombing, which he had earlier warned would be associated with the letter "I" and would go off on Sunday, August 18. "We have postponed our activities," he said, "pending . . . whatever will happen next." Leo Batt, who worked at the newspaper and took the call, asked Rasim, "Well, are you like postponing it from Sunday?" Rasim replied, "Sunday is off. Nothing will happen on Sunday. Nothing. And we hope that the people concerned will read the United States Constitution and will read also the Immigration and Naturalization Law."[62]

Rasim further added, "Pending the outcome we have postponed our activity hoping that something good will happen." Batt was confused. "Pending what?" he asked. Rasim replied, "Pending the outcome of . . . whatever the people's representatives will do." Batt then tried to reason with Rasim: "You know," he said, "that Senator Cranston called us this morning and he asks that somebody communicate with him at a certain telephone number, so that you can, you know, get some help from those government sources. Does that help you in any way?" At that point, the operator interrupted to say, "It is now three minutes." Kurbegovic apparently did not put additional coins into the pay phone he was calling from to continue the conversation. Batt again asked, "Well, does that help you in any way?" Rasim did not respond.[63]

Despite Rasim's assurance that there would not be a bombing on Sunday, the LAPD went on a full-scale alert. They created a one-thousand-man task force to search theaters, churches, parks, and other areas where crowds might gather. The public was also asked to help prevent another attack. "Our officers will stop by churches and alert the members to do their own searching," said Commander Hagan. The FBI and private security forces also set up rigid screening procedures at many public events throughout the city. "We have no way of knowing whether he is telling the truth," Hagan said. "He could be sincere, but then again it could be a ruse. We just can't afford to take any chances."[64]

With everyone on edge for a possible bombing on Sunday, the city was rocked by a massive explosion Saturday night at a downtown trucking company warehouse. Four people were injured in the blast, which leveled a block of the industrial district and caused $5 million in damages. Windows were shattered within a half-mile radius of the blast, which was heard and felt up to twenty-five miles away. Thousands of fans at a Los Angeles Rams–Kansas City Chiefs exhibition football game at the Los Angeles Memorial Coliseum four miles away watched as a ten-story ball of flame rose skyward. "It looked like an atom bomb," said one spectator at the game. "Then about five seconds later, a huge jolt shook the Coliseum."[65]

Could this be the work of the Alphabet Bomber? Many people, including law enforcement personnel, jumped to that conclusion, since the blast had occurred in the industrial district of Los Angeles and could therefore be the "I" bomb. Adding to the fear caused by the possibility that the Alphabet Bomber had struck again was that he was escalating each attack: first an eleven-pound bomb at LAX, then a twenty-five-pound bomb at the

Greyhound bus depot. This new blast near the Coliseum appeared to be even more powerful than the previous bombs. Mayor Tom Bradley and City Councilman John Ferraro were on the scene within an hour, and both promised a full-scale investigation of the blast.[66]

In the midst of all of this, Rasim called the *Herald Examiner* the next day to claim credit for the explosion. "This is T-225," he said, using the code word to let the newspaper know this wasn't a crank call. "Last night, the work on 7th and Mateo [where the blast occurred] is delinquent leftovers from our activities one week ago," he said. "Our promise to keep you next few days clean of fireworks [is] still in effect; and we want some public reaction, on behalf of public representatives in order not to shorten those few days." Jack Brown, the *Herald Examiner* employee who took the call, asked Rasim, "What reaction would suit you?" Rasim replied, "What we have asked. We want action in our favor; legislative, judicial, everything."[67]

By this time, however, investigators had determined that the blast at the Star Trucking Company warehouse was due to the accidental detonation of a five-ton truckload of benzoyl peroxide. Angelinos, however, still stayed home on Sunday, scared that the Alphabet Bomber would strike again. Only thirty-five hundred people showed up for a Watts Summer Festival concert at the Coliseum, which featured music superstar Stevie Wonder, among other performers. A crowd of seventy thousand had been expected. Similarly, a sold-out crowd of eighteen thousand was expected to attend a sermon by New York evangelist Frederick Eikerenkoetter II, popularly known as the "Reverend Ike," at the Forum in Inglewood, but only six thousand went.[68]

The small turnout for the Watts Festival was devastating for its organizers. They ended up with a debt of $150,000 and could not pay their bills. The festival, which had grown out of the Watts riots of August 1965, was seen by some "as a remedy against lingering hostility and pro-riot activism" in the African American community. The financial losses caused it to be suspended for several years.[69]

Police had their hands full that Sunday, searching everywhere for a possible bomb. Complicating matters was a deluge of bomb threats made in phone calls to police switchboards, newspapers, and businesses. Police had to be sent to investigate any address given in the warnings. At LAX, approximately one thousand people were evacuated from the terminal serving Pacific Southwest Airlines, Hughes Airwest, and Continental Airlines following a bomb threat. Delta Airlines also received a bomb threat, forcing the evacuation of the terminal serving it. Evacuations also occurred at the Shrine Auditorium in Los Angeles following a report of a suspicious item, which turned out to be a bag of raisins. Other places named by callers claiming that there were bombs there included the Inglewood Forum, the Coliseum, several local radio and television stations, bus facilities, and Will Rogers State Historic Park.[70]

True to his word, Rasim didn't set off any bombs that day. But he had single-handedly shut down an entire city. It had been an incredibly stressful weekend for the LAPD, beginning with the bomb placed in the locker at the Greyhound depot Friday night and the bomb threats throughout the city on Sunday. The police were frustrated, angry, and more determined than ever to capture this elusive terrorist. But thus far, all leads led nowhere.

The playing of portions of one of Rasim's taped messages at an LAPD press conference on August 16 in the hope that someone might recognize the voice only produced dead ends. Not surprisingly, the police received numerous calls by people claiming to know who the Alphabet Bomber was. Typical of these was one woman who called to say that she recognized the voice to be that of a young man with dark hair and blue eyes who was from Czechoslovakia. She gave his name and said that she had more information about him but did not want to reveal it over the phone. She said she was leaving to go on vacation in a couple of hours. Police therefore had to quickly go to her home to interview her, which wasted precious time and produced no useful information.[71]

In another call, a woman said that she and her boyfriend had been in Tijuana, Mexico, the last week of June 1974 and that she was shopping by herself when a Mexican man approached her and began talking to her. He said his name was Isaac Rozene, although she wasn't sure of the spelling. He spoke in broken English and was upset that Americans came to Mexico to take advantage of Mexicans by purchasing their goods at very low prices. He expressed contempt for Americans but then asked her out on a date.

The woman left and didn't think anything of the meeting until she heard the name "Rasim" mentioned in the media in connection with the LAX bombing. She then called the police with this information, which, like all the tips and calls coming into the police and the FBI, did not produce any meaningful results.[72]

Linguists who analyzed Rasim's taped messages and recorded phone calls couldn't agree on the origins of his accent. First, it was believed to be Middle Eastern. Then it was identified as Hungarian, Lithuanian, or possibly Russian.[73] However, Nancy Watson, the judge in Kurbegovic's criminal trial, recalled that linguists were indeed able to pinpoint exactly where the accent came from. "They not only figured out that he was Yugoslavian," she said, "but where he came from [within Yugoslavia]."[74]

Profiles of Rasim were also constructed. One compiled by the FBI believed him to be probably over forty years old with a Baltic, Slav, Arabic, or North African ethnic background.[75] Another one by the FBI listed Yugoslav as one of the strong possibilities for his nationality.[76] As is true of some profiles, though, they only provide general information, such as the age, ethnicity, marital status, and personality of the perpetrator of a crime, which, even if accurate, may not significantly reduce the number of potential suspects. But there have been some famous cases in which profiling helped catch a criminal. One of these was actually the first time profiling was used by law enforcement. It involved an individual known as the "Mad Bomber," who, like the Alphabet Bomber, terrorized a city and frustrated law enforcement in their efforts to catch him.

George Metesky planted thirty-three improvised explosive devices, of which twenty-two exploded, in public settings including movie theaters, libraries, and train stations in New York City between 1940 and 1956.[77] There were no fatalities, but fifteen people were injured by the bombings. The first bomb, which did not explode, was left at the utility company Consolidated Edison (also known as Con Ed) in November 1940, with a note calling the company "crooks." Metesky had worked there and had been denied disability benefits, despite being injured on the job. A second, similarly constructed pipe bomb without a note was discovered nearly a year later, lying on the street a few blocks from the Con Ed offices. Then there was a hiatus for many years. Metesky wrote letters stating that he was halting his bombing campaign out of patriotism for U.S. involvement in World War II. Years later, in March 1950, an unexploded bomb was found in Grand Central Station. Police were beginning to think that Metesky never intended to have his bombs explode. That belief was proven wrong when additional bombs that he placed in Grand Central Station and the New York Public Library exploded in 1951. Over the next several years, many more bombs exploded, including one inside the Paramount Theatre in Brooklyn in December 1956 that injured several people.

Frustrated with their inability to catch the Mad Bomber, police turned to a psychiatrist, Dr. James Brussel, shortly after the Paramount bombing to produce a psychological profile. Brussel surmised, based on the many letters the bomber had sent to newspapers, police, and Con Ed over the years, as well as the phallic construction of the bombs and other facts of the case, that the bomber was a single man between forty and fifty years old, disinterested in women, an introvert, unsocial but not antisocial, egotistical, moral, honest, and religious. He was portrayed as a skilled mechanic, an immigrant or first-generation American, and a present or former employee of Con Ed, with a possible motive for the bombing being that he had been discharged or reprimanded. Brussel also concluded that the bomber's resentment kept growing and that it was probably a case of progressive paranoia. Some of the other characteristics in Brussel's profile included that the bomber was meticulous and feminine, possibly homosexual, and most likely living with his parents or sisters. Brussel also predicted that when the police finally caught up with the Mad Bomber, he would be wearing a buttoned, double-breasted suit. (Metesky was arrested at home in his pajamas but changed into a buttoned, double-breasted suit for the ride to the police precinct!)

Brussel urged the police to publicize the profile in newspapers as a way of goading the Mad Bomber to communicate with the authorities. This worked, as Metesky fell into the trap of responding to a request from the *New York Journal-American* to write to the newspaper about his grievances. He did so, providing enough information, including the dates he worked at Con Ed, to permit the authorities to identify him. Police had no trouble locating him, since he was still living with his sisters at the same Waterbury,

Connecticut, address listed in his work file. The fifty-three-year-old Metesky was arrested in January 1957.

The Mad Bomber was therefore caught by falling into the trap placed for him with the invitation to write about his motivations in the newspapers. Still, the profile gave the authorities a better idea of whom they were dealing with and contributed to the psychological campaigns aimed at getting him to make a mistake. In the case of "Rasim," the investigators also had a good idea of the person they were dealing with, as he had been providing a wealth of information in his many taped messages and recorded phone calls. There was no need to prod him to communicate; he was doing it on a regular basis. The communications provided investigators with information regarding his beliefs and possible motivations for his terrorist activities. One of the challenges, though, was determining what was real and what might have been said to throw law enforcement agencies off his trail. While there were rambling passages in several of the tapes, the LAPD never thought they were dealing with a "mad bomber" because, according to Commander Hagan, Rasim demonstrated remarkable intelligence.[78]

Foremost among Rasim's messages was anger at U.S. immigration and naturalization laws:[79]

Those who are rightfully or wrongfully arrested for any reason never become citizens and, ah [sic] great number of them are deported to countries they sometimes never knew. We believe that immigration and naturalization laws of this country are great insult to the dignity of this nation, and we believe them to constitute treason.

In the past we have approached several political leaders and appealed to their moral, religious, and patriotic conscience, but have always been totally ignored. We have discovered this land and built it into an economic giant. As a reward for our work we were awarded with immigration and naturalization laws which are in relative historical space more vicious than Gestapo laws regarding Jews. What our children and grandchildren have failed to realize, however, is that whoever had the strength and ingenuity to build his nation, he also must have equal ability to destroy it once he realizes that it has become his worst enemy.[80]

There were also several references to the need to eliminate all laws relating to sexual conduct. He demanded in one taped message that "all sex laws must disappear."[81] On another tape, he complained, "A man is prohibited to exercise his God-given nature in the matter of sex, thus again losing his most fundamental freedom."[82]

Antireligious and anticommunist themes were prevalent in many of Rasim's communiqués. On one of his tapes, he stated:

> We, the Aliens of America, are not willing to live a life where Bible is shoved down our throat by force. Our desire to live a free life from anybody's religious terror, especially religious terror crystallized into legalities such as sex laws of this country, is as strong as our desire to live free of Communism. And we shall fight to the last drop of our blood to see this nation free of religionism, Communism, and all other pornographies of human mind. Freedom to us does not mean that [evangelist] Billy Graham is free to become a millionaire in the name of the Lord. Freedom to us means that John Doe has a right to open a hot dog stand and survive.[83]

On that same tape, Rasim also criticized U.S. policy toward the Soviet Union and Israel:

> Recently, due to the absence of foreign-born people in United States Government, this nation has engaged in signing meaningless pieces of paper with Communists, living an insane illusion that Communists will honor their signature. The only reason Communists negotiate is to find the soft and weak points of his adversary so that he can more successfully kill him when the right time comes. Instead of letting Soviet Communism collapse to its natural decay, the inexperienced leadership of this nation is intending to give it the free man's technology so that it can use it to enslave more people. On the other front, this nation is supporting the insanity of Zionism and insisting that 200 million Jews have a right to immigrate to Israel. Israel is a very small country. Just where are all those people going to go? Or are they going to spill over into Arab land?[84]

Rasim stated on that tape that the letter "O" in the name "Aliens of America" would stand for "oil refinery" but that he would spare Standard Oil Company from attack because it "has courageously taken a stand of reasoning before American people on the matter of Israel."[85] He did not elaborate on this, but in July 1973 the chairman of Standard Oil Company of California, Otto N. Miller, had sent a letter to stockholders and employees urging American support for Arab aspirations and that the United States should work with Arab governments "to build and enhance our relations with the Arab people."[86]

Rasim's messages also had a global revolutionary theme. As mentioned in chapter 2, he issued an ultimatum to all governments of the world to surrender to Aliens of America and stated that his objective was to bring about a society free of nationalism, religion, fascism, racism, and communism.[87]

The Herald Examiner, which had access to most of the tapes since Rasim made several calls to the newspaper directing them where to find the cassettes, ran a story in its August 17 edition titled "Isaac Rasim: A Collage of Hate": "Bit by bit," the story read, "the character of Isaac Rasim is developing as an embittered terrorist. Whether Rasim is an individual or the leader of a band of similarly embittered men is not known. This much is known. He or they are violently anti-Christian, anti-Jewish, anti-communist and opposed to the United States immigration and naturalization laws. Aliens of America (AOA) of which Rasim claims to be 'chief military officer,' is strongly anti-Christian believing this nation to be organized as a Christian nation rather than that which the Constitution decrees—a nation of all men and creeds."[88]

But the authorities weren't sure if Rasim believed everything he was saying on the tapes. If he was an activist for any or all of the causes he talked about, then police would have to spend time trying to identify all the individuals who had taken part in pro-immigration rallies or protests, attended anti-Israel and anticommunist demonstrations, written letters to newspapers regarding various issues, and so forth. That would be an exhaustive search that could prove fruitless and a waste of resources and time. And time was the one thing the police and the FBI did not have on their side, since Rasim had proven he could kill people with his bombs and was promising to continue his terrorist activity "until our name has been written on the face of this nation in blood."

Where the communications by Rasim proved most valuable to investigators was in the names of people he mentioned. On the tape recovered on August 12 (which had actually been dropped off sometime in late July or early August), Rasim boasted that he had set fires to the homes of police commissioners Emmet McGaughey and Margaret Justice and had placed an incendiary plastic bottle into the gas tank of McGaughey's car. This was the first time he mentioned McGaughey and Justice. He next mentioned McGaughey's name in the August 13 call to the *Herald Examiner*. Since the attacks on McGaughey and Justice were not front-page news or known by a large segment of the public, it was therefore likely that the person taking credit for the fires would in fact be the person responsible for those incidents. Investigators now knew that the Alphabet Bomber was the same person they'd been so desperately looking for since the November 9, 1973, house fires.[89]

On that August 12 tape he also said, "Judge Campbell reaches an orgasm when he sentences an innocent alien."[90] Rasim had now named all three house fire victims. The problem, though, was that the police could never find a common link between McGaughey, Justice, and Campbell. The two police commissioners knew each other, but they only knew Campbell by reputation and not personally or even professionally. Interviews with the three victims also did not turn up any suspects. Investigators spent a lot of time checking police commission records, as well as Judge Campbell's personal files and daily diary, for people who might be holding grudges against all three victims. They checked commission board meeting minutes, commission hearing minutes, and related files. Investigators couldn't find any common link.[91]

After the arson attack on McGaughey's car on June 3, 1974, investigators once again carefully went through police commission files and Judge Campbell's records to see if they had missed anything. The results were the same as before. There were no suspects who could be linked to the police commission and Judge Campbell. At one point Campbell told investigating officers about some "bad actors," but Kurbegovic's name was not among them. Investigators attempted to connect the names Campbell gave them with police commission activities or complaints, all to no avail.[92]

The August 12 tape caused the LAPD to essentially start from scratch and conduct yet another exhaustive search of the police commission and Judge Campbell's records, since Rasim had mentioned McGaughey, Justice, and Campbell on the tape. He also mentioned the name of the police commission investigator, Captain George Milemore, on the August 13 call to the *Herald Examiner*, claiming that Milemore and McGaughey were responsible for the killing of two Mexican nationals. It was Rasim's accusation that Campbell sentenced "an innocent alien" that particularly caught investigators' attention. Rasim (i.e., Kurbegovic) had never been identified as a possible suspect in the arson fires, because investigators had been looking for someone with a possible revenge motive against all three victims. Since Kurbegovic had been acquitted in his lewd conduct trial in Campbell's court, his name did not appear on the list of suspects who might want to take violent action against the judge. But now Rasim was mentioning Campbell as someone who had sentenced an innocent alien. The investigators decided to once more look through all of Campbell's records, even searching for names of aliens who had been acquitted. They also examined the police commission records once again. Since these were the days before most criminal records were computerized, the police would have to again check and cross-reference thousands of cases by hand.[93]

Time was running out, with Rasim stating on the tape recovered August 16 that the "I" bomb had already been planted somewhere in Los Angeles.[94] The urgency of establishing the identity of the Alphabet Bomber was increasing with each day that went by. That the LAPD played one of the taped messages from Rasim at a press conference on August 16 illustrates their frustration in not catching him. They were appealing to the public in the hope that someone would recognize his voice. Assistant Police Chief Gates said at the time that the authorities knew nothing about "Aliens of America" and that checks of police, FBI, and INS records hadn't uncovered anyone by the name of "Rasim."[95]

The amount of time, resources, and manpower the police spent searching for the Alphabet Bomber and trying to prevent another attack wasn't lost on the FBI. Although the FBI was also involved in the investigation and cooperated with the LAPD, it was later revealed that the federal agency believed the police were too focused on the Alphabet Bomber case to the detriment of trying to find Patty Hearst and other members of the SLA whom the FBI believed might still be in Los Angeles. (Hearst and the surviving SLA members had actually fled to Northern California soon after the May shoot-out at the SLA safe house in Los Angeles.) The bureau thus quietly intensified its hunt for the SLA in hopes of cracking that case. Some LAPD officers believed the FBI withheld information from local police, including leads on Hearst's possible whereabouts. "There was more activity by the FBI on the Hearst case during the three weeks we were looking for the bomber than at any time during the last two months," said an LAPD investigator. "Maybe it was just a coincidence, but the Los Angeles police were not aware of what the FBI was doing."[96]

Some FBI officials believed that they would do a better job than the LAPD in avoiding another shoot-out should they find Hearst and the other SLA members. The May shoot-out was, at the time, the biggest display of firepower in Los Angeles police history. More than 5,300 bullets and 115 tear gas grenades were fired into the SLA safe house. The FBI reportedly feared that if the police found Hearst and the other fugitives, another confrontation might occur. "We're looking for three fugitives [Hearst and Bill and Emily Harris] and if we can bring them in alive, we'll get the answers to a lot of questions," said one FBI source.[97]

Although the LAPD was also looking for Hearst and her cohorts, they couldn't be blamed for putting most of their energy and resources into the search for the Alphabet Bomber. The SLA hadn't killed anyone in Los Angeles. The Alphabet Bomber had. This was the biggest terrorist event in LA history since the 1910 bombing of the *Los Angeles Times* building. They needed to solve this case and prevent any further carnage in the city.

The task for making yet another run at all the data and information from police commission records (and anything else that was pertinent) fell to Lieutenant Max Hurlbut, a veteran LAPD officer with a keen analytical mind who was one of the investigating officers for the police commission. If anyone would be able to find that needle in the haystack and crack the case, Hurlbut would be that person. He had a master's degree in police administration and an insatiable curiosity about solving problems. He was also the type of person who wouldn't stop until he found the answers he was looking for.

Hurlbut formed a task force of four investigators and two clerks who volunteered to work on their days off. They worked for almost forty-eight hours without sleep beginning on August 16, the day Rasim notified the authorities on a cassette tape where they could find the "L" bomb and that the "I" bomb had already been planted.[98]

Hurlbut and his team read the minutes of the police commission hearings and meetings for the previous five years and examined hundreds of "packages" (i.e., case files) of potential suspects. Whenever someone applied for a permit, he or she was given a package number. If there was a criminal record, it was inserted in the package. The police commission investigator, which in the case of Kurbegovic was Captain Milemore, would write a report on the person's background, including financial and sometimes personal information. Many people, such as neighbors and former business associates, would be interviewed and their statements included in the file. Negative data, like arrests, had to be evaluated for suitability and a potential danger to the public if the police permit was granted.[99]

Hurlbut and the task force had their work cut out for them, as the clock was ticking toward another possible bombing in the city. Case files were strewn everywhere in piles on the floors and squad tables of the cramped two small rooms he was given to work with at Parker Center, the LAPD headquarters building. Hurlbut directed his people to look for certain "descriptors"—key words or phrases that would point to possible suspects. Today, a Google search might take seconds to obtain results. Back then, however, without computerized records, it was tedious, laborious research that had to be done by hand. Among the descriptors he chose were "alien," "sex offenders," "disgruntled applicants," "quarrels with the Commission," and other words and phrases related to the information Rasim had provided in his phone calls and taped messages to the media. Since Rasim had accused McGaughey and Milemore of killing two Mexican nationals in a Skid Row apartment, key words related to that incident, such as "Mexicans" and "Skid

Row," also had to be searched. Because that accusation wasn't true, Hurlbut later wrote, "[it] threw a monkey wrench into some of our descriptors."[100]

Still, after working day and night, Hurlbut was able to identify seven possible suspects. One, however, stood out.[101] He was a male alien who had an arrest record for lewd conduct and a letter written to him from Milemore, informing him of the decision to deny him a permit to open a taxi dance hall because he had "a bad moral character." Hurlbut and his team also saw in the file that Emmet McGaughey had made the motion to deny the permit and that Marguerite Justice seconded the motion. It suddenly seemed to make sense why Rasim, who was now identified as Muharem Kurbegovic, was full of hatred and rage and why he railed against the police commission members and investigator on his tapes.

Hurlbut notified the LAPD's Criminal Conspiracy Section (CCS), which was in charge of the Alphabet Bomber investigation, about his findings. Sergeant Charles Ross, the principal investigating officer for CCS, and his team then read through Kurbegovic's police commission file and determined that he had appeared in a trial in Judge Campbell's court. CCS officers who had been going through Campbell's records to try to discover who might have a grievance against the judge now had a specific name to investigate. They then asked the judge and his bailiff if they had any recollections of what happened in court with Kurbegovic, and both recalled the negative interactions between the judge and Kurbegovic.[102]

The police felt confident they finally had their man. While there were still other suspects, as well as the possibility that Kurbegovic was not acting alone, he was nevertheless the only suspect who could be linked to McGaughey, Justice, Milemore, and Campbell. During the afternoon of August 19, investigators ran his name through the Department of Motor Vehicles records and uncovered two addresses for him in Los Angeles, one from his automobile registration and a different one from his driver's license.[103]

Early that evening, the decision was made to not immediately arrest Kurbegovic but rather place him under twenty-four-hour surveillance. The LAPD wanted to find out whether he had others helping him, whether "Aliens of America" really existed or was just a figment of his imagination, and whether (and where) he'd planted other bombs. Following him around could provide answers to these questions. They also wanted to catch him in the act of committing another crime, such as building a bomb or even trying to plant one somewhere, which would make prosecution of the case much easier.

This would be a perilous surveillance operation, but the LAPD had a small and highly trained unit that relished the challenge of following and bringing down the city's most dangerous offenders, ranging from terrorists and serial killers to bank robbers and other criminals. It was an elite unit, the detectives' equivalent of the SWAT team.[104] Kurbegovic didn't know it, but his days were now numbered.

4

The Homemade Explosives Factory

The name seemed innocuous enough: Special Investigation Section. While the word "Special" might give it more prominence, most people would probably think it was a division in an insurance, credit card, or phone company that investigates fraud or other related offenses. Or perhaps a law enforcement unit that does the routine legwork after a major crime has been committed—interviewing witnesses, victims, and possible suspects; gathering evidence; and producing an endless stream of paperwork when writing up their findings.

It was therefore surprising—shocking, actually—when the *Los Angeles Times* published an exposé in October 1988 about a unit in the LAPD with that very name that did anything but routine police work. "Special Investigations [*sic*] Section: Watching Crime Happen: LAPD's Secret SIS Unit: Citizens Terrorized as Police Look On," the story's headline read.[1] What followed was not a flattering portrait:

> The secretive, 19-man unit watches armed robbers and burglars but rarely tries to arrest them until after the thieves have victimized shopkeepers, homeowners and others. . . . In some cases, the detectives have

overlooked existing arrest warrants. Instead, they have waited for dozens of criminals to commit actual armed robberies and burglaries—felonies that carry longer sentences and are more easily prosecuted because the detectives can testify as witnesses. The *Times* found no cases in which innocent victims were killed by criminals during surveillance by the SIS. However, the investigation documented numerous instances in which well-armed teams of SIS detectives stood by watching as victims were threatened with death and, sometimes physically harmed by criminals who could have been arrested beforehand.[2]

Not surprisingly, Daryl Gates, who had by then become police chief, vehemently denied the accusations against the SIS in the story and claimed that the *Times* was just biased against the LAPD. "Our Medal of Valor winners get an inch in the paper. This gets three pages," he said in an interview with the newspaper. "If that doesn't expose The Times, I don't know what does." Gates was also upset about accusations that the SIS was a secret unit. "There's been nothing secret about it," he said. "Certainly we haven't broadcast it to the felon community, although we now have The Times to thank for doing that. It has accomplished a great deal.... When you suggest we deliberately put people in danger, that is nonsense."[3]

Gates was at least correct in pointing out that the SIS was not a "secret" unit. The *Times* itself had written about the unit in a more positive vein eight years earlier, in an article regarding the accidental shooting death of an SIS member. The newspaper described the officer as "one of the outstanding members of the Los Angeles Police Department's highly regarded Special Investigations Section (SIS), which specializes in trailing suspects believed to be about to carry out dangerous crimes."[4] The 1980 article stated that Mayor Tom Bradley, who was a former LAPD lieutenant, ordered all flags at city buildings lowered to honor the slain SIS officer. Despite this, Bradley later claimed that he didn't know the SIS existed until he read about it in the *Times* exposé in 1988. "I doubt that the [Police] Commission is even aware of this special unit," he said at the time.[5]

Gates was wrong, however, in claiming that victims were not placed in danger while the SIS waited for a crime to occur. The SIS was formed in

1965 without any public announcement and was envisioned to be a squad of "professional witnesses" who could offer in court "irrefutable evidence" against criminals by watching them break the law.[6] But in subsequent years it was the SIS itself that faced a number of accusations that its members also broke the law. In one case, a federal grand jury looked into an incident that occurred in February 1990 to determine whether nine SIS officers should be indicted for violating the civil rights of four robbery suspects. The SIS had been following one of the suspects for nearly three weeks in connection with a series of robberies of McDonald's and other fast-food restaurants. On the evening of February 12, they saw him meet with three accomplices in the Venice Beach area of Los Angeles. They then followed the suspects as they drove to a McDonald's in Sunland in the San Fernando Valley. The SIS team waited outside while two of the men broke into the closed restaurant at approximately 1:30 a.m. and were joined by their accomplices. They then tied up the manager and forced her to open the safe at gunpoint. All the while this was happening, the SIS unit waited outside the restaurant.[7]

It wasn't until the robbers tried to flee in their car that the SIS moved in. They rammed the vehicle and confronted the suspects. Police claimed the suspects pointed guns at them, which later turned out to be pellet guns. The SIS officers fired twenty-three shotgun blasts and twelve shots from their handguns at the men who were still in the car. Three died, and one was wounded. The surviving suspect claimed no one had aimed a pellet gun at the police.[8]

The federal grand jury hearing the case declined in 1995 to indict the SIS members on the violation of civil rights charge. Federal prosecutors said there was insufficient evidence to pursue the civil rights charges. But earlier, in 1994, a federal jury found that the officers acted without cause in firing on the suspects and awarded $44,000 in damages in a civil suit to the families of the dead men and the lone survivor.[9]

This was just one of many controversial incidents involving the SIS. When William Bratton became LAPD's police chief in 2002, he soon changed the way the SIS operated. No longer would they be allowed to wait to catch suspects in the act before making arrests. They also cut back on the use of deadly force and began calling for backup from uniformed officers. "This is not your grandfather's SIS," said Captain Kyle Jackson, head of the Robbery-Homicide Division, who oversaw the SIS during Bratton's tenure as police chief. "This is the SIS for the 21st century. . . . Scores and scores of operations occur without a single use of force. If they didn't have reverence for life, I wouldn't allow them to be there."[10]

But in 1974, the SIS was still a fairly new and little-known unit, operating with virtually no guidelines or constraints. If Muharem Kurbegovic was indeed the Alphabet Bomber, capturing him would be their biggest success story thus far. But how much rope were they going to give Kurbegovic to incriminate himself? Were they going to wait until they could catch him in the act of making another bomb? Or perhaps even planting one in an "I" or "E" location as he worked his way through the spelling of his fictitious group's name? These would be uncharted waters for the SIS, which up till now had dealt with bank robbers and other criminals armed with guns, not bombs. A confrontation with the Alphabet Bomber could result in the deliberate or accidental detonation of a bomb the suspect might be carrying. This would place not only the police in danger but also anyone else who happened to be near the scene at the time.

As the detectives of the SIS gathered at Parker Center early in the evening of August 19 to map out a strategy, they didn't know how long they would be following Kurbegovic. It could be days, weeks, or even months. They hoped, however, that the terror that had gripped Los Angeles might now be coming to an end.

You Saved My Life

It was 7 p.m. on Monday, August 19, when Sergeant Charles Ross from the Criminal Conspiracy Section briefed the SIS team on the information that led them to identify Kurbegovic as the prime suspect in the LAX bombing and subsequent threats. They were given mug shots of Kurbegovic from his prior arrest in 1971 so they would be able recognize him. They were also given the following description from his "rap" sheet: "Male/Yugo (dob 6-1-43) 5-11, 200 lbs." A portion of one of Rasim's taped messages was played so the officers could familiarize themselves with Kurbegovic's voice. They were told that when the tapes were found, each was wrapped in a paper-type towel. His car was described as a 1970 Volkswagen, color unknown, with license plate 707 CZI. The two different addresses for Kurbegovic that were obtained from the Department of Motor Vehicles were also provided to the SIS team.[11]

With all that information at hand, the stealth unit was ready to spring into action. The original nine-member SIS unit from 1965 had by now grown to sixteen members. A command post was established at police headquarters in Parker Center. Officers there would be in communication with the SIS teams in the field, who would be wearing disguises and dressed in street clothes and also driving unmarked police cars. The eight cars used by the SIS were of different makes and models in order to prevent their being identified by criminals on the lookout for the typical unmarked police vehicle. Some of the cars were two-doors with fancy hubcaps. The two-man SIS teams would be in communication with each other using small handheld radios and walkie-talkies.[12]

At 7:30 p.m. the SIS teams drove to the two addresses they'd been given. One was 3050 West Seventh Street, the address Kurbegovic listed on his driver's license, while the other was 1332 Shatto Street, which came from the car registration for the Volkswagen. The Seventh Street address turned out to be B & J Answering Service, which also served as a mail pickup. When the officers saw no lights on in the building and that its hours of operation were from 9 a.m. to 5 p.m. during the week and 9 a.m. to 1 p.m. on Saturdays, they decided there was no point to remain there. Plans were made to return in the morning in case Kurbegovic showed up then.[13]

Meanwhile, other SIS detectives had gone to the Shatto Street address, which they now assumed was his residence, but did not find Kurbegovic's vehicle parked there. They continued the stakeout until midnight, when they were relieved by additional SIS teams who remained there throughout the night and into the morning. Some of those units had earlier driven around downtown Los Angeles looking for Kurbegovic and his car but had been unable to find him.[14]

The stakeout at the Shatto Street address would also turn out to be futile. The police learned the next morning that Kurbegovic had moved several months ago, and no one interviewed knew of his new address. The SIS, therefore, abandoned the Shatto stakeout but maintained surveillance of the B & J Answering Service.[15]

At 9 a.m. on August 20, two SIS detectives went to RPM Industries to interview people there about Kurbegovic. The police had learned the night before in a phone call to the Immigration and Naturalization Service that Kurbegovic had listed McCulloch Corporation as his place of employment. A phone call there led them to RPM, which was the spinoff company Robert McCullough formed after selling his McCulloch Corporation in 1972.[16]

When the SIS members arrived at RPM, which was located just a few miles from LAX, they drove around the immediate area looking for Kurbegovic's Volkswagen. After not finding it, they went inside to talk with people at RPM. They were informed that Kurbegovic had been terminated four days earlier, on August 16. The reasons given to Kurbegovic for the termination were that he had been absent from work several times recently and that there had also been a diminishing amount of business for the company. RPM officials, however, told police that the real reason for his dismissal was that they were worried that he was too interested in explosives and that something bad might happen at work. "I was afraid he was going to blow this place away," said Alan Bell, who had hired Kurbegovic.[17]

Indeed, Bell and others at RPM had good reason to be worried. Even though Kurbegovic was well liked and had excellent performance reviews, he was reckless sometimes with the chemicals he experimented with. Bell told investigators that on one occasion Kurbegovic made a gaseous substance that appeared to be poisonous. The lab had to be evacuated until the gas cleared. On another occasion, a coworker saw Kurbegovic put a substance on the ground in the parking lot and light it. That substance, which Kurbegovic said was nitrocellulose, fizzled and burned out.[18]

Upon learning this, the SIS team requested that members of the CCS come to RPM to conduct a search of the premises for components similar to those used to make bombs. Arleigh McCree, who was in charge of bomb investigations, arrived and discovered that all the necessary chemicals and containers to make the LAX and Greyhound bombs were available at RPM and that there were also duplicates of the Greyhound bomb container there.[19]

The police, though, could not obtain any leads on Kurbegovic's whereabouts from RPM officials. The only home address RPM had for Kurbegovic was the old one on Shatto Street. The news that Kurbegovic had been fired must have made the detectives very uneasy. They had identified the man they believed to be the Alphabet Bomber, but now he might have yet another grudge: being fired from his job. Perhaps he would spiral out of control and begin a new wave of attacks. He had explosives. He had expertise. And he was nowhere to be found.

Meanwhile, the stakeout at 3050 West Seventh Street, the B & J Answering Service, continued. This was the SIS's last hope to try to locate Kurbegovic. But what if Kurbegovic was no longer using that service? At 10:45 a.m., however, the SIS got the break they were hoping for. Kurbegovic was spotted at the Seventh Street address, driving his light blue Volkswagen with the matching license plate number. He parked the car and entered the building, exiting just a few minutes later. He then drove a short distance to the intersection of Westmoreland and Sixth Street, all the time being followed by the SIS. Kurbegovic parked his car on Westmoreland and walked to an apartment house at 3109 West Sixth Street. Sergeant Michael Sirk followed him on foot and watched as Kurbegovic entered the building. After approximately one minute, Sirk went into the building and observed Kurbegovic using a key for apartment 5. Sirk then looked at the mailbox for that apartment number and saw the name "Kurbegovic." He conveyed that information to all the other units, which by now had converged on the West Sixth Street address.[20]

Kurbegovic exited his apartment at 11:35 a.m., walked to his car, and drove away. The SIS followed him, rotating cars the whole time so that no one vehicle would look suspicious to Kurbegovic. "In our surveillance work," Sirk explained, "we usually don't follow somebody for any length of time period, because they eventually turn around and notice you. So one . . . [unit] will follow for a short time and then someone else will take over." The SIS members also wore many different articles of clothing during a surveillance so as not to be recognized by their target.[21]

Kurbegovic drove to an unemployment office in Santa Monica, arriving at 12:05 p.m. He was there only a few minutes, most likely to pick up forms for unemployment benefits. He left the office carrying papers, which he put in his car, and then walked a couple of blocks to an Arby's fast-food restaurant. He looked at the menu on the wall and, not finding anything he liked, walked away. There was a Jack in the Box fast-food restaurant nearby, and Kurbegovic walked there and had lunch inside. He finished lunch about a half hour later.[22]

He then walked along Santa Monica Boulevard, looking inside business windows and at vehicles that were on display at used car lots. The next stop for Kurbegovic was the Santa Monica Public Library, where he thumbed through one of the card catalogs. He left the library at 1 p.m. and walked back to his car, where he took out the papers he had put in there earlier. Then he went again to the unemployment office. He spent some time there, presumably filling out the forms and waiting in line. At 1:45 p.m. he drove back to his apartment in Los Angeles.[23]

Thus far, everything seemed routine in terms of Kurbegovic's actions. There was nothing to make the SIS teams believe they were going to catch him in the act of committing a crime or doing something that would give them more information about possible additional bombs that might have been planted or would be planted in Los Angeles. They also thus far had no indication that Kurbegovic might have others working with him. But it was still very early in the surveillance. They were prepared to wait as long as necessary.

In the meantime, at the command post in Parker Center, a psychoanalyst who was a police buff and liked to help out the LAPD was telling officers there that Kurbegovic was a paranoid schizophrenic and pyromaniac who felt omnipotent. He told them to expect to find his bomb paraphernalia not very well hidden all around his house.[24] The police, however, did not yet want to search Kurbegovic's apartment, since that would alert him to the fact that they suspected him of being the Alphabet Bomber.

Shortly after 4 p.m., Kurbegovic left his apartment and drove to the beach area in Pacific Palisades, just north of Santa Monica. He entered a pay parking lot on the ocean side of the Pacific Coast Highway at 4:50 p.m. He parked his car in the middle of the lot and walked over to an embankment, where he looked up and down the beach. He then returned to his car and sat in the front seat, unaware that Sergeant Robert Sauter, the field supervisor for the SIS, was watching his every move through binoculars from a trailer parked nearby. Sauter could see that Kurbegovic held some papers in his hand, and it appeared that his lips were moving.[25]

At the same time that Sauter was observing Kurbegovic, another SIS member, Officer Martin Dorner, walked into the lot and approached the Volkswagen from the rear. He walked by the passenger side of the vehicle at a distance of about six feet. He confirmed that Kurbegovic's lips were moving as he read from several pieces of paper that he was holding against the steering wheel. Dorner could hear words but couldn't make them out. He also saw an object on the passenger seat, which later turned out to be a tape recorder. He then cut in front of the car and walked away.[26]

The presence of another person made Kurbegovic nervous. Upon seeing Dorner, he put the papers down and watched him walk across the parking lot. After a short while, Kurbegovic started up his car and drove to another point in the parking lot, closer to the highway. He continued there to talk into the tape recorder.[27]

Kurbegovic left the lot around 5:15 p.m. and drove home, arriving about a half hour later. He stayed in his apartment for thirty-five minutes and then walked to a phone booth, where he dialed a number and spoke to someone for about one minute. He then returned to his apartment. Dorner went into the booth and tore off the pages from the phone book that were turned open. There were some lines written around the name of a person who had at one time been associated with the CBS station in Los Angeles but had just been transferred to CBS in New York.[28]

The next time the SIS detectives saw Kurbegovic was at 7:15 p.m., when he exited from the rear door of his apartment building. Joining the SIS surveillance for the first time that day were two FBI agents. Kurbegovic was now wearing a green army fatigue jacket. He drove to the Hollywood area and parked near Sunset Boulevard. He then began walking along Sunset, looking around a lot, both behind him and around on the streets. This was something the SIS hadn't noticed him doing during their prior surveillance of him. They could also see that he was in disguise, having put on a red wig. The SIS knew he was up to something but weren't sure exactly what.[29]

When Kurbegovic reached the intersection of Sunset Boulevard and Western Avenue, he crossed the street and entered a Carl's Jr. fast-food restaurant. Before going in, he put on a pair of sunglasses, another indication that he didn't want anyone to be able to identify him for whatever he was about to do. Following him into the restaurant was SIS member Sergeant Curtis Hagele. Kurbegovic walked past the counter, through the dining room, and into the restroom. Hagele waited a moment and then also entered the restroom. He went to the washbasin and could see through a small crack in the door of the toilet stall Kurbegovic's green army fatigue jacket. He could also see that Kurbegovic's shoes were pointing toward the back wall of the stall area. Hagele left the restroom and went into the dining area.[30]

Kurbegovic exited the restroom shortly afterward. After watching him walk out of the restaurant, Hagele went back into the restroom and looked around the stall area where Kurbegovic had been. He found a green towel folded up just inside the outer edge of the container holding sanitary seat covers for the toilet. He unfolded the towel and saw a cassette tape. He then left the restaurant with the tape and walked across the street to a parking lot for another business. He contacted Sergeant Sauter and asked him to meet him there.[31]

Sauter arrived shortly afterward in his car with the two FBI agents who had recently joined the surveillance. Sauter played a portion of the tape in a recorder that he had with him. Both he and Hagele recognized the voice as the one that had been played for them at the briefing the previous day at Parker Center. They now had evidence that Kurbegovic was the "Rasim" who had made all the threats and admissions on the previous tapes.[32]

They decided, though, after conferring with officers at the command post, not to arrest him yet. They still wanted to know whether he had other bombs planted around the city or anyone else working with him. They continued their surveillance as Kurbegovic walked back to his car. But for some unexplained reason, once he got into his car, instead of driving away, Kurbegovic drove back to Carl's Jr. and parked in front of the restaurant. He then went inside and ordered a cup of hot chocolate. He took it to a booth near the restroom and sat down for a couple of minutes. He then went back into the restroom.[33]

Hagele, who had been watching him the whole time from a window outside the restaurant, notified Sauter that Kurbegovic had reentered the restroom and was going to find out that the tape was missing. He recommended that they should immediately arrest him, since he would now be aware that the police were on to him. Sauter agreed, saying over the radio and the walkie-talkies, "Let's take him."[34]

This was the moment the SIS had been waiting for. It was now shortly after 8 p.m. Their long day of tailing Kurbegovic was about to come to an end. Hagele ran into the restaurant followed by other SIS detectives, including Sergeant Sirk. A cook, not knowing these were policemen, thought they were causing trouble and jumped over the counter, trying to intercept them. Bad decision on his part. Sirk struck him with his fist in the chest and neck area and continued on through the restaurant. Hagele entered the restroom and found Kurbegovic standing in the back by the open stall door. He pointed a gun at him and ordered him not to move, telling him they were police. Another SIS member held Kurbegovic's hands up against the wall, while still another officer handcuffed him. Hagele, meanwhile, was holding the gun at the back of Kurbegovic's head. They then took Kurbegovic outside, and soon afterward he was driven to police headquarters at Parker Center.[35]

Despite Kurbegovic's arrest, the LAPD couldn't yet celebrate the end of the Alphabet Bomber's reign of terror. His capture had come before they could determine whether he had planted additional bombs around LA or had others working with him. It is not clear why they believed that once Kurbegovic discovered the cassette tape missing he would assume the police had found it and that they were now following his every move. He could have just as easily believed it was another patron of the restaurant who found it instead, since it wasn't hidden in a very good place. Anyone using the sanitary toilet seat covers could have reached down and accidentally discovered the green towel with the cassette tape inside. Kurbegovic might therefore have decided to go back into the restroom to retrieve the tape and place it somewhere else before calling the media to alert them to its location.

The authorities, though, now had to hope they could obtain information from Kurbegovic himself regarding additional bombs or possible collaborators. Kurbegovic, though, was not talking when questioned by the police, pretending again to be a mute. When he felt like it, he would answer their questions by writing notes or just nodding his head. In one exchange, Sergeant Ross promised Kurbegovic that he would not be prosecuted for any additional bombs he might have planted as long as he told the police where they were:

> You know what we'd like to really find out, Muharem. I don't think we actually need anything from you to complete our case as we see it. What we would really like to know is if you have left . . . anything out there someplace that we don't know about. . . . If there's some more stuff out there, that have people on a potential danger, we would like to know, just to save them. Do you have anything else out planted around that you couldn't retrieve?[36]

Kurbegovic nodded his head, prompting another officer to say, "When you shake your head yes like that, does that mean that yes, you do, or you're just nodding your head?" Kurbegovic didn't respond. Ross then continued his questioning of the suspect:

> We really feel it's important to get it back if you have stuff out there. See, as of the moment you were arrested—or prior to the time you were arrested, we were all a little fearful because of what had been happening around here for the past couple of weeks, in all honesty. Once you were arrested, our fears and worries were transferred from you to maybe somebody else out there that doesn't know what might be about to happen to them. How about if I guaranteed you never to use it against you?[37]

Apparently amused by Ross's efforts, Kurbegovic wrote on a piece of paper, "I admire your stile [sic]." Ross took it as a compliment. "Thank you," he said. "I really mean it." Ross continued to try to pry Kurbegovic for information: "Do you have anything out there now that is a danger to somebody, that should be taken in off the street? I guarantee you it will never be mentioned if you do. I swear. I give you a blood oath." Kurbegovic then decided to have some fun with the officers. He wrote, "It's in Vandenburg [sic] Airforce Base 7 thermonuclear toys." Not taking any chances, Ross wanted more information: "Is it in a position that nobody knows it's there? Is it hidden up there? Could you direct us to it? Would you? I mean on paper? Muharem, you just wrote something a little scary right now. I don't know if you're even capable of making something like that, but if you are, we would certainly like to [know]. I don't want to go up and retrieve it. . . . But I'd sure like somebody to know about it. How can we find them up there? Draw us a map or something."[38]

Kurbegovic drew a diagram with the words "start" and "think" and ending with an arrow pointing to the words, "I want to have a lawyer present." Realizing that his strategy to get Kurbegovic to talk wasn't working, Ross became angry: "You mean this is all bullshit? . . . Well, it must be. You can't get any security clearance. You couldn't get one at the last place you tried to get a job at. So how could you get on Vandenberg? I guess it's bullshit, huh? Okay. I'll tell you what. . . . [T]he next time we'll see you is at your murder trial."[39]

The search for possible additional bombs continued for several weeks. None were found, but the prospect that there could still be bombs or other devices out there, including chemical weapons, greatly worried a lot of people, including prosecutor Dinko Bozanich: "[Kurbegovic] talked about gas, chemicals, and putting that into air-conditioning systems," Bozanich said. "You don't know how much that used to gnaw at me. Six months after he's in custody, a year after he's in custody. . . . Because you don't know. Something like that could have been done. If there is someone else that's complicit, they could do something to trigger it. Even if there is no one else that's complicit, there may have been some timing mechanism that had either been set to wait a year or had just not gone off immediately, but could go off. It was defective; still could go off."[40]

In an effort to pry some information from Kurbegovic, the police planted one of their own, Sergeant Sirk, in a jail cell with him the night of his arrest. This despite the fact that Sirk was a member of the SIS team that followed Kurbegovic around all day and was one of the officers who went into Carl's Jr. to arrest him. He even sat for a while in a car with Kurbegovic after the arrest. They were confident, however, that Kurbegovic wouldn't recognize Sirk due to the different disguises he and the other members of the SIS team wore. Kurbegovic also never looked up at Sirk while they were together in the car. In addition to hoping Kurbegovic might reveal some key information, the police were also hoping to get more evidence, beyond what they'd observed at the beach—namely, that Kurbegovic was faking being a mute and could actually talk. But Kurbegovic wasn't communicating with anyone that night, and Sirk was removed from the cell after a couple of hours.[41]

Gas, Guns, and Explosives

Although the police didn't find additional bombs or chemical weapons planted around Los Angeles in the days and weeks following Kurbegovic's arrest, or for that matter uncover anyone else working with him, they did find an arsenal of weapons, chemicals, improvised devices, and other materials in his apartment that shocked them and made them realize they were lucky to have found Kurbegovic when they did. His residence was a homemade explosives factory.

At the time the SIS was closing in on Kurbegovic, Charles Ross had spoken by phone with Deputy District Attorney Mike Marcus regarding obtaining a search warrant for Kurbegovic's apartment. While he was on the phone, the arrest took place at Carl's Jr. Ross was told that it could be six to eight hours before a search warrant could be obtained. He recalled Marcus telling him, "You have enough for a search warrant. If you feel in your own mind that there is a danger to the public, you would be on safe grounds going in immediately on the public safety type search."[42]

Ross and other officers at the LAPD believed there was indeed a danger to the public presented by the likely presence of bombs and other materials in Kurbegovic's apartment. A bomb going off there, either accidentally or deliberately, could cause death and destruction in the neighborhood. One particular concern they had was the possibility that Kurbegovic, fearing he might be caught, had constructed a self-destructing device that would go off if he didn't return to his apartment within a given period of time. There was also the possibility that if there were other people involved, they could gain access to any bombs and other devices in the apartment.[43]

The search of Kurbegovic's apartment thus begun shortly after his arrest.

Arleigh McCree was one of the officers to search the residence. At one point during the search, McCree, who at times was using an electronic stethoscope to allow for sounds to be amplified, heard a ticking sound coming from a box in a closet in the living room area. He let everyone know about this, and the other officers immediately ran out the door. McCree stayed and determined it was not a bomb but rather a timer with wires, a lightbulb, and a battery on it. The officers returned, and the search continued throughout the one-bedroom apartment.[44]

Just as the psychoanalyst who was helping the LAPD had predicted, there was a lot of bomb paraphernalia out in the open. "I observed all sorts of tape and chemicals and improvised fuses on top of the refrigerator," said McCree. "And this was just . . . an initial observation, just something that you could just stand back and look around you and see."[45] Kurbegovic had also placed various items in closets, cabinets, and other places. A methodical search by McCree and his fellow officers uncovered a stash of chemicals and other materials for making and containing explosives. These included Freon cylinders; a live pipe bomb; improvised percussion detonators; black and smokeless powders; improvised blasting caps; packages of fire starters; two cans of kerosene; two gas masks; a circuit board and light assembly with four batteries and capacitor; liquid mercury; ammonium nitrate prills; dinitrobenzene; picric acid; mercury fulminate; an empty bottle labeled "nitric acid"; and many other chemicals and devices.[46]

The search also uncovered a Browning Hi Power semiautomatic pistol loaded with thirteen rounds of ammunition on a sofa in the living room; a Browning 9 mm semiautomatic pistol with three magazines and two extra barrels, fully loaded, in the bathroom closet; and a Browning .22 semiautomatic long rifle, loaded with nine cartridges, also in the bathroom closet.[47]

In addition to the weapons, chemicals, and various devices found in the apartment, McCree also discovered that Kurbegovic wasn't kidding when he'd said in one of his taped messages that the "FBI cannot catch us . . . because we studied the same books as FBI did, and we studied the same books as U.S. Army did."[48] Kurbegovic had indeed compiled an impressive library of books and manuals on explosives, unconventional warfare, law enforcement operations and strategies, and chemical and biological weapons. Some of the manuals were declassified military publications. Among the titles were the following:[49]

Explosives and Demolitions
Guide to Germ Warfare
Guide to Chemical and Gas Warfare
Unconventional Warfare
Military Explosives
Devices and Techniques
Defense Tactics For Law Enforcement
Hand-to-Hand Combat
Criminal Investigation
Improvised Munitions Handbook
Pistols and Revolvers
Booby Traps
Grenades and Pyrotechnics

There was also a package of twenty library call slips for books on explosives and chemicals.[50] It was quite a haul for the police. LAPD and FBI spokesmen stated that "almost a truckload of explosives" was found in the apartment."[51] McCree felt that the search was as thorough as it could be: "I believed that I had found everything that was anywhere near in the open or I just did not believe there was anything else present. . . . [W]e pretty much took all the cabinets and shelves and things in the hallway and kitchen apart and ran the [explosive detection] dog through the area. It was a very extensive and methodical, I believe, search."[52]

Still, McCree and the rest of the LAPD were shocked to learn two years later that their search had not been as extensive and methodical as originally assumed. During proceedings in November 1976 to determine Kurbegovic's competency to stand trial, the Alphabet Bomber, who was now no longer pretending to be a mute, stunned the courtroom by claiming he still had plenty of explosives hidden in his apartment. "I want the LAPD to remove approximately 100 pounds of strategic materials, explosives, from my apartment. They have been searching my apartment and they have found only what was in front of their feet. They have not been searching my apartment properly."[53] Prosecutor Dinko Bozanich could not believe what he heard: "There's probably no case in American criminal history that has involved something like what . . . happened in court," he said, "where he makes the statement, in effect, laughing at LAPD . . . [claiming] they didn't find very much."[54]

Bozanich wasn't sure whether what Kurbegovic had said was true. After all, why would he want to incriminate himself further? Perhaps it was to demonstrate to the court that he was not competent to stand trial, since only a crazy person would tell the police that he had more explosives hidden in his apartment. Or maybe it was to show how much smarter he was than the LAPD, since they hadn't been able to find what he had hidden two years earlier. Or perhaps he had a crisis of consciousness and was now concerned that the explosives would go off and kill people in the apartment building. No matter the reason, and even if Kurbegovic was just bluffing, Bozanich didn't want to take any chances. He contacted the Criminal Conspiracy Section of the LAPD and told them what had happened in court: "I know you guys are gonna think I'm [crazy] . . . and I can't tell you what to do, [but] I think you should consider [conducting another search]."[55]

Not believing they could get a search warrant based only on what had been said in court, the police contacted the tenant who was now living in Kurbegovic's former apartment. They told him that there were explosives there and that they would like to have his consent to search the residence. Ros Rouix gave them consent and sat in his living room as another search was conducted.[56]

As the investigators worked their way through the apartment again, they discovered a hidden room behind the medicine cabinet in the bathroom. Kurbegovic had provided more information regarding where the additional explosives and materials could be found, and the police could see through an opening behind a shelf leading down to a room with cans and various items on the floor. One of the officers was lowered into the hole and began lifting things out. A human chain was then formed, with one officer passing items to another and so forth until all the items were placed in the living room, where they were photographed and tagged.[57] All the time this was happening, Rouix sat there, watching in astonishment and probably wondering, "What kind of a place have I been living in?" It is not clear whether he knew before the police contacted him that the Alphabet Bomber had once lived in the apartment. It certainly wouldn't be something a landlord would advertise. Amazingly, though, Rouix did not move to a new place after the police search and was still there as of 1980, when he testified at Kurbegovic's criminal trial.

Meanwhile, Bozanich, who wasn't sure whether Kurbegovic was telling the truth about more explosives in his apartment, received a call from the investigators. "You can't believe the stuff we found," they told him. "You're kidding!" Bozanich replied. They told him there were enough explosives to blow up the Golden Gate Bridge in San Francisco. Among their findings in this second search were canisters labeled "red ferric oxide" and "aluminum powder," as well as bottles, cans, and jars labeled "picric acid," "potassium permanganate," "sodium chlorate," "sodium peroxide," "acetone," "carbon tetrachloride," "precipitated sulfur," "cupric chloride crystal," "chloroform acs," "m-dinitrobenzene," "HNO3" (nitric acid), "stearic acid," "precipitated sulfur," "smokeless powder," "shotshell powder," "methanol," "phosphoric acid," and "Mallinckrodt aluminum nitrate." There were also mechanical timers, fuses, and a Browning 9 mm pistol with a magazine and twelve cartridges.[58]

The police also found a twenty-five-pound blue metal drum labeled "sodium cyanide."[59] This was another indication that Kurbegovic was thinking about building and using chemical weapons, and may have actually gotten quite far with those efforts. McCree, the LAPD's bomb expert, would years later tell a reporter that all but one ingredient needed to build a rudimentary nerve gas bomb had been discovered in the first search of Kurbegovic's apartment. The last item, an organophosphate, "was just waiting to be picked up," according to McCree.[60] It is likely that the nerve gas McCree was referring to was sarin, since Kurbegovic had threatened in many of his taped messages to use sarin and claimed that he was already conducting experiments with it. Had he used it, the results would not have been pretty. Nerve agents such as sarin, soman, tabun, and VX interfere with the transmission of nerve impulses, causing convulsions and death by respiratory paralysis.[61]

The amount of sodium cyanide found in the second search was startling. Kurbegovic may have been planning future threats and actions involving the nerve agent tabun, of which sodium cyanide is a chemical precursor, or the use of sodium cyanide to release lethal cyanide gas.[62] Since he stated in one of his taped messages that he had acquired the plans of the air-conditioning systems of thirty major skyscrapers, he may have been thinking about using sodium cyanide in a future attack on such a target.[63] He might also have thought about using sodium cyanide in a bomb. The judge who sentenced the perpetrators of the 1993 bombing of the World Trade Center in New York, which killed six people and injured more than a thousand others, mostly due to smoke inhalation, believed that sodium cyanide was used in the twelve-hundred-pound urea nitrate bomb that exploded in a rental van in the parking garage beneath the north tower. "You had sodium cyanide around, and I'm sure it was in the bomb," said Judge Kevin Duffy. "Thank God the sodium cyanide burned instead of vaporizing. If the sodium cyanide had vaporized it is clear what would have happened is the cyanide gas would have been sucked into the north tower and everybody in the north tower would have been killed. That to my mind is exactly what was intended."[64]

The discovery of nitric acid in both searches, and of carbon tetrachloride and chloroform in the second search, suggests that Kurbegovic may have been experimenting with the choking agent phosgene, since these chemicals, among others, are used in its manufacture.[65] No lone wolf terrorist before or after Kurbegovic is known to have acquired such an extensive and diverse an array of chemicals that could be used to manufacture chemical warfare agents. And few, if any, had the expertise and motivation to use these weapons of mass destruction on populated areas.

The Alphabet Bomber was escalating his violence during his summer of terror. He had started several months earlier with firebombing the homes of Emmet McGaughey, Marguerite Justice, and Alan Campbell in November 1973, three people he held grudges against. He'd then moved on to placing an incendiary device in McGaughey's car. This was followed by the detonation of an eleven-pound bomb at LAX in an indiscriminate attack against travelers. He then built a twenty-five-pound bomb that he put in a locker at the Greyhound bus station, again aimed at killing innocent people. All indications were that he was learning fast how to build more powerful weapons, and it was most likely only a matter of time before he became the first lone wolf in history to disperse chemical agents upon a city's population.

The night before Kurbegovic's arrest, a local news station (KTTV) had interviewed a psychologist to learn about the mental health of the Alphabet Bomber. Dr. Irene Kassorla was asked why someone would set off a bomb at LAX. She responded by saying that a person would have to be psychotic in order to do that.[66] This caught the attention of Kurbegovic, who planned to have the news station receive his next taped message, the one he made at the beach and later placed in the restroom at Carl's Jr. "On August 19, 1974," the recording began, "your news team 'On Target' has carried an article on so-called 'Alphabet Bomber.' Realizing that On Target team has in the past displayed great quality in journalism and that it is in our interest to point [out] to them that they obviously do not have facts before them, we have decided to make a tape available to them which will obviously, inadequately, but hopefully significantly, shed some factual life on to the organization of Aliens of America. Please understand that you are not dealing with a mad bomber or his psychiatrist. You are dealing with a dynamic . . . group called 'Aliens of America.'"[67]

But was Kurbegovic actually a "mad bomber"? That question would dominate the courts for years, as the fate of the Alphabet Bomber became a contentious battle fought by a colorful array of experts, lawyers, judges, and a defendant who believed he was smarter than everyone else.

FIG. I. Muharem Kurbegovic entered the United States during the late 1960s, when anti–Vietnam War protests were sweeping the nation. Here, a large crowd is gathered in Washington DC in October 1967. Kurbegovic did not want to be drafted into the army during the Vietnam War, so he pretended to be mute in order to obtain a 4-F classification, which was given to a person who was not acceptable for military service due to physical, mental, or moral conditions. Photographer, Warren K. Leffler, Library of Congress, Prints and Photographs Division, LC-U9-18187-4A.

FIG. 2. A group of women waiting to be asked to dance in one of the taxi dance halls in Los Angeles in the 1970s. Kurbegovic frequented these halls, which were places where male customers paid money to dance with hostesses hired by the club. Photographer, Ken Papaleo, Herald Examiner Collection, Los Angeles Public Library.

FIG. 3. Passengers were allowed to place luggage and other items in lockers that were located outside security-checked zones at Los Angeles International Airport (LAX). It was in a locker like one of these that Kurbegovic placed a homemade bomb that exploded on August 6, 1974, killing three people and injuring thirty-five others. Photographer, John Malmin, Los Angeles Times Photographic Archive, Library Special Collections, Charles E. Young Research Library, UCLA.

FIG. 4. Shattered lobby of the Pan American World Airways overseas passenger terminal at LAX after the August 6, 1974, bombing. Photographer, Mike Meadows, Los Angeles Times Photographic Archive, Library Special Collections, Charles E. Young Research Library, UCLA.

FIG. 5. Shortly after the explosion, LAX received numerous bomb threats, and explosive detection dogs were used to search the airport. Herald Examiner Collection, Los Angeles Public Library.

FIG. 6. LAPD crime lab experts examine debris from the bombing. Herald Examiner Collection, Los Angeles Public Library.

FIG. 7. LAPD assistant police chief Daryl Gates (*left*) and William Sullivan, the assistant director in charge of the FBI Los Angeles office, listen to one of Kurbegovic's taped messages. Kurbegovic claimed to be the leader of a group he identified as Aliens of America. "This first bomb was marked with the letter A, which stands for Airport," he said on the tape. "The second bomb will be associated with the letter L, the third with the letter I, etc., until our name has been written on the face of this nation in blood." Herald Examiner Collection, Los Angeles Public Library.

FIG. 8. The LAPD bomb-disposal truck (*arrow*) in which a bomb was loaded after Kurbegovic alerted authorities that he had placed the bomb in a locker at the Greyhound bus terminal in downtown Los Angeles. Police estimated that had it gone off, one hundred people would have been killed. Although Kurbegovic disclosed the location of the "L" bomb—claiming in a taped message that since his activities had been generating publicity, he'd decided to let "L" stand for "life"—he also warned that the "I" bomb had already been planted. Photographer, Bob Steiner, Herald Examiner Collection, Los Angeles Public Library.

FIG. 9. Headline in the *Los Angeles Herald Examiner* on August 15, 1974. Reprinted with permission of *San Francisco Chronicle*, Hearst Corp.

FIG. 10. Headline in the *Los Angeles Herald Examiner* on August 17, 1974. Reprinted with permission of *San Francisco Chronicle*, Hearst Corp.

FIG. 11. The upstairs apartment where Kurbegovic made his bombs and stored explosives, chemicals, guns, and other weapons. Herald Examiner Collection, Los Angeles Public Library.

FIG. 12. Kurbegovic was arrested on the evening of August 20, 1974, at a fast-food restaurant in Hollywood where he had planted an audiotape. Photographer, Guy Goodenow, Herald Examiner Collection, Los Angeles Public Library.

FIG. 13. Deputy District Attorney Dinko Bozanich spent more than six years on the Alphabet Bomber case, from the time shortly after Kurbegovic was arrested, in 1974, to his conviction in 1980. Herald Examiner Collection, Los Angeles Public Library.

FIG. 14. Deputy District Attorney Lea Purwin D'Agostino assisted Bozanich in the prosecution of Kurbegovic during the 1980 criminal trial. Kurbegovic called her the "Dragon Lady," a moniker she was proud of. Courtesy *Los Angeles Daily Journal*.

FIG. 15. Judge Nancy Watson's UCLA law school graduation photo, 1958. Watson presided over Kurbegovic's criminal trial in 1980. Courtesy Marcia Goodman.

FIG. 16. Judge Nancy Watson's court photo, 1972. Watson endured continual insults, shouting, and other erratic behavior by Kurbegovic, who acted as his own lawyer, during the eight-month trial. "I really felt beaten down after a while," Watson would later say. Los Angeles Times Photographic Archive, Library Special Collections, Charles E. Young Research Library, UCLA.

FIG. 17. (*above*) Illustration of a costume Kurbegovic sometimes wore in court. The seven-headed cobra symbol on the back of his vest is identical to the insignia that had been used by the Symbionese Liberation Army, the group that kidnapped Patty Hearst in 1974. Illustrator, Gene Cannoy, reprinted with permission of *San Francisco Chronicle*, Hearst Corp.

FIG. 18. (*opposite*) Kurbegovic held up this sign at a sentencing hearing after his conviction. He said that a life sentence was too vague and asked Judge Watson to change it to a thousand years in prison so that he had "something to look forward to." Photographer, Ken Hively, Los Angeles Times Photographic Archive, Library Special Collections, Charles E. Young Research Library, UCLA.

5

I Shall Return!

"I am cut off from all the outside help and on top of that I was a friendless person to begin with," Muharem Kurbegovic wrote in a letter from his cell in the Los Angeles County jail shortly after his arrest. "I don't like people to help me, but sometimes every man can fall into a deep hole from which he can come out only if he cries for help. This is one of those times."[1]

The letter was addressed to Robert McCulloch, the rich and colorful industrialist who'd formed McCulloch Corporation and then RPM Industries, where Kurbegovic had worked until recently. "I know that your family has engaged itself in support of many worthy causes in the past," Kurbegovic wrote. "Most of these causes were immediately gratifying. Supporting this cause would not be immediately gratifying. It indeed might be painful and awkward experience supporting an unpopular cause. But I am innocent sir, innocent not only technically but morally of all charges levied against me. You can help me prove my innocence by taking interest in this case."[2]

Kurbegovic wrote this letter on September 26, 1974, the day after a grand jury indicted him on twenty-five counts: three counts of murder (the victims of the LAX bombing), six counts of arson, one count of willful and malicious burning of personal property, and fifteen counts of violation of the dangerous weapons' control law, which, among other things, included the intent to murder Emmet McGaughey, the causing of great bodily injuries to Rev. Rhett Patrick Shaughnessy and Arturo Trostl Jr., the causing of bodily injuries to the other victims at LAX, and the possession of destructive devices.[3]

Kurbegovic knew that McCulloch was a generous man with a good heart, oftentimes helping those in need. He had offered to help find doctors who might be able to cure Kurbegovic's muteness (not knowing that Kurbegovic was faking the disability). Now, Kurbegovic was seeking McCulloch's help in finding a top lawyer to take his case. "It is clear to me that you might feel that my employment at RPM Industries was a regrettable experience due to these charges," he wrote, "but I also want you to know that I am innocent and I would consider it appropriate and a matter of RPM Industries self defense if you would help me financially to prove my innocence by convincing some of big lawyers to represent my case." It was a shrewd move by the savvy Kurbegovic, combining his cry for help with a veiled hint that RPM Industries would be tarnished in reputation and perhaps even the target of lawsuits by victims and their families for having employed the Alphabet Bomber and possibly providing him an environment where he learned how to make explosives.[4]

Although McCulloch was fond of Kurbegovic, he didn't think finding him a top lawyer was a good idea. He figured it would be a waste of money. He told prosecutor Dinko Bozanich in an interview at RPM that based on what he had read and heard about the case, he figured Kurbegovic was indeed the Alphabet Bomber, that the police must have caught him "red handed," and that nothing could be done to establish that Kurbegovic was not the bomber. He thought that even though Kurbegovic seemed normal when he worked at RPM, he must have some "screws loose," and therefore the best way to help him was to find a top psychiatrist to meet with him. He contacted Dr. Frederick Hacker, a psychiatrist he knew who had been treating McCulloch's daughter for several years. "I do not wish to become involved in the matter of his guilt or innocence," McCulloch wrote to Hacker on October 23, "and believe he is in all probability in good hands with the Public Defender. However, if he should need help or psychiatric consultation, I can think of no one more qualified than you to be of assistance."[5]

Hacker had experience working on famous cases. He had been a court-appointed expert in the trial of Charles Manson and his cult followers, the "Manson family," who brutally murdered pregnant actress Sharon Tate and several other people near Hollywood in 1969. He was also at the time McCulloch contacted him serving as an adviser to the Hearst family as they dealt with the kidnapping of their daughter, Patty Hearst, by the SLA.[6] Hacker visited Kurbegovic at the county jail a month after receiving McCulloch's letter. He told McCulloch afterward that Kurbegovic "was a mixed-up guy who thinks there is a plot between Yugoslavia and the United States to do something to him." McCulloch relayed this information to Bozanich when they met at RPM.[7]

The involvement of psychiatrists such as Hacker in the case did not surprise Bozanich. He anticipated this from the beginning. He felt confident he had a slam-dunk case based on strong circumstantial evidence, including Kurbegovic being seen dropping off the tape that corresponded with other taped messages sent by the Alphabet Bomber, the discovery of bomb-making materials in his apartment similar to those used in the LAX bombing and the Greyhound bus bomb, and many more pieces of evidence. Everyone expected Kurbegovic's defense to be either "not guilty by reason of insanity" or "diminished capacity."[8] The main difference between the two is that "while 'reason of insanity' is a full defense to a crime—that is, pleading 'reason of insanity' is the equivalent of pleading 'not guilty'— 'diminished capacity' is merely pleading to a lesser crime."[9]

If Kurbegovic were to plead "not guilty by reason of insanity," he would have to convince a jury that at the time of the LAX bombing and other violent acts, he did not know what he was doing or he did not know that it was wrong. This was known as the M'Naghten rule, which the American and British courts generally followed as the test of criminal insanity. The M'Naghten rule derived from a case in Britain in 1843. Daniel M'Naghten, a Scottish woodworker, believed that he was the target of a conspiracy between the pope and British prime minister Robert Peel. He attempted to assassinate Peel but mistakenly shot and killed the prime minister's private secretary, Edward Drummond. M'Naghten was acquitted based on his lawyers' successful argument that their client was insane.[10]

This verdict infuriated the British public and government as well as Queen Victoria, who, a few years earlier, had herself been the target of an assassin found not guilty by reason of insanity. The House of Lords and the queen, along with many other people, felt that Britain needed a clear and strict definition of criminal insanity. Therefore, the House of Lords (along with a panel of judges) ruled that a defendant could use an insanity defense only if "at the time of committing of the act, the party accused was labouring under such a defect of reason, from a disease of the mind, as not to know the nature and quality of the act he was doing; or, if he did know it, that he did not know he was doing what was wrong."[11]

If a jury found Kurbegovic not guilty by reason of insanity, he would be committed to a state mental hospital rather than sent to prison. Another possible defense that Bozanich had to anticipate was diminished capacity, which, if successful, could result in Kurbegovic being convicted of a lesser offense and obtaining a reduced sentence. A diminished capacity defense does not argue that a defendant is insane but rather "because of mental impairment or disease, [is] simply incapable of reaching the mental state required to commit a particular crime."[12] In other words, "Due to emotional distress, physical condition or other factors [a defendant] could not fully comprehend the nature of the criminal act he/she is accused of committing, particularly murder or attempted murder. It is raised by the defense in attempts to remove the element of premeditation or criminal intent and thus obtain a conviction for a lesser crime, such as manslaughter instead of murder."[13]

While he was at Atascadero State Hospital, Kurbegovic found a book in the library there that contained several pages on diminished capacity.[14] Always the fast learner, he became an expert on that type of defense. "He was more skilled in that than even . . . [the majority] of attorneys in California," said Bozanich. If Kurbegovic were to offer a defense of "not guilty by reason of insanity" or "diminished capacity," Bozanich knew he would have to cross-examine psychiatrists who would be called as expert witnesses for the defense. And he couldn't wait to do that. In fact, one of the main reasons Bozanich was assigned the case was his stellar reputation for dealing with psychiatrists in court. He was head of the Los Angeles County district attorney's medical-legal section and was a rising star in the legal profession. A tall, eloquent, and dogged prosecutor, Bozanich, whose family was originally from Croatia, relished cross-examining psychiatrists. He did not have a high opinion of them: "People in forensic psychiatry, the kindest way I can phrase it, based upon my experience, as with any profession, there's a top, a bottom, and in the middle," he said. "Those who obtain medical degrees, the bottom of that barrel becomes psychiatrists. The bottom of the barrel of the ones that become psychiatrists are the ones that become forensic psychiatrists." He conceded, though, that despite his assertion, "There are some good ones."[15]

Meanwhile, Kurbegovic continued his quest for a prominent lawyer. In addition to writing to McCulloch for financial assistance to hire one, he also wrote to the Los Angeles Times to request an interview. "So far I was unable to get in contact with an attorney who is cut out for this case," he wrote. "I am thus forced to ask the news media to help me find such an attorney." The interview was granted and held at the county jail on October 1. He wrote notes in answers to questions and to make his points. When asked how other inmates were treating him, he replied, "I am together [in a cell] with a 'hit man.' He likes me. Very nice fellow." Kurbegovic was specific about the type of lawyer he wanted: "I need a young attorney who has a lot of political awareness. Has a minimum of 5 years experience and can take this case for just what government pays him."[16]

It's not surprising that Kurbegovic thought the media could help him. He had played the media expertly during his reign of terror in Los Angeles, manipulating them with tantalizing taped messages and phone calls that generated front-page news. Now he would use them to help in his defense. Ironically, Kurbegovic already had the top lawyer he was looking for representing him, Deputy Public Defender Gerald Chaleff, a young and ambitious attorney who'd graduated from Harvard Law School and would go on to become one of LA's most famous criminal defense lawyers, handling several high-profile cases. An article published in Los Angeles Magazine in 1998 described him as follows: "If you kill someone and [Johnny] Cochran can't squeeze you in, murder specialist Gerald Chaleff can help."[17] Chaleff would also serve as president of the LA Police Commission and become president of the Los Angeles Bar Association. Kurbegovic, who was facing the death penalty at the time (since California had recently reinstated it before he set off the bomb at LAX), either could not see the talents and potential of Chaleff or perhaps felt it was beneath him to be represented by just a public defender. After all, he was the Alphabet Bomber and felt he deserved better.

The Ping-Pong Strategy

When Kurbegovic was brought to court, the judge who was scheduled to preside, Raymond Choate, expressed doubt as to his competency to stand trial, as defined by section 1367 of the California Penal Code: "A person cannot be tried or adjudged to punishment while such a person is mentally incompetent. A defendant is mentally incompetent for purposes of this chapter if, as a result of mental disorder or developmental disability, the defendant is unable to understand the nature of the criminal proceedings or to assist counsel in the conduct of a defense in a rational manner."[18] One of the court-appointed psychiatrists who examined Kurbegovic had written to Choate that he believed Kurbegovic "is presently insane" and that "due to a paranoid psychosis he is not competent to stand trial." Kurbegovic had told this psychiatrist (through writing notes) that he believed he'd been arrested again for lewd conduct, not for the LAX bombing.[19]

A competency hearing was scheduled for January 1975 before another judge, William Keene. A distinguished, bright, and ambitious man, Keene had been in the first graduating class of UCLA law school in 1952. He then became a deputy district attorney and after that went into private practice. He was appointed a municipal court judge in 1963 by Governor Pat Brown and promoted by Brown two years later to the Los Angeles Superior Court. He had hoped to be appointed by the Board of Supervisors to the position of district attorney in 1970, but the board chose another individual instead. During that same year, Keene had achieved a degree of national fame by presiding over part of Manson's murder trial. He was eventually replaced after Manson filed an affidavit of prejudice. (Any defendant can file at least one affidavit of prejudice against a judge and have him or her removed from the case without giving a reason.) After he retired from the bench in 1984, Keene became a television star as the judge on the popular show *Divorce Court*.[20]

Having Keene as the judge for Kurbegovic's competency hearing greatly worried Bozanich. Keene "was so bright that he would end up reducing any case that came in front of him," Bozanich said. "He would quickly size it up, what it was worth and the way it should work out. The attorneys were reduced to hod carriers; it wasn't really an adversary system. You either played ball or he would really take it out on you."[21]

Not wanting to leave the determination of Kurbegovic's competency in Judge Keene's hands, Bozanich requested and was granted a jury trial, which was to be held in January 1975. Chaleff remained Kurbegovic's lawyer for that trial. Bozanich was able to convince the jury that Kurbegovic had tricked all four court-appointed psychiatrists who'd examined him and that while Kurbegovic was a disturbed man, he was feigning an inability to understand the charges against him or to cooperate with an attorney. In cross-examination, Bozanich showed the psychiatrists the letter Kurbegovic had written to McCulloch seeking financial assistance in hiring a lawyer, an articulate and eloquently written letter the psychiatrists had not seen before. In that letter, Kurbegovic also wrote, "I was arrested and charged with the L.A. Airport bombing, attempted murder on L.A.P.D. commissioner, firebombing of three homes, etc.," clearly demonstrating that he understood the charges against him. After reviewing the letter, the psychiatrists acknowledged that Kurbegovic had no hallucinations, delusions, or misunderstanding of the charges.[22]

During this competency trial, Kurbegovic acted in a manner he probably hoped would convince the jury that he was not competent to stand trial, thus avoiding a murder conviction that could send him to the gas chamber. In court, he flicked imaginary dust from his clothes and made wild gestures. He also emitted loud grunts and attempted to wear a tricornered paper hat. From time to time he sat in the Lotus position on his chair. Most of the time, though, he sat with his head cradled in his folded arms. One time, he tried to escape. When left alone in a locked attorney conference room, he put a chair on top of a table and punched a hole into a drop ceiling. He then crawled in and eventually kicked his way out into an unlocked anteroom just outside the courtroom. The bailiff heard the noise and ran over to see Kurbegovic's feet coming out of the ceiling. He ordered him down and, pointing a gun at him, had him lie on the floor.[23]

The jury determined that Kurbegovic was competent to stand trial, but Judge Keene granted a defense motion for a judgment notwithstanding the verdict and found Kurbegovic not competent.[24] He was thus sent to Atascadero State Hospital located on California's Central Coast. Within forty-eight hours of being there, Kurbegovic began to speak. Chaleff accused the hospital of forcing him to do so by denying him water and keeping him strapped to a bed. The hospital denied these accusations.[25]

While at Atascadero, Kurbegovic usually kept to himself and spent his leisure time watching television or reading. When he did interact with other patients, he tried to teach them hand-to-hand combat techniques, which the hospital staff naturally frowned upon and told him to stop doing. Once, he was found with a three-foot piece of one-eighth-inch-thick rope. When asked by a staff member what he planned to do with it, he responded, "I was going to hang you." He also made other threatening remarks toward the staff, such as "I want you to know that I have been trained to cut off people's heads."[26]

Although not likely influenced by these threats and a desire to rid themselves of him, the superintendent of Atascadero nevertheless certified in October 1976 that Kurbegovic was now competent to stand trial. A second competency trial began that month. It was during this second competency trial that Kurbegovic revealed that he had more than one hundred pounds of explosives still hidden in his apartment that the police had failed to find in their search two years earlier. He also requested that he be allowed to act as his own attorney. Judge Keene tried to dissuade him, telling him that he had an excellent lawyer representing him, but Kurbegovic, having seen Bozanich in action in court before, didn't think Chaleff was up to facing Bozanich again. "Mr. Bozanich is, in my opinion, a very strong lawyer," Kurbegovic told Keene. "Mr. Chaleff is an extremely intelligent lawyer but if Mr. Chaleff would represent me I'm afraid that Mr. Bozanich would beat me. On the other hand, I am confident that I can beat Mr. Bozanich because I have great respect for that man's ability and I know what that man is able to do, and his ability and his tactics. Mr. Chaleff does not and I can beat Mr. Bozanich and Mr. Chaleff cannot."[27]

Keene decided to allow Kurbegovic to act as his own lawyer but warned him that it was not an ongoing privilege and that he would take it away if he felt Kurbegovic was not capable of competently representing himself. It didn't take long for Keene to do just that, as Kurbegovic immediately began telling the judge in a long, rambling speech that he was indeed the Alphabet Bomber, but not because he set off bombs in an alphabetical order. Rather, it was because "I am destined to find the construction of the thermonuclear bomb in the alphabet itself." After listening to Kurbegovic for some time, Keene ordered that Chaleff be reinstated as his attorney. This time, the jury returned a verdict that Kurbegovic was not competent to stand trial, and he was returned to Atascadero.[28]

In November 1978 criminal proceedings were reinstated against Kurbegovic, but the court again declared doubt concerning his competency to stand trial. Therefore, yet another competency jury trial began in January 1979. By this time, it appeared that Kurbegovic might never face criminal charges—and that was in fact his intention. He was using a "ping-pong" strategy. He believed that if he could convince a jury three or four times that he was incompetent, the charges against him would have to be dismissed. He planned to do this by claiming to be the Messiah during competency trials, which he believed a judge or jury would find as evidence of incompetence, because only someone mentally ill would claim to be the Messiah. He would then be returned to Atascadero, where he would stop being the Messiah so he could be returned to court, at which time he would again become the Messiah and repeat the process. He believed that if competency could not be determined several different times and if he could prove he was not a danger to himself or others, he would be released.[29]

That is what Bozanich feared. "It wasn't just a question of seeing that this guy be convicted," said Bozanich. "The first problem, and the problem that existed for the first five years off and on, was getting him to trial. Would we ever get him to trial? 'Cause until and when he would be found competent, there's no way a conviction can occur because you will not have even been able to try the guy.... It did reach a ping-pong point where even the defendant realized it, that there might be a crack he might have slipped through and never face a guilt [criminal] trial jury. That would have been terrible, I think, in the overall scheme of things."[30]

By the time of the third competency trial, William Keene was no longer presiding over the proceedings. Another key player gone was Gerald Chaleff, who had left the public defender's office to go into private practice. Kurbegovic was therefore assigned a new attorney, Michael Adelson. However, not surprisingly, Kurbegovic said that he could not get along with Adelson and wanted him replaced. Judge Paul Breckenridge, who would preside for just a brief time over the proceedings, told Kurbegovic that Adelson was a fine lawyer. Sensing that the judge would refuse his request, Kurbegovic came up with another idea: *Why not punch my attorney right here in the courtroom? That way, they'll have to get me a new lawyer.* So, without warning, Kurbegovic punched Adelson on the side of his face, knocking him to the floor. "Are you okay?" a startled Judge Breckenridge asked Adelson. "I'm all right," he said.[31] Kurbegovic was removed to his jail cell, and the court proceedings continued.

There had been several incidents of defendants punching their public defenders in Los Angeles County courtrooms in the weeks preceding Kurbegovic's attack. It was a tactic used to force the removal of one attorney and obtain a different one. But whereas in the other cases the public defenders were replaced, Adelson indicated he could continue to be Kurbegovic's lawyer. Judge Leslie Light, who would preside over the rest of the third competency jury trial, told Kurbegovic: "Well, the mere fact that you punched him, either to create an apparent conflict or not, or for other reasons, doesn't matter to me at this point, Mr. Kurbegovic. I don't relieve an attorney simply because a defendant has punched him." The judge's ruling, along with Adelson's decision to remain as Kurbegovic's attorney, put an end to the rash of punchings, as other defendants realized the tactic might not work anymore.[32]

The jury in the third competency trial found Kurbegovic competent to stand trial. Kurbegovic then made a motion to waive counsel and represent himself (known as *propria persona*, or simply *pro per*) in his forthcoming criminal trial, which Judge Light granted, telling him, "You've been found to be competent so the presumption is that you can represent yourself." The Court of Appeal agreed with Light's decision, stating, "Kurbegovic was a model of ability: He had successfully defended himself previously on a criminal charge, he had a university education, was very intelligent and had done a great deal of legal research." Even Dinko Bozanich admired Kurbegovic's legal skills: "If he wasn't such a jerk," he said, "and half a bubble off, he could have been a good trial lawyer."[33]

It would not be until early 1980 that the criminal trial began. This displeased Kurbegovic, who wanted to go to trial right away.[34] He relished the opportunity to be the man of the hour, to take center stage in what promised to be a media-covered and high-profile trial. A showman, a terrorist, and perhaps "half a bubble off," the Alphabet Bomber would try to turn the courtroom upside down with wild theories, vitriolic accusations, and odd behavior while at the same time possessing an uncanny ability to effectively cross-examine some of the top experts in their respective fields. He would also continually test the patience of a pioneering judge and engage in confrontations with her never before seen in a courtroom. It would become one of the most fascinating criminal trials in history.

I Really Felt Beaten Down after a While

By the time Kurbegovic came to trial in February 1980, five and a half years had passed since his arrest. Many people were perplexed over the delay. "What took so long?" a reporter for the *Los Angeles Times* wrote. "Can the criminal justice system be doing its job if it takes less time to go through college than it did to bring one man to trial?"[35] Bozanich blamed it on Judge Keene, who, after the jury in Kurbegovic's first competency trial found him competent to stand trial, granted a judgment nothwithstanding the verdict and found him incompetent. "If he had just let the adversary system operate, the case would have been tried in 1975," Bozanich told the reporter.[36] Keene disagreed, stating, "I don't think there was anyone in the courtroom at the time—the press, attaches or knowledgeable legal minds—who didn't think that to put that man to trial at that time would have been an absolute farce."[37]

The jury, however, didn't think it would be a farce. When the media asked the jurors how they could have found Kurbegovic competent, one of them said, "What do you people know? You waltzed in here [courtroom], you took a look, [heard] the [psychiatrists say] he's incompetent, and then you walked out. You didn't hear any of the cross-examination, you don't know what the evidence was to show that this guy was deceiving people, including the [psychiatrists]."[38] Meanwhile, Keene's granting of the defense motion for a judgment notwithstanding the verdict was reversed by the Court of Appeal.

Much had changed in America during the ensuing years. Watergate had become a distant memory for many people, with Richard Nixon long gone and his successor in the presidency, Gerald Ford, out of office by 1977. America's stature in the world took a major hit during the years of the Jimmy Carter administration, with Americans taken hostage in their own embassy in Iran in November 1979 and Russia invading Afghanistan a month later. A failed attempt to rescue the hostages in April 1980, which resulted in the death of eight U.S. servicemen, added to the depressed mood in the country.

The one bright spot for America occurred the same month that Kurbegovic's trial began. In what is considered one of the biggest upsets in sports history, the U.S. Olympic ice hockey team, composed mainly of college hockey players, defeated the powerful (and quite professional) Soviet Union team at the Winter Olympics in Lake Placid, New York, and went on to win the gold medal. The victory over the Soviets became known as the "Miracle on Ice." It lifted the spirits of the nation and has since been immortalized in books, movies, and documentaries.

Angelinos joined with the rest of the country in celebrating the victory. But they hadn't forgotten about their summer of terror in 1974. The trial of the Alphabet Bomber garnered widespread media coverage. For the key players involved in the trial, the stakes were very high.

The judge for the trial, Nancy Watson, had been born into the legal profession. Her father, Frank Belcher, was a prominent trial lawyer and former president of the State Bar of California and the Los Angeles County Bar Association. A very bright young woman, she graduated from

Stanford University in 1946, but she lived during a time when women were expected to, rather than become lawyers, "get married and have a family." And that is what she did. Watson eventually realized, though, that it would be expensive to put her children through college. Her first husband had been severely injured during World War II and was unable to stay employed for more than brief periods of time. According to one of her sons, he was also "a psychological casualty of the war long before the term PTSD arrived." She therefore entered UCLA law school and earned her law degree in 1958. She then joined her father's law firm and specialized in defending personal injury and other civil cases. She became the only female lawyer among several hundred men in the Southern California Association of Defense Counsel.[39]

Watson's home life was extremely difficult, as her husband was both emotionally and physically abusive. He would beat their two young boys, Brian and Harvey, when their mother was not home and warned them, "If you tell your mother, I'll kill you."[40] They, along with their older sister, Marcia (another daughter, Diane, was born in 1962), also witnessed their father slapping, punching, and whipping their mother on several occasions. One time, he ruptured her spleen, for which she needed emergency surgery. The children did not witness that incident, which their mother blamed on an accidental fall.[41]

Both boys, who went on to become college football stars and have brief careers in the National Football League, fantasized about taking revenge on their abusive father. "We both would think about ways to kill our father," said Brian. "And really, I'm sure if I'd [been much older], I probably would've tried to murder him."[42] Watson served her husband with divorce papers in 1964. He was forced to move out but continued to call her, threatening her life. "I can't wait to get you through the sights of a gun, you and the kids," he would say. Her father hired an armed bodyguard to stay at her home.[43]

Throughout all of this turmoil, Watson was able to advance in her legal career. She became a judge in 1968, when Governor Ronald Reagan appointed her to the Los Angeles municipal court system. She handled traffic court, the arraignment calendar, and preliminary hearings on felony cases. She hoped to eventually be appointed to the Superior Court, but by

1972 she realized that Reagan was unlikely to appoint her to this higher-level court, since he had been in a dispute with her second husband, Los Angeles County tax assessor Philip Watson, over the issue of reducing property taxes.[44] She thus decided to challenge six other candidates that year for an open superior court seat made available by a retiring judge. She won the primary and then won the general election judicial runoff, becoming only one of five women among California's 471 superior court judges. She handled divorce cases and became supervising judge of the Family Law Master Calendar Court.[45]

Nothing in her legal past, though, could have prepared Watson for the trial of the Alphabet Bomber. After the third competency trial for Kurbegovic was completed, the case was assigned to her in May 1979. She presided over various pretrial motions and related matters, with jury selection finally beginning in February 1980. This was going to be one of the most high-profile trials in recent Los Angeles history, and Watson needed to make sure she didn't make any errors that could result in a reversal of a conviction on appeal. She was also representing the small but growing number of female judges across the nation. Any major snafu on her part could set back the progress women were making in the judicial ranks.

The stakes were also high for prosecutor Dinko Bozanich. After all these years of trying to bring Kurbegovic to trial and winning the battle over whether or not he was competent, he didn't want to see a jury somehow acquit the Alphabet Bomber, find he suffered from diminished capacity at the time of the crimes, or not be able to reach a unanimous verdict. He also had to be careful, like Judge Watson, not to make errors that could lead an appellate court to reverse a conviction.

As noted earlier, Bozanich believed he had a slam-dunk case against Kurbegovic. But the fear of a hung jury worried him. He took a risk during jury selection by not using a peremptory challenge on a prospective juror who admitted to having once been convicted of voluntary manslaughter. The man most likely had the conviction erased, or he would not have been allowed to serve on a jury. Bozanich asked him whether, based on his past and the fact that he had been prosecuted by the Los Angeles district attorney's office and served time in Los Angeles County jail, just like Kurbegovic, he could really be a fair juror. The man leaned back in his chair, looked at Bozanich, and said firmly, "I can be the fairest juror you've got." Bozanich interpreted that to mean he would be able to put himself in the mind-set of Kurbegovic, having been where the defendant was now, and see through any lies or tricks Kurbegovic might try to pull during the trial. "I not only didn't bounce him for cause," said Bozanich, "I left him. I passed peremptory challenge. . . . Can you imagine if, after [a] lengthy trial, that jury would have hung up 11 to 1 and he's the guy who hung it up? What people would have thought of me the rest of my life, let alone my bosses?"[46] It was Kurbegovic who immediately used a peremptory challenge, probably thinking the same things Bozanich was about this prospective juror.

Bozanich also faced the risk that the jury somehow, despite what Kurbegovic did, might feel sorry for him or be impressed that he was acting as his own lawyer against the powerful district attorney's office, a David-and-Goliath-type situation. "Typically, you learn at an early stage, when you're a trial lawyer, that the jury does take into account the lawyer for each side," said Bozanich. "How trustworthy is the person? Do they like him? Dislike him? You don't know how that really factors in. So, you could have a defendant who, despite the incredibly serious crimes that he committed, they might at some point start feeling sorry for him, to some extent. Or, [they might believe that] he got screwed by the American system."[47]

The stakes were also high, of course, for Kurbegovic. He was no longer facing the death penalty because California's death-penalty law, which had been in effect at the time of the 1974 LAX bombing, had been declared unconstitutional by the California Supreme Court while Kurbegovic was in custody. Although the death penalty was reinstated by the time his criminal trial began, it was not retroactive and therefore could not be applied to his case.[48] He also wasn't facing a sentence of life in prison without the possibility of parole, since without the option of a death penalty there couldn't be a life without parole option, just a straight life sentence.[49] It was not until 1977 that the California Penal Code was revised to include the sentence of life imprisonment without the possibility of parole, and that too was not retroactive.[50]

Still, a conviction with a life sentence would most likely mean Kurbegovic would spend the rest of his life in prison, since parole for setting off a bomb that killed three people and maimed another would be highly unlikely. For a man who prided himself on being smarter and cleverer than everyone else and who believed he could always beat the system, losing the trial would be devastating. Kurbegovic gambled by choosing not to plead not guilty by reason of insanity, which, at least if successful, would have resulted in his spending the rest of his life in a mental institution rather than prison. So the stakes were high for him to either win an acquittal, which was very unlikely, or have a hung jury, or produce a successful diminished capacity defense that could result in a conviction on lesser charges.

The criminal trial was held in Department 124 on the thirteenth floor of the downtown Criminal Courts Building.[51] Kurbegovic, who now had a receding hairline with long, flowing hair and a beard, put on a show that at times amused, impressed, and offended those in the courtroom. Sometimes he wore a colorful Yugoslav costume that a woman who had become enamored of him and visited him in jail had made. It consisted of green pants, a red shirt, and shoes with the toes curling up.[52] Other times, he wore a brocaded lime pantaloons outfit with a tan leather vest. The vest was embroidered with a dark green seven-headed cobra symbol identical to the insignia that had been used by the Symbionese Liberation Army.[53] He also sometimes just wore jail clothes.[54]

During the peremptory challenges, Kurbegovic knew some prospective jurors probably didn't want to sit on an expected long trial. So he decided to have fun with them. He put pieces of paper with numbers written on them in a shoebox, shook it up, and told them that this was the "scientific peremptory challenger here." He then picked a piece of paper out of the box and exclaimed, "Number six, you are the lucky one!" The prospective juror was then excused. He did that and other, similar gimmicks with the first few peremptory challenges he had.[55]

At one point in the trial, he waved a piece of paper in front of Judge Watson, telling her it was a prayer. "People keep saying I don't have a prayer [to be acquitted] and I want to show them they're wrong," he said. He also asked Watson to be allowed to enter a special plea that he was the Messiah, which she turned down.[56] He presented a green-covered booklet that he had written, titled *An Introduction to Kurbegology by King Muharem*. On the top right corner of the cover was a sticker with the words "Aliens of America," while on the bottom right corner was a sticker with the words "Alphabet Bomber." The first page of *Kurbegology* looked like an advertisement for the movie *Apocalypse Now*, a popular film of the time. The *Apocalypse Now* logo was printed at the top of the page, with images of Kurbegovic and the SLA's cobra insignia just below. Kurbegovic poked fun at the LAPD by also having a movie-like advertisement at the bottom of the same page with the words "Chief Daryl F. Gates Presents *Los Angeles Now*."[57]

Kurbegology contained Kurbegovic's thoughts on various subjects and press clippings about himself and other people. In the foreword, he wrote, "Kurbegology is an exact science of the entire nature, and is an outgrowth of discovery of mathematical relationship between quantity and quality or 'Q-Q formula' and its application on qualitative problems of nature, such as politics, religion, philosophy, literature, etc." He also wrote about reincarnation and told the court that most people are reincarnated in the opposite sex. "Patricia Hearst was Virgin Mary's husband, legal husband, real husband," he said in court. "And I was in my first life Virgin Mary. In other words, we are now both reincarnated, and God has connected us through Symbionese Liberation Army ordeal." He further stated that "Mr. Bozanich is also one of those who has reincarnated in the opposite sex." In the booklet, he lists Bozanich as being the "Virgin Mary's girlfriend" in his first life.[58]

For all his antics and bizarre behavior, though, Kurbegovic still impressed observers with his ability to cross-examine key prosecution witnesses. One of those was Arleigh McCree, the LAPD bomb expert who had gained a reputation as one of the top authorities in U.S. law enforcement on the subject of explosives.[59] "Even if I had nothing else to argue that the guy wasn't nuts," said Bozanich, it was that "he just couldn't resist demonstrating how smart, clever, et cetera, he was. . . . [W]hen it came to handling those exhibits and stuff, and asking McCree questions, it was bomb expert versus bomb expert."[60]

McCree had testified on direct examination about many things related to the LAX bombing, the Greyhound bomb, and the arson devices that were used to firebomb the homes of Emmet McGaughey, Marguerite Justice, and Alan Campbell. He had explained how the chemicals and other items that were found in Kurbegovic's apartment could be made into explosive devices similar to those used in these attacks. But Kurbegovic wanted to poke holes in McCree's knowledge of the manufacturing of explosives:

> KURBEGOVIC: Have you ever observed the manufacture of explosives from raw chemicals?
>
> MCCREE: No I have not. Not in the manufacturing sense you are talking about.
>
> KURBEGOVIC: So you are lacking personal experience in taking chemicals for start, combining them, processing them and ending up with an explosive?
>
> MCCREE: If you are speaking of the process of taking coal and processing toluene or benzene out of that coal and from that making TNT, trinitrotoluene, dinitrobenzene, or trinitrobenzene, no, sir.
>
> KURBEGOVIC: Now, have you at any time received any training by some experienced explosive chemist who would tell you what are the scientific ingredients in the explosive manufacture?
>
> MCCREE: No, sir.
>
> KURBEGOVIC: So is it then true that you are lacking that dimension to your explosive expertise that connects the theory of manufacturing explosives with the final product?
>
> MCCREE: In that sense, yes.[61]

Kurbegovic's cross-examination skills were also evident in the following exchange with McCree regarding the search of Kurbegovic's apartment on the evening of his arrest in 1974:

> KURBEGOVIC: You stated you found explosives in the apartment. What explosives did you find?
>
> MCCREE: Black powder, smokeless powder, material that I believed to be explosive mixture of chlorate and sugar. Other materials that I was not real sure of what they were, residues of ammonium nitrate and nitrobenzene.

KURBEGOVIC: Now, you stated "black powder, smokeless powder."
Aren't you perhaps mistaken that those are called explosives?
Aren't they officially called propellants?

MCCREE: Sure they are propellant. But they are also an explosive.

KURBEGOVIC: Yeah, but are they officially classified as explosives or
propellants?

MCCREE: They are officially classified as propellants.[62]

While exchanges such as these between Kurbegovic and McCree did not damage the prosecution's case, since there was an overwhelming amount of circumstantial evidence indicating that Kurbegovic was the Alphabet Bomber—ranging from the explosives and other materials found in his apartment that were similar to the LAX and Greyhound bombs and the arson devices used in the firebombing of the three homes to the tapes claiming credit for all of the attacks—it was still an impressive display by Kurbegovic in cross-examining one of the nation's top bomb experts.

Acting as his own lawyer also gave Kurbegovic the opportunity to cross-examine the victims of his attacks whom the prosecution had called as witnesses. This wasn't something these victims wanted to experience. The very first witness called by Bozanich was Judge Alan Campbell, who'd presided over Kurbegovic's lewd conduct trial and whose home Kurbegovic firebombed along with those of the two police commissioners, Emmet McGaughey and Marguerite Justice, who'd denied his permit to open a taxi dance hall. Campbell had severely reprimanded Kurbegovic during that trial in which he was acquitted, but now, on the witness stand, his antagonistic attitude toward the defendant was gone. When Kurbegovic held up photographs of Campbell's home during cross-examination, he requested permission to approach the witness. Campbell became alarmed: "Your Honor, please, I believe that I can distinguish each of those photographs if they were held up by Mr. Kurbegovic from where he sits."[63] Kurbegovic remained at the defense table. "Campbell was really nervous," Judge Watson recalled. "He didn't want to be in the same courtroom as Kurbegovic. I thought it was kind of funny."[64]

Another victim of Kurbegovic's violence was Rev. Rhett Patrick

Shaughnessy, whose right leg had been amputated because of injuries he suffered at the LAX bombing. Unlike Campbell, however, he was not nervous at all but rather seemed to enjoy the chance to debate theological issues with Kurbegovic. He told Kurbegovic that he had come to terms with what had happened to him, since God always has a reason for why things occur. "Is it your view, Mr. Shaughnessy, that God has allowed this to happen . . . [and] is also the God who has nailed Jesus Christ to the cross?" asked Kurbegovic. Shaughnessy responded, "Well, your question theologically is incorrect so I can't answer it theologically. God did not nail Christ to the cross. He sent his son to give his life. He did it willingly. But it is the same God who sent his son to die for us who allowed me to be blown up." Kurbegovic could not believe what he was hearing. "In other words, it is such a nice God that nails his son to the cross and blows people up?" he asked. Shaughnessy responded that it is "through suffering we have an opportunity to glorify God." Kurbegovic then wanted to know whether Shaughnessy had ever "asked God why does he have to nail his son to the cross and blow people up." Shaughnessy said he never asked that question.[65]

During the trial, Kurbegovic continually insulted people in the courtroom, including the jury, which was composed of eight men and four women, the majority of whom were African Americans. Kurbegovic tried to convey to them that as an alien, he too was discriminated against in America. But he used the "n-word" constantly to convey that message. Bozanich saw it as a strategy to prove to the jury that he had diminished capacity. "He started it during jury selection," Bozanich said. "Who else but a crazy man could look at a bunch of jurors in a Los Angeles courtroom during the 1970s and start using the [n-]word . . . right, left and sideways, if he wasn't trying to prove that he was nuts? He did it."[66]

One female black member of the jury couldn't take it. Several months into the trial, and after a couple of days of Kurbegovic again using the epithet, Shelia Easley sent a heartfelt and eloquent letter to Judge Watson:

Judge Watson,
As a very conscientious and proud American, I feel this letter to
be very pertinent. These past two days of humiliation, insult and

stereotypical innuendo experienced on this jury has been quite disgusting and distasteful. I have not worked all these years for a betterment in life to be brought down to such a level of ignorance and degradation as this defendant has clearly shown to my race, my pride and my dignity. I thank God that I did not have to experience the injustice and suffering of my forefathers.

This subjection to the derogatory terminology used by this defendant is not far from a past hell black people have known. It is outrageous.

I appreciate the experience of being on jury duty. It is most educational observing the judicial system of America in progress. I have the utmost respect for the bench and the judicial proceeding, but I feel the subjection [*sic*] of the last two days is a turn from the level of professionality.

This letter is not intended as a request to be excused. It is a request for a use of better terminology by the defendant if it is within your ruling or jurisdiction to do so.

I am not sure of the right or acceptability of a juror sending correspondence of this nature. I felt it necessary.

Yours respectfully,

Shelia E. Easley, Juror No. 12.[67]

Kurbegovic moved that the court excuse the juror, claiming that she was a racist! After questioning Easley as to whether she could continue to perform her obligations as a juror in a fair manner, Watson was convinced that she could and allowed her to remain on the jury.[68]

It was Watson, however, who bore the brunt of Kurbegovic's insults. A typical exchange between the defendant and the judge went as follows:

KURBEGOVIC: I at this time move Your Honor to disqualify yourself on the ground you are not intellectually competent to proceed in this particular trial.

THE COURT: I suggest you watch your comments or you will hear the balance of the morning in the lockup. . . .

KURBEGOVIC: It is not being disrespectful of the Court. It is simply a matter of my observation.

THE COURT: If you think I would tolerate that kind of comments from an attorney, you are grossly mistaken. I would cite an attorney for contempt immediately. And I am admonishing you that if you continue with that kind of disrespectful, discourteous comments you will be removed from the courtroom for the balance of the morning.

KURBEGOVIC: I respectfully request a hearing before another judge that is not related by professional connection to Your Honor to hear the issue of Your Honor's intellectual and educational and professional incompetency in relation to this trial....

THE COURT: Sit down and be quiet.

KURBEGOVIC: Is my motion granted or denied?

THE COURT: Denied.[69]

At one point in the trial, Kurbegovic screamed at the judge, "If I had a mother as cruel as you are, I would nail her to the cross." Another time, he requested more money for an investigator to help him with his case. Watson told him that the court had already provided him with thousands of dollars in services. "How much of it has ended up in your own pocket?" he replied. He also claimed that Watson was insane: "In my view as a layman you are insane in relation to me. And one of the reasons why you are insane in relation to me is because I am insane also. And insanity has a way of spreading itself in much the same way as magnetism does. Whenever I am in your presence your Honor is insane, in my view. And I, therefore, move for the hearing where I would show that only when I am in your presence or when person with identical mental condition as I have is in your presence, then you are insane and incapable of rationally judging the facts." Additionally, he once claimed Watson only became a judge because of the influence of her father: "Well, apparently your Honor has been fortunate for a while in your life by your father being a lawyer, having plenty of connections in obtaining your job of a judge. I do not believe that you have any academic qualifications to be a judge even in Iran, not to mention Los Angeles."[70]

Watson took this abuse and a lot more from Kurbegovic, though she removed him from the courtroom several times because his behavior was disrupting the trial. In the event of a removal, he was brought to a lockup, where a speaker was hooked up so he could listen to the proceedings. It was a risky move, since Kurbegovic was acting as his own lawyer, and continuing with the trial without the defendant present could result in a reversal of a conviction upon appeal. "It was gutsy," said Bozanich. "It was something that a lot of judges would not, I think, have been capable of. They might have concluded, 'I got to do it, but I'm gonna get reversed if I do it. It would be too risky to do it.'"[71]

Dealing with Kurbegovic as a defendant for a trial that was going to last eight months took a toll on the well-respected judge. "I really felt beaten down after a while," Watson said. "I remember saying one morning . . . to my husband, 'You know, I've so enjoyed sitting on the bench but I'd rather take a beating than go to court today.' I mean it was just unending with him. Just unending. And I like to think that I kept people in order in a courteous but firm matter. But I'm sure there were a couple of times where I yelled at him and said, 'Sit down!'"[72]

Kurbegovic liked to play tricks on the judge. Walt Lewis, who was the calendar deputy district attorney in Watson's courtroom, recalled one day being in her chambers and seeing a *Playboy* magazine on her desk. He teased her by saying he didn't realize that she subscribed to the magazine. She told him "that (bleep) Kurbegovic had subscribed to *Playboy* in her name and had it sent to the courtroom to embarrass her."[73] Lewis was impressed with Watson: "She didn't take any guff from anyone, but she still had a sense of humor, which kind of softened her, and I don't know anyone who didn't like her and respect her."[74] Lea Purwin D'Agostino, a young deputy district attorney who assisted Bozanich in the prosecution of Kurbegovic, remembered Watson as "a fabulous judge."[75] Bozanich agreed: "I could not have had a better trial judge," he said.[76]

Neither Lewis nor D'Agostino nor Bozanich was aware of the emotional toll the case was having on Judge Watson, since she never let on in the courtroom or in chambers that she was having a difficult personal experience dealing with Kurbegovic. She kept it all in. "You would never know in a million years," said D'Agostino.[77]

Another person frustrated by Kurbegovic's antics was of course prosecutor Dinko Bozanich, who had been dealing with him since 1974. Once, when Kurbegovic kept objecting while Bozanich was questioning a witness on direct examination, the exasperated prosecutor exclaimed, "Sometimes I wish the muteness would return." Another time, there was a discussion over whether a pipe bomb found during the search of Kurbegovic's apartment on the night of his arrest was a live bomb or not. Kurbegovic wanted to have the jury brought to a field to demonstrate "that the item cannot explode under any circumstances period." Watson would have no part of this: "If you think we are going out in the field to blow up a bomb in front of this jury, you are greatly mistaken." Bozanich had a solution: "Your Honor," he said, "perhaps the Court might reconsider, and this being somewhat said tongue in cheek, but I think the defendant could be confronted with the following proposal: That we go out and see him hold it while it is detonated. Then we will determine whether it is a live bomb or not." Kurbegovic shot back, "No, we will have Mr. Bozanich hold it when it is detonated." Watson ordered the pipe bomb removed from the police magazine where it had been stored for years and destroyed, with the destruction videotaped.[78]

Kurbegovic took pleasure in needling D'Agostino. "Mrs. D'Agostino is getting on my nerves," he told Watson, "with her sexual advances to every female in this court and with her laughs. She is getting on my nerves with her personality. She is aggressive toward every woman in this court that I observed . . . sexually speaking."[79] He called her "Dragon Lady," a moniker she proudly used in her later career, which included running (unsuccessfully) for the district attorney job in 1988. "I'm not called the Dragon Lady because I have dark hair and red fingernails," D'Agostino said in a campaign speech. "It's because I'm tough."[80]

Bozanich called scores of witnesses, including LAPD bomb experts like Arleigh McCree, in order to demonstrate beyond a reasonable doubt that Kurbegovic had committed all of the acts charged against him. Kurbegovic himself helped Bozanich's case by presenting an unusual defense that he called a "binary defense."[81] In his opening statement to the jury, accompanied with a handout and diagrams he drew on a blackboard, he said there were two interpretations of the evidence: "One of those interpretations . . . is very close to what Mr. Bozanich will be presenting and that is that I and only I have committed all the acts that I'm charged with." Another interpretation, Kurbegovic told the jury, is "that the organization [Aliens of America] that I am part of, but not necessarily conspirator within has committed all the acts that I am charged with. And . . . my job is entirely and only to go into the courtroom to present something in a courtroom that is both to my advantage, long term advantage as well as to the long term advantage of the association that I belong to."[82]

But when later in the trial Kurbegovic took the stand in his own defense and started asking himself questions about the interpretation that he alone committed the crimes, he gave details that amounted to a confession:

Q: Did you place the bomb at LAX that exploded on August 6th, 1974?

A: . . . Yes I did.

Q: Where did you place the bomb?

A: I placed it in a locker number T225.

Q: When did you place it?

A: Early morning hours of August 6th, '74. Could have been between 5:30 and 6:50 a.m.

Q: Where did you get the components for the bomb?

A: At RPM, RPM Industries.

Q: Where did you get the chemicals for the bomb?

A: At RPM Industries.

Q: Where did you get [the] fuse that you used in the bomb?

A: From Stephen Smith.

Q: Why did you place a bomb in locker T225?

A: I have no idea.[83]

Bozanich was, in the end, able to prove that the chemicals and components used in the LAX and Greyhound bombs were available at RPM and the Erb and Gray supply shop that Kurbegovic went to once with Stephen Smith, his friend and supervisor at RPM, and a few times by himself. Smith testified that he told Kurbegovic how one could make a bomb but never thought Kurbegovic would actually build one himself. He thought they were just having humorous discussions about the subject. "The tone, the expression on Mu's face and my tone of answer was more of a humorous interest in much the way one would on an Agatha Christie murder and plan a new way to do an unsolvable crime," Smith said.[84]

Smith shared many of Kurbegovic's antigovernment views. He was as quirky as Kurbegovic was, and at RPM the two men had engaged in conversations (with Kurbegovic writing but not talking) about scenarios for how to make $10 million by setting off a bomb and then promising not to set off another. They also discussed how they could make IRS records disappear and how to steal gold from Fort Knox. Bozanich at first thought that perhaps Smith knew more about Kurbegovic's plans than he admitted but eventually determined that Smith wasn't involved with Kurbegovic's terrorist attacks. He viewed Smith as a "mad scientist" who "was one of those type [of] people who liked to fantasize about things. Would like to talk about these things. But it was just talk."[85]

Bozanich believed, though, that money was a motive in Kurbegovic's crimes. "I can't exclude that he wasn't gonna [eventually] be doing this [planting bombs] for the money," Bozanich said.[86] A plausible scenario would be to plant a bomb and then extort the authorities or commercial entities for money in order to reveal the location of the bomb before it exploded, or simply promise not to plant any more bombs in exchange for money. "I never did, nor will I ever, subscribe to [the idea] that . . . [his motivation] was solely related to somehow a beef with the immigration laws or sex laws. . . . [H]e threw that out there because he did have some problems with that, but that wasn't the only reason, and the principal reason was . . . money. That's the way I saw it. Still do, and that will never change."[87]

Judge Watson, however, wasn't so sure about the money angle. "I suppose . . . [money] certainly is a possibility," Watson would later say. "It's not one that I would say would occur to me. I never got the impression that he was looking for wealth. He . . . really lived a very kind of bare-bones kind of life. And I think he had like about a one-room apartment. He drove a little VW. . . . It was kind of beaten up. . . . There wasn't anything about him that suggested to me that this guy was looking to live in a grand style, or anything of that kind."[88] Indeed, Kurbegovic never made any monetary demands in his taped messages or phone calls to the media.[89]

Bozanich also believed that Kurbegovic, while not a well person, was nevertheless exaggerating his illness after the arrest in order to first avoid having to face a criminal trial and then, once the trial began, to get a conviction for a lesser offense (or to have the sentence reduced by a judge) due to diminished capacity. When he cross-examined Frederick Hacker, the psychiatrist who had met with Kurbegovic in jail and who believed Kurbegovic was a paranoid schizophrenic, Bozanich was able to get him to admit that a person who is not mentally ill can fake mental illness. He also got Hacker to admit that he had never been tested on his ability to detect deception on the part of a person he was interviewing.[90]

Can It At Least Be a Thousand Years?

By October 1980, the trial was finally coming to an end. No one was happier about this than Judge Watson. There have probably been few, if any, other judges in history who had to endure as much abuse and insults for such a long period of time from a defendant as she did from Kurbegovic. But if she thought she had heard everything possible from him thus far in the trial, she was mistaken. Kurbegovic couldn't resist taking one final swipe at the judge during closing arguments. Watson remembered it as "possibly the most embarrassing moment I ever had on the bench":

> At the end of the trial when he is making his closing argument, he points to the seal, the great seal of the state of California, which is a big thing behind the bench in criminal courtrooms. And he says to the jury, "You see the man there holding the spear?" and the jury is all looking up at this, and he goes, "That's me. And you see the bear in the seal?" He goes, "That's Judge Nancy." Not Judge Watson, Judge Nancy. And then he said, "And I love my bear." I thought I was going to die! The jury of course cracked up. They thought it was very funny.... Personally, I was very embarrassed![91]

It wasn't just the reference to a bear that embarrassed Watson. "There is no question in my mind that his suggestion of a twisted affection for her was nothing short of mortifying for her," recalled her son Harvey. "He also had outbursts of hate toward her. His sociopathic behavior was a tough thing for her to endure. After the trial, he sent letters to her over the years that expressed perverted affection and slightly less than veiled threats."[92] Her daughter Marcia agreed. "I think Kurbegovic was kind of fascinated with her," she said. "He may have even had a crush on her, even though she was like twenty years older. You know, she was an attractive woman, she was very intelligent, [and] she's in this position of power over his life."[93]

Since Kurbegovic presented a diminished capacity defense and the issue of his mental health was pervasive throughout the trial and through deliberations, and because the jury raised a question even after they began deliberations regarding the relationship between mental capacity and malice aforethought, Watson was very specific in her instructions on this matter to the jury:

> Your initial task is to determine whether the defendant had substantially reduced mental capacity, whether caused by mental illness, mental defect or any other cause. If you find such substantially reduced mental capacity existed, it may or may not negate the existence of malice aforethought.
>
> If you find that the defendant's mental capacity was diminished to the extent that you have a reasonable doubt whether he was able to act with either express or implied malice aforethought, you cannot find him guilty of murder.
>
> However, if you find beyond a reasonable doubt that the defendant did act with malice aforethought even though he also had diminished capacity, you may find him guilty of murder.[94]

After deliberating for more than six days, on October 16 the jury returned guilty verdicts for all twenty-five counts, including murder. Kurbegovic, wearing a pair of green satin pants, a multicolored cummerbund, and a black-and-green jacket, never looked at the jurors as the verdicts were announced. At the sentencing hearing a month later, Kurbegovic anticipated he would be receiving a life sentence. He complained to Watson that that would be "too vague" of a sentence. "Well, can it at least be a thousand years so that I have something to look forward to?" he asked the judge. He also turned to a television camera that had been allowed in the courtroom under an experimental new California state law and held up a sign that read "I Shall Return!"[95]

Watson indeed sentenced him to life in prison, saying that if she had the power to do so she "would impose a sentence of life without possibility of parole or I would make all of it life sentences consecutive so that as a practical matter he would never be eligible for parole. But I don't believe the law provides for that." She further stated, "I don't know whether Mr. Kurbegovic is the most dangerous person in custody, but I consider him the most dangerous person in custody that I know of. And I would point out that this case amply demonstrates that this defendant has an enormous capacity for feeling[s] of vengence [sic] and for anti-social acts." She also said that "it was his intention to kill as many people as he could." Bozanich cringed at the notion that Kurbegovic might someday be paroled, stating, "The first person that ever lets this man out of jail, the blood that this guy is going to spread is on that person's hands."[96]

Bozanich didn't need to worry about Kurbegovic being paroled, at least not when he first came before the parole board in August 1987. Two Secret Service agents watched the proceedings, because Kurbegovic had made threats against then-president Ronald Reagan. He had also stated on more than one occasion that he intended to kill Bozanich, D'Agostino, and Watson. In addition, he wasn't exactly a model prisoner at San Quentin, California's oldest prison located near San Francisco, where he was incarcerated at the time of the parole hearing. He was accused of several prison violations there, including possession of explosives and weapons and throwing excrement at prison guards. [97]

At the parole hearing, Kurbegovic pleaded his case to be released. "I'm considered to be a top threat to the United States government," he argued. For that reason, "the people of California can only gain" from his release because, he believed, he would then be immediately deported to Yugoslavia and no longer pose a threat to California and the rest of the country. He also said he should be paroled for humanitarian reasons, claiming that authorities had injected him with the AIDS virus and that he now had only two years to live. He showed the three-member board a bruise on his left arm that he said was caused by Kaposi's sarcoma, a symptom of acquired immune deficiency syndrome. Prison medical personnel, however, said he had tested negative for AIDS.[98]

Not surprisingly, the parole board ruled against Kurbegovic, stating that he would pose an "unreasonable risk of danger to society if [he] were released."[99] He remained at San Quentin for several more years before being transferred first to Pelican Bay State Prison near the Oregon border, then to the California State Prison, Corcoran, in central California, and finally to the California State Prison, Los Angeles County, in Lancaster, about seventy miles north of Los Angeles, where he was as of October 2018. Always the legal maven, Kurbegovic flooded the courts over the years with petitions for writs of habeas corpus.[100] Among other notable assertions, he has claimed in some of these petitions that he represents the terrorist group al-Qaeda, that he understands a divinely inspired predictive code hidden in the alphabet, and that he has been in contact with space aliens and that only he can build a computer to communicate with the aliens before they destroy all of us.[101] All of Kurbegovic's petitions have been denied.

Perhaps the most interesting thing that Kurbegovic said at his first parole hearing was that there was nothing wrong with his mental health.[102] Whether he truly believed that or was trying to deceive the board in the hopes of being pardoned is not known. He had deceived people in the past, first by feigning muteness and later by exaggerating the symptoms of his mental illness to try to be declared incompetent to stand trial, like claiming to be the Messiah and stating that his head was a hydrogen bomb filled with heavy water.[103] But clearly, as Bozanich acknowledged, Kurbegovic was not a well man and was "half a bubble off." He symbolizes one type of lone wolf that exists today: a bright, creative individual who may be suffering from a mental disorder and has had something happen in life that propels him or her to violence. Lone wolves often latch onto an existing ideology or cause, such as Islamic extremism or white supremacy and neo-Nazism, or create one of their own, as Kurbegovic did with his antigovernment and antireligious platform.

A key question, then, that the Alphabet Bomber case raises is how we should deal with the mentally ill lone wolf and what, if anything, can be done to prevent such individuals from reaching a tipping point and launching a terrorist attack.

146

6

Crazy Like a Fox?

"While he superficially seems intact, it is quite apparent to this examiner that Mr. Kurbegovic is psychotic and probably has been psychotic for many years. His high intelligence have [*sic*] enabled him to mask open manifestations of his psychotic disorder." Thus wrote Dr. Franklin Drucker after meeting with Kurbegovic in 1976 before his second competency trial. But trying to figure out the mind-set of the Alphabet Bomber was not an easy task for the psychiatrist: "The precise formal psychiatric diagnosis is not entirely clear in my mind, but Paranoia or Paranoid Schizophrenia would seem most relevant; I am somewhat hesitant about diagnosis because of the brightness and superficial intactness of this obviously psychotic, delusional man."[1]

Bright, psychotic, and delusional: Kurbegovic wouldn't have made it into a terrorist group if that was something he ever desired. Individuals suffering from mental disorders tend to be excluded from membership in terrorist organizations. The last thing these groups want is an unpredictable, disruptive, and uncontrollable member who can jeopardize their operations. The myth that all terrorists must be crazy since they kill innocent people has given way to a better understanding of the varying motivations, strategies, and tactics of the diverse array of terrorist groups that have existed over the years.[2]

But it's a different story when it comes to the lone wolf. Studies have found a higher percentage of mentally ill lone wolf terrorists than mentally ill individuals who are members of a terrorist group. It has also been found that in the pre-9/11 period, when Kurbegovic was active, "fully half of the . . . lone wolves [studied] suffered from a documented mental illness," including schizophrenia, bipolar disorder, manic depression, and/or delusions.[3] Studies of individuals who have assassinated or attempted to assassinate U.S. presidents throughout history have also found the majority to be suffering from some type of mental illness.[4]

As a lone wolf, Kurbegovic was on his own. No group to control him or tell him what to do. He was therefore free to act upon any scenario he thought up. What started out as revenge attacks against specific individuals he felt had done him wrong escalated into the worst terrorist attack ever at a U.S. airport up to that point in time. But were there any early warning signs that Kurbegovic was capable and willing to perpetrate such an attack? And just how crazy was the Alphabet Bomber?

Master of Deception

Kurbegovic was undoubtedly a crafty, savvy, and smart young man who, as Dr. Drucker noted, was able to hide any signs of mental illness from those who thought they knew him. No one at his different jobs thought he needed psychological counseling or any type of help. He got along with most people and performed well at all his places of employment. He was also able to hide the fact that he could talk, fooling his coworkers and supervisors into believing he was mute, all due to his desire to attain a 4-F classification from the draft board, which would make him ineligible to serve in the military, thus avoiding the Vietnam War.

Prosecutor Dinko Bozanich viewed Kurbegovic's behavior as less an ability to hide manifestations of mental illness and more of a long-term plan to deceive people. He called him "a master of deception" during the competency and criminal trials. "The principal thing," recalled Bozanich, "is he's got enough of a grasp on reality that his first and foremost thing is deception. 'How can I get what I want, and what is it that I have to say or do to get what I want?' He's very good at that."[5] In addition to continuing the ruse of being a mute for several years after he received the 4-F classification, Kurbegovic also tried to fool all the psychiatrists who examined him in the criminal process, along with the judges and juries, by claiming to be the Messiah, a strategy he hoped would result in his being found not competent to stand trial.[6]

Kurbegovic was "about as normal a guy as you could get," according to one of his coworkers. There is no evidence that anyone who knew him socially or at work prior to his arrest in 1974, with the exception of the taxi dance hall hostess who once told him to see a psychiatrist for what she thought was his "inferiority complex," was aware of any hallucinations, delusions, or bizarre behavior. That is why Bozanich was convinced that while Kurbegovic "was a disturbed man . . . he was [nevertheless] faking the dramatic symptoms which he presented to the psychiatrists and that he had in fact deceived the psychiatrists."[7] One psychiatrist admitted under cross-examination that Kurbegovic "didn't become clinically ill until after he became incarcerated."[8]

Exaggerating the symptoms of mental illness for a defense against criminal charges is not unusual. According to forensic psychologist Dr. J. Reid Meloy, even when those who are arrested for some crime are in fact suffering from a mental disorder, they can still take advantage of what they may learn in a hospital or in visits with psychiatrists to help their case. "They're gonna learn the therapeutic language, they're gonna learn the diagnostic language, they're gonna learn the language of symptoms," Meloy explained. "When you then add to that criminality or criminal element you have the distinct possibility of the individual who still has a mental disorder but . . . can deliberately use aspects of his mental disorder to influence the outcome of his case."[9]

Even though Kurbegovic seemed normal to many people who knew him prior to his arrest, there were some signs that he needed psychiatric help while living in Los Angeles in the late 1960s. During the summer of 1968 he visited a urologist for impotency treatment, telling the doctor (speaking and not pretending this time to be mute) that he had never been able to perform sexually. The physician, Dr. B. Lyman Stewart, could not find any physical reasons for the impotency. When the doctor asked about his family's history, Kurbegovic told him that his father had died of stomach cancer and that his mother was living but was extremely nervous. Kurbegovic talked to him about his two sisters, and based on that conversation, Stewart believed that one of the sisters had "certain neurotic traits that were what one might expect in a socio-pathologic personality." He also found that Kurbegovic had "many built-in inhibitions from his upbringing, particularly the connection with morals as they are in the church, Yugoslavia and in his home."[10]

Kurbegovic also told Dr. Stewart that he was sure he had bad breath because of the way people looked at him when he talked to them. (Kurbegovic pretended to be a mute at work, but at other places, he talked.) Stewart, who did not detect any bad breath from Kurbegovic, viewed a "paranoic trend" in that type of statement. The doctor became very concerned when Kurbegovic talked about his sexual fantasies, which included "damaging the woman with whom [he] expects to have intercourse." In a letter to a psychiatrist whom Stewart wanted Kurbegovic to see, he wrote: "This type of patient, as far as I am concerned, has a very serious problem and needs to be treated by a full-time psychiatrist such as yourself. This man talks very easily and I think he may come along but the paranoid ideas and the destructive-sadistic tendencies certainly make the prognosis guarded."[11]

There is no evidence that Kurbegovic ever went to see the psychiatrist Stewart recommended or that he sought psychiatric or psychological counseling elsewhere.[12] Despite Stewart's diagnosis, Kurbegovic did not arouse any suspicion or concern in others that something was wrong with him. If there was one person who should have been suspicious of Kurbegovic, at least in the sense of what he was up to, it was his friend and supervisor at work, Stephen Smith. But even here, Kurbegovic was able to deceive Smith into thinking the scenarios they talked about (building bombs, making threats, appearing to be the leader of a group when in fact you're just a single individual, and so forth) were all in fun. Kurbegovic, though, was serious about learning as much as he could from these discussions. Smith never suspected that Kurbegovic was serious about these scenarios or that he was emotionally disturbed.

While no one at work or among the women he met at the taxi dance halls, with the exception of the one dance hall hostess discussed above, suspected Kurbegovic might be mentally ill or capable of violence, that has not been the case for some of the other lone wolf attacks that the United States and other countries have experienced. One in particular stands out for the magnitude of the incident and the fact that despite receiving treatment and medication for his illness, the perpetrator's mental condition did not improve, and he was still allowed to work in a facility where he had access to biological warfare agents.

I Wish I Could Control the Thoughts in My Mind

Shortly after the devastating suicide airplane attacks of September 11, 2001, on the World Trade Center in New York City and the Pentagon in Washington DC, America was rocked again by a major terrorist attack. This time, instead of planes crashing into buildings, it was biological warfare agents being sent through the mail.[13] And the person responsible for what became known as the "anthrax letter attacks" was a renowned microbiologist who was filled with obsession, revenge, and mental illness.

Bruce Ivins began working at the U.S. Army Medical Research Institute of Infectious Diseases (USAMRIID), which is located at Fort Detrick in Frederick, Maryland, in 1980. USAMRIID is the military's premier research laboratory for developing medical defenses against biological warfare threats. Ivins, who earned a doctorate in microbiology from the University of Cincinnati in 1976, specialized in developing a new and more effective anthrax vaccine. He became one of the world's leading authorities on growing anthrax spores.

While friendly and well liked at work, Ivins had a dark side. He was obsessed with the Kappa Kappa Gamma (KKG) sorority, driving three hours or more to visit KKG chapter houses on various campuses, look at the house for approximately ten minutes, and then drive home for another three hours. He broke into the houses on two occasions, once to steal the sorority's cipher, which was a decoding device for their secret rituals, and another time to steal the actual ritual book. He also vandalized the property where an adviser to the sorority lived. When FBI agents later asked Ivins about his interest in KKG, he stated, "Oh, it's not an interest. It's an obsession." What, though, had caused Ivins to focus so much energy on the sorority and want to take revenge against it? All it took was a Kappa Kappa Gamma coed turning him down for a date when he had been a student at the University of Cincinnati.

Although he was a renowned microbiologist, Ivins became very worried by the summer of 2001 that funding for his anthrax vaccine research at Fort Detrick would be drastically cut or even eliminated. The Pentagon wanted USAMRIID to shift personnel and resources away from research on anthrax vaccines and into the research and development of products that could be used against other biological agents, such as glanders, tularemia, and plague. Ivins grew angry when his bosses at USAMRIID approached him about working on glanders, which is a bacterium that kills both livestock and humans. "I am an anthrax researcher!" he told them. "This is what I do." At the time, he was working on a new anthrax vaccine that he had co-invented and expected to collect patent royalties if the vaccine ever made it to market.

The fear of not being allowed to work on anthrax vaccines was cited by the Department of Justice as a motive for his anthrax letter attacks. "Dr. Ivins's life work appeared destined for failure, absent an unexpected event." That event would, of course, be an anthrax attack that created demand for anthrax vaccines.

The attacks came in two waves, with letters filled with anthrax spores sent to media targets on September 18, 2001, and congressional targets on October 9. One letter never recovered is believed to have been sent to the American Media building in Boca Raton, Florida. Five people died from inhaling the *Bacillus anthracis* spores, and seventeen others were infected, some by inhaling the spores and others by absorbing the spores through their skin, which is known as cutaneous anthrax. Ten thousand more people believed to have been exposed to the spores underwent antibiotic prophylaxis. The Environmental Protection Agency spent $27 million from its Superfund program to decontaminate Capitol Hill facilities.

Ivins was put back to work on anthrax vaccines following the attacks. Since the anthrax letter attacks occurred shortly after the 9/11 suicide attacks by al-Qaeda, there was fear throughout the country that the terrorist group had struck again. There was also concern that the United States would now have to deal with the threat of bioterrorism in addition to conventional terrorist attacks such as hijackings, suicide plane crashes, bombings, and assassinations.

It would take the FBI nearly seven years to connect the dots and identify Ivins as the prime suspect. There was strong circumstantial evidence against him, including the findings by the FBI that an anthrax spore-batch (from the Ames anthrax strain) known as RMR-1029 was the parent material for the anthrax letter attacks and that Ivins had created and maintained this spore-batch in his laboratory at USAMRIID. Ivins was also among the few anthrax researchers in the country who had the ability to produce the highly purified spores that were used in the mailings. Additional circumstantial evidence pointing to Ivins as the perpetrator was the fact that the anthrax letters were sent from a mailbox outside the Princeton University offices of the Kappa Kappa Gamma sorority, the same sorority Ivins later admitted he was obsessed with and, as noted above, would drive three hours or longer to visit in different states.

Ivins committed suicide on July 9, 2008, as the FBI was about to bring charges against him. Although he tried to hide his mental illness from his coworkers and friends, he did confide in a former colleague, Mara Linscott, who was an object of his affection. He emailed her in June 2000 that he was seeing a psychiatrist and going to group therapy sessions but that it was not helping. He wrote that even with medication, "the depression episodes still come and go." He believed he could handle his depression, but "what is REALLY scary is the paranoia. . . . Psychosis or schizophrenia—that's a whole different story." In August 2000 he emailed her again: "I wish I could control the thoughts in my mind. It's hard enough sometimes controlling my behavior." He told one of the therapists he was seeing that his impulses to inflict harm were getting stronger and that he wasn't sure he could control them. He had earlier told the therapist that Mara was no longer responding regularly to his emails and that he planned to poison her but changed his mind.

When the therapist reported this to the police, she was told that nothing could be done since no crime had been committed. Although his mental state was deteriorating, Ivins continued to work with anthrax spores at Fort Detrick. A report by a panel of behavioral analysts in March 2011 stated that Ivins's history of mental problems should have disqualified him from obtaining a security clearance and that he should not have been allowed to work with dangerous biological agents at the U.S. Army's research facility.

The Ivins case illustrates how difficult it is to prevent a determined individual from committing a terrorist attack. Even with treatment for his mental illness, Ivins perpetrated the worst bioterrorist attack in U.S. history. Had he been prevented from working at USAMRIID due to his psychological condition, he still might have launched an attack by acquiring biological agents or other weapons of mass destruction on his own. Or he could have used conventional weapons such as bombs or guns to strike out at various targets. Although professional help did not work for Ivins, the same may not be true for other potential lone wolves who are suffering from mental disorders. A key question, then, is what the mental health community can do to try to reduce the risk of lone wolf terrorist attacks.

Are There Any Happy Terrorists?

Muharem Kurbegovic, like Bruce Ivins, was not a happy man. He harbored resentments toward those he believed had done him wrong. This included the police commissioners who denied him a permit to open a taxi dance hall, a judge who had reprimanded him in court, and the U.S. government and American justice system, which, he believed, discriminated against alien residents like himself. He had no meaningful relationships with women and had no friends, with the exception of his boss and coworker, Stephen Smith. He was a loner who found solace in frequenting the taxi dance halls of downtown Los Angeles. Had he sought the psychiatric treatment a doctor urged in 1968, perhaps he would have turned out differently. He had a good job, was bright, and was living in an exciting and vibrant city. He had his whole life ahead of him. Being in continual therapy might have enabled him to handle the major disappointments in his life in a better way. "He could have been a useful member of society," said Judge Watson. "But unfortunately was not. He was a very destructive personality."[14]

There is little, of course, that the mental health community can do when individuals with mental disorders do not seek help on their own or are not persuaded to do so by family, friends, coworkers, teachers, or others. But once they are seen by professionals, the challenge becomes distinguishing between those who are at risk of committing a terrorist attack and the vast majority of mentally ill individuals who are nonviolent.

J. Reid Meloy believes he has the answer. Meloy, who is a clinical professor of psychiatry at the University of California, San Diego, and a consulting forensic psychologist to the FBI, has developed an intriguing screening tool to aid mental health professionals in assessing the risk that a particular individual is likely to commit a lone wolf terrorist attack. He calls the tool the TRAP-18 (TRAP stands for Terrorist Radicalization Assessment Protocol).[15] It starts with a simple premise. "You'll never meet a happy terrorist," said Meloy. "If we scratched the surface, if we peeled away the layers, we'd find [someone] who had a history that suggested failures, alienations, things of that nature."[16]

The TRAP-18 involves eighteen different behaviors and characteristics, ranging from "fixation" and "energy burst" to "personal grievance" and "history of criminal violence."[17] While it would be a challenge for any therapist to measure and assess eighteen different indicators, Meloy believes it could be done and would be beneficial in identifying potential lone wolf terrorists. It "can help the clinician determine whether a patient should be monitored for further concerning behavior, or whether the patient should be actively risk managed to divert him or her from a pathway toward ideologically motivated violence."[18]

Not surprisingly, cooperation and information sharing between the mental health community and law enforcement is a controversial issue. It raises privacy, ethical, and practical concerns. If patients are suspicious that their therapists may report them to the police or to federal authorities, they will then naturally hold back with what they are telling their doctors and likely stop seeking treatment. The same is true if patients believe that law enforcement and intelligence agencies will be granted access to the hospital, clinic, and private doctor records of mental health patients. There is also the risk that many therapists might not be able to identify what exactly constitutes a patient at risk of committing a terrorist attack, despite the TRAP-18 and other studies aimed at assisting them in their assessments. Patients could, therefore, be wrongly reported to authorities.

If the mental health community wants to find examples of successful programs that aimed to prevent individuals, whether mentally ill or not, from following a path leading to terrorism, they will unfortunately be frustrated in their search. One of the more publicized and highly visible programs in recent years that was created to do just that has had a dismal history. The Strategic Implementation Plan (SIP) for countering violent extremism (CVE) was established by the U.S. government in 2011. Led by the Department of Homeland Security (DHS) and the Department of Justice (DOJ), the program's main objective has been to educate and provide resources to communities for preventing violent extremist attacks. Specifically, CVE is "aimed at enhancing the ability of local police and community organizations—including religious, educational, and non-profit entities—to provide information and resources to communities targeted by violent extremists and individuals who may have started down a road to violent extremism. These activities generally aim to provide alternative messages and options to terrorist or violent extremist recruitment and radicalization efforts through civic engagement."[19]

While on the surface that may have sounded promising, a 2017 report by the U.S. Government Accountability Office (GAO) highlighted the problems with CVE.[20] The GAO criticized the government for not having a cohesive strategy or process to evaluate the effectiveness of the program's effort. That effort included forty-four tasks focused on three core CVE objectives: community outreach, research and training, and capacity-building. Among the tasks have been the DOJ "conducting CVE outreach meetings to communities targeted by violent extremism and DHS integrating CVE content into law enforcement counterterrorism training." There have also been efforts by the DHS toward "building relationships with the social media industry and increasing training available to communities to counter violent extremists online." The GAO summed up its view of the CVE program as follows: "Although GAO was able to determine the status of the 44 CVE tasks, it was not able to determine if the United States is better off today than it was in 2011 as a result of these tasks."[21]

Many critics have argued that the United States is not better off due to the CVE program, which has had test runs in Los Angeles, Minneapolis, and Boston. "The beating heart of CVE is collaboration, but the current effort has actually dissuaded collaboration by stoking alienation," writes terrorism scholar Erroll Southers. "Although the strategy is ostensibly designed to address any violent ideology, in practice it has focused primarily on the risk of extremism in Muslim communities." Indeed, there had been reports that President Donald Trump might rename the program "Countering Islamic Extremism" or "Countering Radical Islamic Extremism."[22] The Trump administration decided, however, not to bother with a new name for the program and instead unveiled a budget proposal that would eliminate all funding for the program.[23]

The CVE program has also been criticized for having the DOJ manage the pilot programs. As Southers writes, "A successful program cannot be run by the same arm of government that prosecutes terrorism cases. That demands an unrealistic level of trust on the part of the community. Why would someone participate in such an initiative if they fear their questions, comments and concerns could lead to an FBI agent knocking on their door?"[24] That element of trust, which has eluded the CVE program thus far, is one of the key obstacles the mental health community will need to overcome as it tries to help troubled individuals who may be on a path to terrorism.

Another challenge facing the mental health community, and one that has also been a problem for all government and nongovernment efforts to counter violent extremism, is confusion over what the term "radicalization" means. "Radicalization" has become the new buzzword in terrorism studies, policy statements, counterterrorism strategies, and media coverage of terrorism. This despite the fact that there is no consensus on what exactly radicalization entails. Is it an individual who simply expresses anti–U.S. government or pro-terrorist sentiments? Or is it an individual who is in direct or indirect contact with extremists and their sympathizers? If a patient expresses "radical" sentiments, it may not necessarily mean the person is "radicalized" or intent on carrying out an attack. He could be merely exercising his right to freedom of speech or just fantasizing, venting, or expressing his thoughts for shock value.

The attractiveness of the concept of radicalization for analysts, policy-makers, journalists, and others is that it reduces a complex phenomenon like terrorism to a process that presumably can be observed, as well as possibly managed and prevented under the right circumstances. However, there is no single road a person takes to becoming a terrorist, nor are there always observable signs that someone is becoming "radicalized." As one terrorism scholar notes, "Multiple factors interact in complex ways that cause radicalization to emerge in individual people and groups. As with other complex systems, such as ecosystems, removing one factor does not cause the system to collapse but instead to evolve in ways that may be positive or negative.... International conflicts, social networks, community, ideology, and individual vulnerabilities all combine to let radicalization emerge."[25]

The popularity of the radicalization concept is similar to the wide appeal that the concept of a "terrorist network" had during the 1970s and 1980s. A popular book at that time was Claire Sterling's *The Terror Network*, which argued that the Soviet Union was the main source of international terrorism and the training, financing, and influencing of various terrorist groups around the world. The implication was that if the United States and its allies could counter Soviet influence, then a big part of the terrorist problem would be solved. That, of course, proved to be wrong, as terrorism during that era had many origins and causes, as is true today. But reducing the complex phenomenon of terrorism to a "network" controlled or influenced by the Soviet Union made the threat seem more manageable, or at least provided a visible entity to focus counterterrorism policies on. That is why Sterling's book was well received by President Ronald Reagan, who had referred to the Soviet Union as the "evil empire."[26]

Another problem with the concept of radicalization is that it is not clear what specifically causes a person expressing radical views to take it to the next level and actually commit a violent act. Trigger points could be anything from negative personal experiences or situations such as divorce, debt, or physical illness to anger over foreign or domestic policies, world events, or any other situation that may arise. For some lone wolves, taking violent action in the name of a group or cause can fill a void in their lives and give meaning to an otherwise unhappy existence.

The case of a female lone wolf terrorist, Roshonara Choudhry, illustrates the problem with the idea that radicalization is something that can usually be observed in the words or behavior of another person, and that actions can then be taken to counter it or at least prevent the "radicalized" person from reaching a tipping point that leads him or her to violence.[27] Choudhry, who was not mentally ill, was an excellent student at the prestigious King's College London before unexpectedly dropping out just a few months before graduation in 2010. She then attempted to assassinate Stephen Timms, a British Parliament member who supported the war in Iraq. Choudhry showed no signs of radicalization prior to the attack and gave no indication to her friends, family, or acquaintances that she was sympathetic in any way to those who espoused Islamic extremist views.

However, it was learned after her arrest in May 2010 that she had secretly begun downloading in November 2009 the sermons of Anwar al-Awlaki, the extremist Islamic cleric who was living in Yemen at that time and who would later be killed in a U.S. drone attack in 2011. Al-Awlaki could be considered the godfather of modern lone wolf terrorists, having influenced from afar a diverse array of extremists, including several even after his death, such as the Tsarnaev brothers, Tamerlan and Dzhokhar, who set off pressure-cooker bombs at the Boston Marathon finish line in April 2013, killing 3 people and injuring more than 260 others. Al-Awlaki's sermons have lived on after his death via the Internet. In Choudhry's case, between November 2009 and May 2010, when she carried out the attempted assassination, she listened to more than one hundred sermons by al-Awlaki. She never met, emailed, or talked to al-Awlaki but was motivated solely by his inflammatory sermons calling for violent attacks against the West. She became "radicalized" without anyone ever knowing.

The influence of the Internet today is crucial in explaining the rise of lone wolf terrorism. The Islamic State of Iraq and Syria (ISIS) has effectively used the Internet to inspire individuals to commit terrorist attacks in their home countries. ISIS has used Twitter, Facebook, online videos, and other Internet means to appeal to individuals to ram cars into crowds, shoot and stab people, set off pressure-cooker bombs, or find any other type of weapon to kill the infidels, whom they define as anyone not following their religious ideology. It was an ingenious method of recruitment, similar to spam email, where spammers send out millions of messages and need only a small percentage to take the bait to be effective. For ISIS, and any other extremist group, there is no risk in who the individual is who acts on their behalf. They could be mentally unstable individuals, but since they are not privy to any information about the group, such as plans, operational strategy, and members, the extremist groups can use these people without fear of compromising their organization.

Among the many terrorist attacks by individuals with mental illnesses who were inspired by ISIS or other Islamic extremists and groups have been those of Martin Couture-Rouleau, who rammed his car into two soldiers, killing one, in Saint-Jean-sur-Richelieu in Quebec, Canada, in October 2014;[28] Michael Zehaf-Bibeau, who killed a soldier in Ottawa and then ran through the Canadian parliament building before being shot and killed by the sergeant at arms, also in October 2014;[29] Mohammod Youssef Abdula-zeez, who fired upon U.S. servicemen at two locations in Chattanooga, Tennessee, in July 2015, killing four marines and fatally wounding a navy sailor;[30] and Ahmad A., who stabbed five people on a street in Hamburg, Germany, in July 2017, killing one person.[31]

Mentally unstable lone wolves have been inspired by other ideologies as well and have committed terrorist attacks. These include, among others, Anders Breivik, an anti-Islamic and anti-immigration right-wing lone wolf terrorist who killed seventy-seven people in two attacks in Norway in August 2011, with most of the victims being children and youths attending a summer camp run by the ruling Labor Party;[32] Dylann Roof, a white supremacist sympathizer who shot and killed nine African American churchgoers in Charleston, South Carolina, in June 2014, hoping it would start a race war;[33] and Theodore Kaczynski, the infamous Unabomber, who called for a revolution against the industrial-technological society and sent package bombs or left them at various places over a seventeen-year period beginning in 1978, resulting in the death of three people and injuring twenty-three others.[34]

The diverse array of ideologies and causes that can propel an individual to commit a terrorist attack illustrates the difficult task any mental health worker has in trying to determine whether a patient is on the road to "radicalization" and then terrorism. Nevertheless, there is pressure building in many countries to utilize the mental health community in the battle against terrorism. In France, Interior Minister Gérard Collomb announced in August 2017 that he and Health Minister Agnés Buzyn "would be asking psychiatry experts from both the private and public sector to help the Government identify 'disturbed aspiring jihadists' who are not known to police by reporting any suspicious behavior among their patients."[35] In Australia, a "Fixated Persons Investigations Unit" composed of specialist detectives and mental health experts was established by the police in New South Wales in April 2017. One of the unit's objectives is to "investigate individuals who've made threats of violence and then determine whether they should be arrested and charged or provided with mental health care." Another objective is to "identify people who may be vulnerable to rapid radicalisation or lone-wolf-style attacks."[36]

In October 2016, as the presidency of Barack Obama was coming to an end, the White House announced plans to create "intervention teams" that would be led by mental health professionals, faith-based groups, educators, and others with the objective "to divert a person away from violence before they commit a violent act and without involving law enforcement agencies."[37] Since President Trump wasn't keen on the CVE program initiated by the Obama administration, it is doubtful that he will embrace this new attempt at identifying and preventing lone wolf terrorism.

As noted earlier, efforts around the world to incorporate the mental health community into the battle against terrorism are fraught with difficulties, ranging from the practical (including trying to correctly identify patients at risk of committing a terrorist attack) to ethical and legal concerns (compromising patients' privacy rights and reporting "false positives," or innocent people, to the authorities). Bringing psychiatrists, psychologists, and other mental health workers into counterterrorist watchdog teams in various communities can also compromise the profession's integrity and reputation of presumably being doctors there to help people suffering from various mental disorders. "We will not spy on our patients," wrote a psychiatrist and a psychologist in a blog for *Psychology Today*. "We do not read minds, and we know that none of us can predict the future."[38]

Still, there is no denying that mental illness is a characteristic found in many lone wolf terrorists. The skills and expertise of the mental health community are therefore needed to try to reduce the risks of terrorist attacks committed by emotionally troubled individuals. There are ways that the mental health community can help without creating the perception that they have become an arm of the authorities in trying to identify the lone wolves who live among us.

One important way is to work with a patient's family when that option is available. Families are often the first to notice, or be told about, extreme changes in the behavior, thinking, attitudes, and so forth of other family members. Facilitating avenues for family members to be able to contact therapists about other family members they are concerned about, or therapists themselves making contact with family members of patients they suspect may be on the path to violence, could help.

For example, Tamerlan Tsarnaev, who along with his brother, Dzhokhar, perpetrated the Boston Marathon bombing in April 2013, confided to his mother, Zubeidat, around 2008 that "he felt like 'two people' were inside him."[39] When she told a close friend about this, the friend said that Tamerlan might need psychiatric care. Whether being in therapy might have changed Tamerlan and prevented his terrorist attack years later cannot, of course, be determined. But his mother was opposed to any psychiatric care for Tamerlan and instead "believed that religion would be the cure for her son's inner demons and growing mental instability, and pushed him deeper into Islam."[40]

In cases where family members and friends might want to intervene on behalf of those they believe are on the path to potential terrorist activity but do not know what to do or say to the person, mental health workers could be of assistance.[41] Either through group sessions with the individual and those people he or she trusts or admires, or through just talking informally with the family members and friends, mental health workers might, in some instances, be able to create a support network for the person in question and reduce the risk that the individual will commit a terrorist attack.

In addition, family and friends can at times play a role in helping to catch a lone wolf terrorist after an attack. For seventeen years, Theodore Kaczynski, the Unabomber, eluded the FBI and other law enforcement agencies that were trying to apprehend the unidentified individual who was sending package bombs throughout the country. Despite their efforts, Kaczynski was not captured until his manifesto was published in the *Washington Post* in September 1995. His brother, David, saw a resemblance between letters he had received from Theodore over the years and the writing style and ideas expressed in the published manifesto. He contacted the authorities, and this led to Kaczynski's arrest in a remote Montana cabin in April 1996.[42]

The irony regarding the case of the Unabomber is that had the Internet been accessible and widely used during the Unabomber's reign of terror from 1978 to 1995, Kaczynski probably would have been caught a lot sooner. Kaczynski desperately sought an outlet for the dissemination of his anti-technology and anti-industrial views. That's why he demanded that newspapers publish his manifesto. He very likely would have used the Internet instead to post the manifesto online early in his terrorist career, despite his distaste for technology. The same scenario that played out years later, with his brother turning him in after reading the manifesto in the newspaper, would likely have occurred once his brother read it online. Subsequent attacks could have therefore been prevented.

Addressing the threat of lone wolf terrorism will remain a top priority for governments and societies in the coming years. There will undoubtedly continue to be calls for mental health workers to play an active role in trying to identify potential lone wolf terrorists. For all the reasons discussed above, there will also continue to be resistance from psychiatrists, psychologists, and others toward compromising patients' privacy rights in order to assist law enforcement and government agencies in the battle against terrorism. In the end, however, it may actually be in the performance of their everyday jobs that the mental health community can make its most important contribution to dealing with the terrorist threat. For each person they see who is suffering from depression, anxiety, paranoia, schizophrenia, or any other mental disorder and for whom they are successful in helping to improve their lives, the risk of that person committing a terrorist or any other type of violent act may indeed be reduced.

Whether mental health professionals could have helped the Alphabet Bomber is not known. Muharem Kurbegovic was a master of deception, and he fooled many psychiatrists who saw him in the years following his arrest, exaggerating his symptoms in order to help his own defense during his competency and criminal trials. Without any counseling or therapy prior to his terrorist activity, he was free to descend into a vicious cycle of blaming everything wrong in his life on other people or events. His story is a tragic one, and one that holds many lessons for today.

7

What the Story of the Alphabet Bomber Can Teach Us

When Muharem Kurbegovic arrived in Los Angeles in 1967, I was finishing my senior year at Midwood High School in Brooklyn, New York. I had been in the honor society, although I don't remember any activities or meetings that we had. However, we did take a group picture for the high school yearbook. In that photo were two female classmates who would soon have experiences with the type of terrorism that was prevalent in those days. One would become a hostage in the most spectacular hijacking in terrorism history at that time, when the Popular Front for the Liberation of Palestine seized four planes on the same day in September 1970. My other classmate would join the leftist terrorist group the Weathermen and is currently serving time in a New York state prison for her part in a 1981 Brinks armored truck robbery and murders in Nyack, New York. Both women's experiences with terrorism were indicative of the terrorism of the times—namely, attacks perpetrated by organized groups with clearly stated objectives.

The term "lone wolf terrorism" had not yet been invented. That would not occur until the 1990s, when white supremacists Alex Curtis and Tom Metzer called for "lone wolf" actions by their followers in order to evade detection by the authorities.[1] Eventually, the term "lone wolf" would be used to refer to any individual with a political, religious, or social objective who committed terrorist attacks alone, with no assistance from other individuals or groups.

The lone wolf phenomenon revolutionized the world of terrorism. By the second decade of the twenty-first century, it was considered by many law enforcement and intelligence agencies, government officials, policymakers, academics, and the public to be one of the most serious terrorist threats facing the global community. No longer was the enemy only known groups with communications that could be intercepted or members who could be arrested to learn of impending plots. The enemy now could be just one person, anywhere, with a weapon and a cause.

Muharem Kurbegovic foreshadowed this new type of terrorist. He was savvy, cunning, creative, and dangerous. There is much we can learn from his terrorizing a city more than forty years ago.

Lone Wolf Terrorism Is a Diverse Phenomenon

Perceptions of terrorism can sometimes be misguided. That has been the case in the United States in recent years. The prevailing view among the media, politicians, and the public is that the domestic terrorist threat in America stems primarily from Islamic extremism. This despite the fact that from September 12, 2001 (the day after the 9/11 attacks), to December 31, 2016, there were eighty-five deadly attacks in the United States by violent extremists, with most of them (sixty-two) perpetrated by far-right violent extremists. Islamic extremists were responsible for twenty-three attacks.[2]

Portraying the terrorist threat as primarily stemming from Islamic extremists, however, gives a face to this diverse and complex phenomenon. This was what happened with Claire Sterling's thesis regarding the Soviet Union being behind most of the organized group terrorism plaguing the West during the 1970s and 1980s. Yet lone wolf terrorism, just like group terrorism, cuts across the entire political, religious, and social spectrum. There have been right-wing, left-wing, Islamic, Jewish, single-issue, and idiosyncratic lone wolf terrorist attacks throughout the world. Among just some examples of the diversity in lone wolf attacks in the United States and other countries are the following: far right/white supremacist/neo-Nazi (Dylann Roof, Anders Breivik, Robert Bowers); left wing (James Hodgkinson); Islamic (Nidal Malik Hasan, Tamerlan and Dzhokar Tsaranev, Syed Rizwan Farook and Tashfeen Malik, Omar Mateen); Jewish (Baruch Goldstein, Yigal Amir); single issue (Eric Rudolph [anti-abortion], Joseph Stack [anti-tax]); and idiosyncratic (Muharem Kurbegovic, Theodore Kaczynski).[3]

The idiosyncratic category is the wild card in lone wolf terrorism. Although the idiosyncratic lone wolf may commit attacks in the name of some cause, that cause is usually irrational and unattainable, such as the Unabomber's call for an end to the "technological-industrial" society we live in and Kurbegovic's call for the abolition of all immigration, naturalization, and sex laws. As is true for the idiosyncratic lone wolf, Kurbegovic created his own ideology, a mixture of antigovernment, antireligious, and anticommunism sentiments. The combination of personal grievances (the denial of a permit to open a taxi dance hall and likely delays and the possible denial of his application to become a naturalized U.S. citizen) along with his own ideological beliefs and perceived failures in life resulted in his terrorist attacks.

The diversity in the causes and motivations of lone wolf terrorists will continue to make this form of terrorism a difficult one to deal with. No single cause or movement has a monopoly on this growing international threat.

Terrorists and the Media Use Each Other for Their Own Benefit

It was pointed out in the Introduction that there is a symbiotic relationship between terrorists and the media, with each needing the other to achieve their objectives. Terrorists need the media to gain publicity for their cause and to spread fear beyond the immediate target of their violence. Terrorist groups also can win new recruits via the publicity they generate from their threats and attacks. The media, in turn, needs terrorist crises to increase viewership and circulation.

The Internet has revolutionized this relationship, as terrorists can now bypass traditional media and use websites, chat rooms, tweets, Facebook pages, and so forth to achieve the same objectives. ISIS perfected the use of social media to recruit individuals to come to Syria and Iraq to join their group and also to call upon people to commit lone wolf attacks in their home countries. Along with al-Qaeda, they've also published online magazines containing instructions on how to build homemade bombs.

Terrorists, however, still like to have their actions, causes, and messages publicized by traditional media, since not everyone gets all of his or her news via social media and the Internet. And since newspapers and television networks all have a presence on the Internet via their own websites, terrorists can achieve additional publicity when traditional media covers their threats and activities. These traditional media outlets, in turn, can attract more people to visit their websites when they report on terrorist events through multiple channels.

The traditional media, therefore, still plays a role in how terrorist events are portrayed to the public. Kurbegovic demonstrated how a savvy, clever, and diabolical individual can exploit the media to spread fear throughout a city, and how the media allowed this to happen. At first his threats were ignored by the media, as there was no reason to believe that anything he was saying was true. That is why there was no mention in newspapers or broadcasts by television news stations of the tape that he left near the lobby of the *Los Angeles Times* building on July 5, 1974, and similar tapes he had sent to the Washington DC bureau of the United Press International news service and to the British and Soviet embassies in Washington, claiming to be the leader of a new terrorist group, "Aliens of America," which had developed four nerve gases and had already tested them on animals and humans. Outlandish boasts of having planted the nerve agents in several cities in the United States and other countries, as well as his issuing an "ultimatum to surrender" to governments everywhere and calling for an "end to all Nationalism, Religionism, Fascism, Racism, and Communism," made it easy for the media to ignore the tapes.

But all this changed after the bombing at Los Angeles International Airport on August 6, 1974. When he called the *Los Angeles Herald Examiner* later that night again claiming to be the leader of this new terrorist group and gave the correct publicly undisclosed information regarding the number of the locker in which the bomb had been placed, Kurbegovic now had to be taken seriously. While the *Los Angeles Times* and other newspapers reported on this phone call from Kurbegovic and his subsequent threats and actions in the following days, it was the *Herald Examiner* that took the lead in covering the story, sometimes in an exploitative manner that only scared people more than necessary. Headlines such as "L.A. BOMBER PLEDGES GAS ATTACK" and "RACE AGAINST TIME TO FIND THIRD BOMB" were chilling reminders to the public that a terrorist was on the loose and that people should be very worried.

The Kurbegovic case raises two questions that are often heard regarding the proper role of the media in reporting on a terrorism event. How much coverage should the media give to a terrorist incident, and does it play into the terrorists' hands by reporting on the event? Various proposals have been made regarding how the media should cover a terrorist story. These include, among other things, limitations on interviews during hostage incidents; delays of the release of inflammatory or sensitive information; minimum intrusiveness in the course of terrorist incidents; and balanced and noninflammatory coverage of such incidents.[4]

Freedom of the press, however, makes any enforced restrictions on the media difficult, if not impossible, to implement. Self-imposed guidelines would also be difficult for any television network or newspaper to follow, since there is competition to be the first with a story and to be the forum providing the most detailed, vivid, and dramatic account of the events. Furthermore, any effort to reduce news coverage of a terrorist event or provide guidelines for how to cover it due to concern for the media's impact on the event could open a floodgate of censoring of other stories in which similar concerns are raised. Former ABC News correspondent Sam Donaldson expressed the views of many in the media regarding the perils of any form of censorship of the press:

> [We] want to continue to report that story right through to the end. Giving it as much coverage as—again, reasonable editors can differ— but as much coverage as would normally be given a story. And I don't think you scrimp on it. I don't think you say, well, this is a terrorist attack. The terrorists want to engage the news media, therefore we won't give them what their objective is. That seems to me to fly in the face of

everything we stand for. It is not up to me to decide what is good for my audience. It is up to me to report the news. It is up to the audience, the individuals, to decide how to think about it, what to do with it. . . . We get on awfully dangerous ground when we decide to play censor because we think it is not in the best interest of American people or any other people to have a particular cause publicized.[5]

For his part, Kurbegovic played the media like a maestro in front of his orchestra. He telephoned newspapers and television and radio stations, dropped tapes off at different locations in Los Angeles, and threatened to kill more people with each new threat. He also, however, pulled back at times, such as when he revealed that the "L" bomb was in a locker at the downtown Greyhound bus station, saying that because his cause was getting publicity, he had decided to let "L" stand for "life." But in the same tape, he warned that the "I" bomb had already been planted.

Kurbegovic manipulated the media creatively, using the alphabet to tease the authorities about his next target. He likely got the idea to drop off tapes for the media from the SLA, which had recently kidnapped Patty Hearst. The SLA, though, did not threaten to set off bombs or target crowds of innocent civilians in their messages to the media. Instead, they tried to appeal for public support by demanding a program to distribute food to the poor. The SLA was more of a curiosity item for the public than a real threat. The public's fascination with the group stemmed more from their high-profile hostage, Patty Hearst, and how her fate would turn out than from any fear about the SLA.

Kurbegovic, however, had the entire city of Los Angeles in fear, beginning first with the LAX bombing and then from his continual flow of taped messages and phone calls promising more violence. He took the SLA's idea of sending messages to the media to a new level and demonstrated how a clever lone wolf can keep the public and the authorities on edge with the help of the media, thereby sustaining a terrorist crisis.

Lone Wolves Love to Talk a Lot

The story of the Alphabet Bomber illustrates a phenomenon we are witnessing today—namely, the tendency for lone wolf terrorists to talk a lot.

This is surprising, because one of the advantages that lone wolves have over groups and cells is that there are no communications among members of a group for the authorities to intercept that can lead to the identification and arrest of the terrorists. One would think, therefore, that lone wolves would guard this advantage and be careful not to reveal their plans or motivations to anyone. But the human need to communicate is too strong even for lone wolves to resist.

Today, lone wolves do their talking primarily on the Internet, usually giving clues as to what they are about to do via blogs, Facebook pages, online manifestos, and so forth. For example, Anders Breivik, the Norwegian lone wolf who massacred scores of youths at a summer camp in July 2011, posted a manifesto on the Internet shortly before embarking on his violent rampage. In the manifesto, he wrote, "Once you decide to strike it is better to kill too many than not enough, or you risk reducing the desired ideological impact of the strike." Similarly, Joseph Stack, who flew a plane into a building containing offices of the Internal Revenue Service in Austin, Texas, in February 2010, wrote in his online manifesto shortly before his suicide attack that "violence not only is the answer, it is the only answer."[6]

During Kurbegovic's time, there was no Internet where a lone wolf could do his or her talking. Other means had to be used. Although Kurbegovic had enough self-control to fake being a mute for years at work and converse only by writing notes, he could not resist the temptation to boast about the LAX bombing and warn of more attacks in the taped messages he left for the media. Yet it was his desire to continue to taunt the Los Angeles Police Department with his messages that ultimately led to his downfall. If he hadn't named various people whom he felt had done him wrong, he might never have been caught. The information he provided on one of the tapes eventually enabled investigators to identify Kurbegovic as the Alphabet Bomber.

The same was true for George Metesky, the Mad Bomber who terrorized New York with a bombing campaign in the 1940s and 1950s. It was only after he was encouraged to write to a newspaper about his grievances that he unwittingly revealed that he had a workman's compensation claim that had been denied by Consolidated Edison, the New York utility company.

Then, investigators were able to check the company's records and discovered his identity and arrested him. And Theodore Kaczynski, the Unabomber, was caught when his manifesto was published in a newspaper and his brother, David, recognized the writing style and ideas expressed in it as those of his brother. David notified the authorities, leading to Kaczynski's eventual arrest.

Whether it be through traditional media such as newspapers (as in the cases of Kurbegovic, Kaczynski, and Metesky) or through blogs, tweets, emails, or manifestos posted online (as is the case today with many lone wolves), the urge to talk is a major advantage for law enforcement in its battle against this form of terrorism. "What really did him in," said Judge Nancy Watson, who presided over Kurbegovic's criminal trial, "was [that] he couldn't resist being heard."[7]

Lone Wolf Terrorists Can Be More Creative and Innovative Than Terrorist Groups

The Alphabet Bomber was a smart and creative terrorist. He epitomized why lone wolves are sometimes more innovative than many organized terrorist groups. Lone wolves tend to think outside the box, since that is how they live, as loners and outsiders not constrained or obligated to follow what might be considered socially accepted norms of behavior. Lone wolves are free to act upon any scenario they may think up, because they are accountable only to themselves. There are no group decision-making processes or intergroup dynamics at play to stifle their creativity in formulating plans and operations. That is why lone wolves have been responsible for the first vehicle bombing (1920), major midair plane bombing (1955), hijacking (1961), airport bombing (1974), product tampering (1982), and anthrax letter attacks (2001) in the United States.[8]

Kurbegovic was the first person to bomb an airport anywhere in the world. It is not known how he came up with the idea. He might have seen the lockers when he was at the airport one day and observed that there was no security around that area. In doing something no individual or terrorist group had ever done before, he was guaranteed widespread publicity for his cause. When he was later asked by a psychiatrist why he or his group exploded one bomb at LAX and placed another at the Greyhound terminal, Kurbegovic responded, "Number one is to say we are here . . . Aliens of America . . . That we exist . . . In all conflict between military forces, people get killed, property get[s] destroyed. . . . Number two [is] making a military impact on the entire establishment."[9]

Of course, it isn't just lone wolves who need to do something spectacular or different to ensure that they are taken seriously. The same is true for terrorist groups. As noted in chapter 2, when people and the media become desensitized to the "normal" flow of terrorism, such as daily car bombings, hijackings, and shootings, there is an incentive for terrorists to escalate their attacks. By killing more people than they have in the past or perpetrating a new type of attack, they are guaranteed the publicity and reaction that their previous attacks generated but no longer do. Also, for a new terrorist group or faction that has broken away from an existing group, a spectacular attack can achieve the purpose of announcing their presence.

However, terrorist groups, unlike lone wolves, usually have constituencies that they are appealing to for support, whether that be financial, political, or logistical. These constituencies may not approve of the violence but nevertheless support the cause. That is why terrorist groups are usually aware of certain boundaries regarding "acceptable violence." That might be the reason why any number of domestic terrorist groups active during the 1960s and 1970s did not do what Kurbegovic did—namely, explode a bomb in a crowded airport terminal, killing innocent civilians. Kurbegovic illustrated the indifference that lone wolves have to the public's reaction to their attacks when he said in one of his tapes, "We do not ask American people to support us; in fact, we don't give a damn whether they like what we have to offer or not."[10]

The "success" of Kurbegovic's bombing of LAX wasn't lost on other terrorist groups. In December 1975 a bomb exploded in a locker at the baggage claim area at LaGuardia Airport in New York, killing eleven people and injuring seventy-five others. It was as though the only people who'd learned lessons from the LAX bombing were the terrorists and not the authorities, as unsecured, coin-operated lockers were still permitted in crowded areas at airports. No one was ever arrested for the LaGuardia bombing, although

Puerto Rican and Croatian extremist groups were among the suspects. Even in Los Angeles in the aftermath of the LAX bombing, unsecured lockers were still in place at the downtown Greyhound bus station, allowing Kurbegovic to place yet another bomb in a locker in a crowded public area. However, since that occurred less than two weeks after the airport bombing, it may be that the authorities didn't have enough time or resources to remove and secure all the lockers at the bus station.

Why It's Important to Anticipate and Prepare
for New Types of Terrorist Attacks

The LAX bombing caught everyone off guard. That should not have been the case. Airlines had been popular targets for terrorists around the world before the LAX attack, with many hijackings occurring during the late 1960s and throughout the 1970s. The United States experienced several hijackings both overseas and at home, as well as a midair bombing of a domestic flight in 1955. There were numerous bombings by terrorists of various targets in the United States, including government and law enforcement buildings. That no one anticipated a target could be the crowded lobby at an airport reflected the tendency that still exists today: to think about terrorism from the perspective of what has happened in the past rather than thinking "outside the box" as to what may occur in the future.

The history of terrorism teaches us that terrorists continually strive to find new and more devastating ways to perpetrate their violence. That is why the 9/11 suicide airplane attacks in the United States shouldn't have been surprising. There had already been numerous suicide attacks on the ground, such as the car and truck bombings that occurred in Lebanon in the 1980s and a suicide attack at sea against the USS *Cole*, a navy destroyer, in Yemen in 2000. It was therefore only a matter of time before terrorists escalated their violence to include suicide attacks from the air.

The failure to anticipate terrorist attacks and take precautions was the focus of lawsuits filed by the heirs of one of the victims who was killed in the LAX bombing, George Moncur, and by one of those who had been injured and lost a leg, Rev. Rhett Patrick Shaughnessy. The plaintiffs in both cases essentially argued that the City of Los Angeles, which operated LAX, was negligent for failing to take safety precautions in restricting access to the rental lockers, which were located in an area where people did not have to go through security checks and where a bomb could easily be placed. They charged that the city had knowledge "of the prevailing climate of violent activity by extremists and the fact that airplanes and airport facilities are favorite targets of these extremists."[11] The trial court dismissed the lawsuits, but the plaintiffs appealed.

The Court of Appeal affirmed the trial court's decision in 1977, in effect stating that the bombing at LAX was an unforeseen event and therefore the city was not negligent:[12]

If there is a common factor that exists in the varied acts of terrorism which appears to be increasing in frequency it is the dogged but irrational determination of the perpetrators. There is a myriad of possibilities which can be readily suggested as to how a determined bomber could introduce an explosive into an airport. There are toilet facilities and trash receptacles which provide obvious places for such activity. In fact, an ordinary piece of luggage sitting unattended next to a bench in an airport terminal would attract little notice.

How then can it ever be said that the availability of a rental locker outside of the security screen was the "cause" of a bomb being exploded in the terminal? How can it be said that "but for" the presence of the unsecured locker, the bomber would not have done his dastardly deed?

That a locker happened to meet the peculiar requirements of the bomber in this particular case is not enough even by maximum use of hindsight to turn the locker into a dangerous condition of the property.

Furthermore, although one may be able to foresee the likelihood of aberrant behavior in these turbulent times and perhaps divine with reasonable success the general behavioral form which it will take, the precise means which a deranged person or a fanatic will employ is based upon too many variables for accurate prediction.

In brief, while it is known that fanatics and lunatics can be harmful to others, their devices and stratagems are as diverse as the variety of mental ills or compulsive radicalism which prompt their behavior. To follow plaintiffs' argument to its logical extreme the City would have to place a security screen at least at the doors of the entire terminal or more likely at the point of vehicular access to the entire grounds. . . .

The complaints here set forth no facts which give rise to the duty on the part of the City to expand its policing of the airport terminal. Nor do the complaints allege facts from which it could even be inferred that the condition of the terminal was the "cause" of the explosion. This tragic event was solely the result of the criminal conduct of a third person unaided by any act or omission on the part of the City.[13]

This was a stinging rejection of the idea that terrorist attacks and the way they might unfold can be foreseen. While it is true, of course, that no one can predict where, when, or how the next terrorist incident will take place, it is still the job of security planners, intelligence analysts, law enforcement agencies, and others to try to envision plausible scenarios for terrorist attacks and then take action to try to prevent them from occurring. It isn't clear whether this was ever done prior to the airport bombing. If it had, then lockers in unsecured areas should have raised some red flags.

While the first responders, including fire, police, and emergency medical personnel and others, did an excellent job in the aftermath of the LAX bombing—arriving on the scene shortly after the blast, attending to the injured, and performing other essential tasks—there was no contingency planning for the other type of terrorist attack that Kurbegovic had pledged to do in his taped messages: unleashing chemical warfare agents such as sarin gas upon civilian populations. It appears that the authorities and others did not believe that this type of attack was possible. There had never at that point been a terrorist attack with chemical weapons that targeted civilians. It would not be until 1995 that the Japanese cult Aum Shinrikyo released sarin gas into the Tokyo subway system.

This failure to plan for a new type of terrorist attack, even when it is spelled out by the potential perpetrator, became a source of criticism years later in an assessment of how the City of Los Angeles and the U.S. government dealt with the Alphabet Bomber's threats to use chemical weapons. The authors of the article wrote, "Politicians and particularly the medical structure did not anticipate and were unable to control substantial public anxiety about a chemical attack within the U.S." There were no medical experts or other spokesmen who came forward to try to calm the public's fears about a massive chemical terrorist attack: "Local, state, and federal medical systems were not prepared to provide a coherent and organized presentation to the public about the (medical) validity of the threats or to offer any useful suggestions for medical preparation." Furthermore, there was "no evidence that any local hospital had undertaken specific preparations for a large-scale chemical event."[14]

Not preparing for public anxiety over a new type of terrorism and not preparing for mass casualties in the event of such an attack continue to be problems today. Although there have been numerous exercises and simulations of a terrorist attack involving a chemical or biological agent, the public has basically been left in the dark about what to do or where to go in the event of a major attack. Furthermore, the ability of the medical community to treat potential victims of an attack that has utilized a weapon of mass destruction still remains an issue. A bipartisan, congressionally appointed commission found in 2010 that the United States was lacking in its preparation for a bioterrorist attack. Among the major problems were the lack of a capability to rapidly recognize, respond, and recover from a biological attack and not having a national plan to coordinate federal, state, and local efforts following a bioterrorist incident.[15] In 2015, former senator Jim Talent, who had co-chaired the commission, testified before Congress that the situation had not improved since the report was issued. "First and foremost," he said, "the lack of sufficient medical countermeasures (MCMs) in our Strategic National Stockpile (SNS), and the lack of a system to quickly develop and produce MCMs during a crisis was our number one concern . . . [when we issued the report] and remains so today." He also said that dispersing the MCMs quickly remained a major problem: "We may be confronted with a situation where we have countermeasures but can't get them to the people who need them, when they need them."[16]

Although the Alphabet Bomber case involved the threat of chemical, and not biological, weapons, it nevertheless exposed vulnerabilities in our preparations for, and responses to, a potential terrorist attack with a weapon of mass destruction. Those vulnerabilities, unfortunately, still exist today.

Lone Wolf Terrorists Are Candidates to Use
Chemical and Biological Agents

In addition to demonstrating how Los Angeles and the rest of the country were not prepared for new types of terrorism, such as bombs exploding at airports or chemical warfare agents being released over a city, the Alphabet Bomber case also illustrates why lone wolves are candidates to acquire and use weapons of mass destruction.

Kurbegovic exhibited some of the main characteristics necessary for an individual, or a group, to use chemical or biological agents. These include a general, undefined constituency whose possible reaction to a chemical or biological attack does not concern the individual or group; a perception that conventional terrorist tactics are no longer effective and that a higher form of violence or a new technique is needed; and a willingness to take risks by experimenting with and using unfamiliar weapons.[17]

Lone wolves like Kurbegovic only answer to themselves, so there is no concern about alienating supporters by killing too many people with a chemical or biological terrorist attack. He was also escalating his attacks prior to his arrest. At some point, he might have become frustrated that his conventional terrorist tactics such as placing bombs in crowded areas were not getting the attention and reaction that he wanted from the government, like acquiescing to his demands to abolish all immigration, naturalization, and sex laws in the country. A decision to use a higher form of violence or a new weapon, such as chemical warfare agents, would likely have been the next step. He had already been threatening to do so for some time.

The fact that after Kurbegovic's arrest police found in his apartment books and manuals on germ and chemical warfare, gas masks, and all but one ingredient (an organophosphate) needed to build a rudimentary nerve gas bomb (and something Kurbegovic was about to pick up) points to his serious consideration of launching a chemical agent attack. The discovery more than two years later of a fake wall where Kurbegovic hid more chemicals and explosives, including twenty-five pounds of sodium cyanide, which is a precursor for the nerve agent tabun and which can also be used to release lethal hydrogen cyanide gas, further lends weight to Kurbegovic's diabolical future plans.

Kurbegovic also had no fear about experimenting with dangerous or unfamiliar weapons, as illustrated by his producing a poisonous gaseous substance once at RPM Industries where he worked, forcing the lab to be evacuated until the gas cleared. What was remarkable about Kurbegovic, and which has implications today for lone wolves interested in acquiring and using chemical or biological warfare agents, was how fast he was able to learn new things. This was in the days before the Internet and the wealth of information that can now be found quickly through various search engines. Yet Kurbegovic, by checking out books from the library, reading whatever he could get his hands on, communicating with his coworker (Stephen Smith), using his technical expertise as an engineer, and so forth, was able to learn in a relatively short period of time how to make bombs and synthesize homemade nerve agents. What took him months to learn back in the 1970s can now be accomplished even faster today and by more people due to the Internet.

While Kurbegovic did not threaten to use biological warfare agents, it would not have been beyond his capabilities to learn how to produce and use these weapons as well. The threat of a lone wolf unleashing biological agents such as anthrax, botulinum toxin, ricin, or other agents upon civilian populations is a major concern. With his wave of anthrax letter attacks in 2001, Bruce Ivins demonstrated that a lone wolf could do just that. One doesn't even have to be as technically and scientifically proficient as Ivins was to be able to produce biological agents. As one microbiologist has observed, "Today, anyone with a high school education can use widely available protocols and prepackaged kits to modify the sequence of a gene or replace genes with a microorganism; one can also purchase small, disposable, self-contained bioreactors for propagating viruses and microorganisms. Such advances continue to lower the barriers to biologic-weapons development."[18]

The creativity that is a characteristic of many lone wolves can also be used for thinking up new ways to use chemical or biological agents in an attack. Kurbegovic demonstrated this with his ingenious hoax regarding placing nerve agents under the stamps of postcards that he sent to all the U.S. Supreme Court justices. He initially claimed in one of his taped messages that there was nerve gas under the stamps but then admitted it was a hoax after the stamps got caught in the canceling machine at the Palm Springs post office and it was revealed that there was actually a nontoxic substance on the postcards. But hoaxes can give ideas to other terrorists who might copy or improve upon the technique and actually place nerve agents or other dangerous substances under stamps and send them to various targets.[19]

Don't Make the Mentally Ill the Scapegoat for Lone Wolf Attacks

In the aftermath of the worst mass shooting in U.S. history, which occurred on October 1, 2017, in Las Vegas, Nevada, when Stephen Paddock killed 58 people and injured more than 500 others at an outdoor country music festival, President Donald Trump described Paddock, who killed himself before he could be arrested, as "a sick man, a demented man. Lot of problems, I guess."[20] However, there was no evidence at the time that Paddock suffered from any mental disorders.

President Trump reflected the natural tendency after a horrific incident like the Las Vegas mass shooting to assume that the perpetrator was mentally ill. This sentiment, unfortunately, continues to stigmatize mentally ill individuals, the vast majority of whom are nonviolent.[21]

Muharem Kurbegovic, of course, was a violent individual, and he was mentally ill. The jury, however, found that his mental illness was not sufficient to reduce his criminal responsibility for murder. Prosecutor Dinko Bozanich was convinced that Kurbegovic was exaggerating the symptoms of mental illness after his arrest in order to help his case in the three competency trials and in the criminal trial. One of the psychiatrists who testified on Kurbegovic's behalf admitted under cross-examination that a person who is not mentally ill can still fake mental illness, while another psychiatrist admitted that Kurbegovic did not become clinically ill until after he was incarcerated. And Nancy Watson, the judge in the criminal trial, said that "certainly Kurbegovic isn't insane, legally. Because that means you don't know right from wrong. And he knew right from wrong. He just doesn't give a damn."[22]

Portraying the Alphabet Bomber as crazy plays into the hands of those who want to paint a broad picture of the mentally ill as potentially dangerous individuals. As we saw in the previous chapter, questions about the connection between mental illness and lone wolf terrorism have led to calls from government, law enforcement, and other entities for the mental health community to play a role in trying to identify those individuals with mental disorders who might commit terrorist attacks. Many in the mental health community have resisted this call on legal, ethical, and practical grounds, arguing among other things that it would compromise their patients' privacy rights and, without specific reasons to believe a patient is intending to commit a terrorist act, could lead to reporting innocent people to the authorities.

While it is true that a significant percentage of lone wolf terrorists have some type of mental disorder, the majority do not. Giving a segment of the population that is already suffering from mental illness, and in many cases trying to get better, the extra burden of labels such as terrorists or mass shooters seems unfair, unjust, and wrong.

8

It's a Horrible Shame What
He's Done with His Life

Today, Muharem Kurbegovic wouldn't recognize the section of downtown
Los Angeles that he frequented in the 1970s. Gone are the taxi dance halls,
nightclubs, and car dealerships that filled the area. In their place are luxury
hotels, condominiums, and apartments; skyscrapers; the massive Staples
Center sports arena; and an entertainment and dining complex known as
"L.A. Live," containing trendy and expensive restaurants.[1] It would not be
a place the eccentric Kurbegovic would be comfortable in.

His homes since his conviction in 1980 for the LAX bombing and other
violent acts have been several state prisons in California. These have included
San Quentin, Pelican Bay, Corcoran, and most recently California State
Prison, Los Angeles County.[2] Kurbegovic, who turned seventy-five in June
2018, hasn't lost his sense of humor during his many years of incarceration.
He has continued to think up ways to embarrass former prosecutor Dinko
Bozanich. On one occasion, he wrote an angry letter to the Campbell Soup
Company, claiming that the Bozanich family had become sick after eating
Campbell's alphabet soup (no doubt a play on his own infamous name)
during a Thanksgiving Day dinner. He signed it "Dinko Bozanich" and used
the prosecutor's home address on the letter. Bozanich was at work the next

week when he received a telephone call from his wife informing him that a representative from Campbell's was at their front door with a caseload of alphabet soup! The representative apologized for all the problems that his company's soup had caused the Bozanich family.[3]

Another time, Kurbegovic wrote to every person with the name Bozanich in California and other states, advising them that Dinko Bozanich's father had died and that there would be a meeting to divide up the estate. Kurbegovic told them to contact Bozanich to find out how much money they were going to get. Bozanich was flooded with calls from all over the country.[4]

Kurbegovic didn't leave Lea Purwin D'Agostino, the "Dragon Lady" who assisted in the prosecution, alone either. He took out scores of subscriptions in her name to magazines such as *Men's Health*, *Flex*, *New Beauty*, *Money*, *Rolling Stone*, *Car and Driver*, *The Hockey News*, and *Playboy*, among others. She had to write to all of them to cancel the subscriptions, but still she received past-due bill notices. That Kurbegovic had found her unlisted address in order to subscribe to the magazines unnerved her but did not surprise her. "If he'd put all of this ingenuity to use he could have—God only knows what he could have accomplished," she said, "because he's very ingenious, he's very bright, he's very knowledgeable, he knows how to get things done, he knows how to find things. It's a horrible shame what he's done with life." But she still saw him as extremely dangerous: "I would never want to be in a room with him alone. Very, very scary what he could do."[5]

Even from prison, Kurbegovic has been able to raise concerns about future terrorist attacks by lone wolves. In one of his many petitions for writs of habeas corpus, he claimed to be a representative of al-Qaeda, the Islamic terrorist group responsible for the 9/11 attacks. This was taken seriously by the city of San Fernando in Los Angeles County. The minutes of one of its city council meetings in 2015 reflect their concern: "It is unlikely that San Fernando will be targeted by international terrorist groups, but it is very possible that a local community could be targeted by individuals claiming allegiance to international terrorist groups. The LAX Alphabet Bomber Muharem Kurbegovich recently wrote from prison that he now claims allegiance to the Al Qaeda terrorist organization."[6]

As is true for most terrorist attacks, lives are changed forever. The LAX bombing was no exception. Rev. Rhett Patrick Shaughnessy's right leg had to be amputated as a result of the bombing, but his survival renewed his faith in God, whom he believed "let this happen for a purpose" and "will take care of me." He remained devoted to his church in Phoenix, Arizona, where he remained pastor until his retirement in 1987, after which he continued to be active teaching, speaking, and conducting other religious activities. The bombing, however, made him realize how precious life was, and he began spending more time with his family after the attack. He also tried to cheer up other amputees he visited with. "Things happen to us so we can be benefit to others," he said. "There are four thing we can do with our hurts: nurse them, curse them, rehearse them or reverse them. I'm trying to reverse mine."[7]

"The Great Arturo" also tried to reverse his hurts. Unfortunately, he was not as successful as Shaughnessy in this effort. Arturo Trostl Jr. had been a famous trapeze artist when his career was ruined by the LAX bombing. He suffered burns, thigh and chest injuries, and had shrapnel lodged in his face, neck, and bladder. Although he tried to perform again, this time billed as "The Indestructible Arturo" (a reference to his surviving the bombing), he wasn't as daring or as good on the trapeze as he used to be. According to his manager, Arturo had lost his confidence. He eventually quit performing and tried other careers, including becoming a theatrical touring event agent, a builder of race cars, and an owner of a tool business. It was while engaged in the tool business that he suffered yet another horrific injury when his legs and back were crushed in an accident.[8]

Things got worse for Trostl when he became consumed with mounting debts and unable to pay the rent at his residence in Australia. He was faced with eviction and realized he would soon become homeless. He then sought help from the Australian Red Cross, which obtained emergency financial and food relief for him and also advised him on how he could get out of debt. "You start to regain your self esteem," Trostl said in 2014. "Once you start to feel like there are people out there helping you, you yourself start to get involved. You start to take control."[9]

Taking control is what Nancy Watson, the judge in Kurbegovic's criminal trial, had tried to do during the eight-month-long court proceedings.

Her experience in dealing with Kurbegovic was a nightmare for her, as he continually insulted her, interrupted the proceedings, and did other things to wear her down. She requested and received a transfer from the criminal courthouse to the civil courthouse shortly after the end of the Alphabet Bomber trial, not wanting to relive that experience again with another criminal defendant like Kurbegovic. She retired from the bench in 1984. Her name is inscribed on the Criminal Justice Wall of Fame at the Clara Shortridge Foltz Criminal Justice Center building in downtown Los Angeles. She died in February 2004.[10]

The one person who had to deal the most with Kurbegovic, from the days right after his arrest to his conviction more than six years later, was Dinko Bozanich. It was the longest case of his stellar legal career, and he felt it was his duty to make sure that Kurbegovic was deemed competent to stand trial and held accountable for what he did during that summer of terror in Los Angeles in 1974. When asked more than forty years later what he would say to the Alphabet Bomber if he were to speak to him today, the former prosecutor replied that whatever he said to him "would fall upon deaf ears and could also give him something that he would twist and respond in some way that would either cause laughter, derision. So, I don't know that I would say anything to him."[11]

However, there are plenty of questions that Bozanich would like to ask Kurbegovic, but he would not expect to receive an answer—or if he did, it wouldn't be an honest answer. "One question would be when was he [going to] make his extortion demand. [I] wouldn't ask him, 'Were you going to make one?' [but rather] 'When were you [going to make one]?'" Bozanich remains convinced that Kurbegovic all along had extortion as the main motive for the LAX bombing and the subsequent threats of additional bombings.[12]

Another question Bozanich would like to have answered is whether Kurbegovic actually traveled to Washington DC and entered the Supreme Court while it was in session with the intention of assassinating the justices, as he stated in one of his taped messages. According to Bozanich, given "the way things were in terms of security back in those days," it is possible, although improbable, that Kurbegovic might have made an attempt to do that.[13]

The bomb that Kurbegovic placed in a locker at the Greyhound bus station has also puzzled Bozanich over the years. What exactly was Kurbegovic trying to do with that bomb? Did he reveal the location of the bomb in a possible attempt to have it explode when the bomb squad arrived at the station to remove it? "The thing that's always been in the back of my mind is [whether] that bomb . . . was designed to blow up the bomb squad. Now, if that had happened, talk about a state of panic in the city of Los Angeles, 'cause the bomb squad didn't have that many people. . . . So, I can't exclude that he did it for that reason. Again, that would be a question [I would ask him]."[14]

Bozanich admits that if he were to have a conversation with Kurbegovic, he wouldn't be able to resist the temptation to needle him: "I would say, 'You know, you really blew it. Everything else that you did to try to convince people you [were] crazy. . . . You sure blew it when you . . . tried to show up Arleigh McCree [the LAPD's top bomb expert] on the witness stand, and you proved it was bomb expert versus bomb expert, and that you weren't crazy. You're crazy like a fox.'"[15]

Meanwhile, the Dragon Lady would have just one thing to ask Kurbegovic if she were to talk with him today. "I think I would probably ask him," said D'Agostino, 'Why on Earth, with what this country has given immigrants, especially an immigrant such as [you] who had a wonderful job, who has a good education . . . why would [you] do something like this—to kill people? Why on Earth would you want to kill people like that?' I can't think of anything else to ask him."[16]

It may never be known why Kurbegovic killed innocent people with his bombing of Los Angeles International Airport or why he threatened to kill more "until our name has been written on the face of this nation in blood." Perhaps it was due in part to his mental illness or to his belief that he was discriminated against because he was an immigrant, despite his having a good job and a good income. Maybe he just wanted to lash out at society for perceived injustices. Perhaps it was because he believed his lewd conduct trial (for which he was acquitted) would follow him for the rest of his life and deny him opportunities, including becoming an American citizen, that he felt entitled to. Or perhaps it was to eventually extort the city of Los Angeles or other entities for money in exchange for not setting off more bombs or doing other violent things. He might even have done this just to become famous.

The answers to any lingering questions about why the Alphabet Bomber did what he did lie with an aging, lonely man who will likely see his final days locked up in a California prison. Even if he were to explain the motivations and objectives for his terror campaign more than four decades ago, one could never be quite sure, based on his track record, whether he was telling the truth.[17] Questions are therefore likely to always remain regarding one of the most enigmatic, creative, and dangerous lone wolves in history.

Where there is no doubt, however, is in his foreshadowing the rise of the lone wolf terrorist as the formidable adversary that governments and societies now have to deal with. Muharem Kurbegovic showed how a determined and smart individual working alone can hold a city in fear, manipulate the media, build powerful and destructive homemade explosives, and even experiment with weapons of mass destruction. The story of the Alphabet Bomber is one that will continue to resonate in a world where the threat of terrorism has become a permanent fixture in all our lives.

NOTES

All books, articles, and interviews listed in the bibliography appear in the notes with abbreviated citations. Depositions, appellate decisions, and miscellaneous court filings appear in the notes as full citations on first mention in each chapter and then as abbreviated forms thereafter. The same is true for newspaper articles and transcripts of the audiocassette tapes that Muharem Kurbegovic made during the summer of 1974. Court reporter's (or court reporters') transcripts are abbreviated throughout the notes as follows:

1971 RT   1971 Reporter's Transcript (Misdemeanor Trial), *People v. Kurbegovic*, No. 383707 (Los Angeles Municipal Court, May 1971)

1974 RT   1974 Reporter's Transcript (Grand Jury Proceedings), *People v. Kurbegovic*, No. A 311331 (Los Angeles Superior Court, September 1974)

1976 RT   1976 Reporter's Transcript (Second Competency Trial), *People v. Kurbegovic*, No. A 311331 (Los Angeles Superior Court, October–December 1976)

1978–79 RT   1978–1979 Reporters' Transcript (Third Competency Trial), *People v. Kurbegovic*, No. A 311331 (Los Angeles Superior Court, October 1978–February 1979)

1980 RT   1980 Reporters' Transcript (Criminal Trial), *People v. Kurbegovic*, 2nd. Crim. No. 39123 (also No. A 311331, Los Angeles Superior Court, February–October 1980)

INTRODUCTION

1. Al Martinez, "Two Killed, 36 Hurt as Bomb Rips L.A. Airport Waiting Area," *Los Angeles Times*, August 7, 1974.

2. Martinez, "Two Killed."

3. 1980 RT at 11,341–55.

4. 1980 RT at 5,821.

5. 1980 RT at 7,847–48.

6. 1980 RT at 7,856–62.

7. *People v. Kurbegovic*, 138 Cal.App.3d 731 (1982) at 737.

8. 1980 RT at 6,184–89.

9. Transcript of tape recovered on August 9, 1974, in Maywood, California, following call to CBS (Los Angeles Police Department Item No. 1340, files, Los Angeles County District Attorney's Office).

10. 1980 RT at 4,384.

11. Transcript of tape recovered by FBI on August 12, 1974, from Glenn Evans after initial recovery by Evans in late July–early August 1974 in area of radio station KPFK (Los Angeles Police Department Item No. 1341, files, Los Angeles County District Attorney's Office).

12. Transcript of August 13, 1974, telephone call to Conrad Casler (*Herald Examiner*) (Los Angeles Police Department Item No. 1342, files, Los Angeles County District Attorney's Office).

13. *Los Angeles Herald Examiner*, August 15, 1974.

14. *Los Angeles Herald Examiner*, August 17, 1974.

15. Transcript of tape recovered by FBI on August 12, 1974.

16. Transcript of tape recovered by FBI on August 12, 1974.

17. *People v. Kurbegovic* (No. A 311331) (microfilm record located at the Clara Shortridge Foltz Criminal Justice Center, Los Angeles Superior Court, roll 352); Simon, "The Alphabet Bomber," 85–86.

18. George Lardner, "Terrorist Reportedly Sent a Justice Toxic Chemicals," *Washington Post*, December 20, 1983.

19. Bozanich interview by the author, December 23, 1997; U.S. Congress, Office of Technology Assessment, *Technologies Underlying Weapons of Mass Destruction*, 24.

20. Transcript of tape recovered on August 9, 1974.

21. Transcript of tape recovered on August 16, 1974, at Eleventh and Los Angeles Streets (Los Angeles Police Department Item No. 1345, files, Los Angeles County District Attorney's Office).

22. Transcript of tape recovered on August 16, 1974.

23. Simon, "The Alphabet Bomber," 71.

24. Simon, *Lone Wolf Terrorism*, 21. Unless otherwise indicated, page numbers refer to the 2013 edition.

25. Transcript of tape recovered on August 20, 1974, at Sunset and Western (scene of arrest) (Los Angeles Police Department Item No. 1338, files, Los Angeles County District Attorney's Office).

26. Simon, *Lone Wolf Terrorism*, 21–22.

27. Simon, *Lone Wolf Terrorism*, 78.

28. Simon, *Lone Wolf Terrorism*, 99.

29. Cited in Crenshaw, "The Causes of Terrorism," 126n13.

30. "About 40 Percent of Lone-Wolf Terrorists Are Driven by Mental Illness, Not Ideology," Homeland Security News Wire, December 22, 2014, http://www .homelandsecuritynewswire.com/dr20141222-about-40-percent-of-lonewolf -terrorists-are-driven-by-mental-illness-not-ideology-researchers.

I. THE MAKING OF A TERRORIST

1. Rapoport, "Fear and Trembling," 660–64; Mackay, *Memoirs of Extraordinary Popular Delusions*, 371–400.

2. Simon Kuper, "Sarajevo: The Crossroads of History," *Financial Times*, March 24, 2014, https://www.ft.com/content/293938b2-afcd-11e3-9cd1-00144feab7de; Jon Henley, "Enemies in Life, Comrades in Death: A Century to Count the Cost of War," *The Guardian*, August 4, 2014, https://www.theguardian.com/world/2014 /aug/04/st-symphorien-first-world-war-centenary-dead-honoured.

3. Sylvia Poggioli, "Two Decades after Siege, Sarajevo Still a City Divided," *NPR Morning Edition*, April 5, 2012, http://www.npr.org/2012/04/05/150009152/two -decades-after-siege-sarajevo-still-a-city-divided; Chris Leslie, "Sarajevo: A Portrait of the City 20 Years after the Bosnian War," *The Guardian*, December 14, 2015, https://www.theguardian.com/cities/ng-interactive/2015/dec/14/sarajevo-portrait -city-20-years-bosnian-war-dayton.

4. Greble, *Sarajevo*, 2; Hoare, *The Bosnian Muslims*, 282–83; "Timeline: A Short History of Sarajevo and Region," *Los Angeles Times*, July 25, 2014, http://touch .latimes.com/#section/-1/article/p2p-80903508/.

5. Greble, *Sarajevo*, 210–11.

6. 1980 RT at 14,697, 14,703, 14,758.

7. Greble, *Sarajevo*, 238. The population of Sarajevo in 1948 was 36 percent Serb, 35 percent Muslim, and 24 percent Croat.

8. 1980 RT at 20,714.

9. 1980 RT at 14,693–94.

10. 1980 RT at 14,693–94, 14,722–23; files, Los Angeles County District Attorney's Office.

11. Files, Los Angeles County District Attorney's Office.

12. Files, Los Angeles County District Attorney's Office.

13. 1980 RT at 14,711–13. Dinko Bozanich, the prosecutor for Kurbegovic's 1974 grand jury proceedings and 1974–80 competency and criminal trials, believed that Kurbegovic left Yugoslavia in order to avoid being drafted into the Yugoslav Army. Bozanich interview by the author, November 30, 2016.

14. Files, Los Angeles County District Attorney's Office.

15. 1980 RT at 14,711–14.

16. Files, Los Angeles County District Attorney's Office.

17. Hacker, *Crusaders, Criminals, Crazies*, 21.

18. 1980 RT at 20,001–4, 6,267–68.

19. 1980 RT at 14,714, 14,724–25.

20. Files, Los Angeles County District Attorney's Office.

21. 1980 RT at 14,730.

22. The Weathermen changed their name to the Weather Underground in 1970.

23. Simon, *The Terrorist Trap*, 320. Unless otherwise indicated, page numbers refer to the 1994 edition.

24. Simon, *The Terrorist Trap*, 169, 321.

25. Simon, *The Terrorist Trap*, 314.

26. Simon, *The Terrorist Trap*, 371.

27. Toobin, *American Heiress*, 11.

28. Bozanich interview by the author, July 28, 2017.

29. 1980 RT at 11,542, 11,558.

30. Files, Los Angeles County District Attorney's Office. Muteness was a physical condition that would lead to a 4-F classification. Prosecutor Bozanich could never prove that avoiding the draft was the reason Kurbegovic faked being mute. There was, however, evidence to suggest that was the reason. "One [thing] that became very important," Bozanich said, "but it became impossible to nail down with the type of precision that I would have liked, but there was enough to proceed with it, and that was the tying it to a scam to beat the draft. At that time, if you were legally here, although not a U.S. citizen, you were subject to the draft. We already knew that probably the principal reason he left Yugoslavia was to avoid conscription. . . . We did have somewhat of a record of him trying to go see a doctor, and the doctor was no longer available [to be interviewed at the time of Kurbegovic's arrest in 1974]. [We] had enough to say that [Kurbegovic] had done something to be able to get a 4-F rating, which was, at that time, [what] everybody who didn't want to get in the service [tried to obtain]. So, he was 4-F. Once you arrive at that factual conclusion, or at least have evidence to be able to legitimately argue that point, you now have a motive: not a nut motive, but a rational and criminal

motive. The last thing you want to do is now start talking at work and somehow the U.S. [government] gets knowledge of that [and that] you engaged in some chicanery to avoid the draft." Bozanich interview by the author, November 30, 2016.

31. Bozanich interview by the author, December 23, 1997.

32. Files, Los Angeles County District Attorney's Office.

33. Files, Los Angeles County District Attorney's Office.

34. Files, Los Angeles County District Attorney's Office.

35. Files, Los Angeles County District Attorney's Office.

36. Files, Los Angeles County District Attorney's Office.

37. 1980 RT at 11,554.

38. In addition to lying to the draft board, Kurbegovic also lied on his immigration form when he wrote that he was a mute. Files, Los Angeles County District Attorney's Office. Kurbegovic likely knew before he entered the United States that he would be eligible for the draft. "So, it would not be surprising that he could put something on his entry that would not show any physical disability, it would place mute," said Dinko Bozanich. Bozanich interview by the author, July 28, 2017.

39. Files, Los Angeles County District Attorney's Office.

40. Files, Los Angeles County District Attorney's Office.

41. Files, Los Angeles County District Attorney's Office.

42. Files, Los Angeles County District Attorney's Office.

43. Files, Los Angeles County District Attorney's Office.

44. Bozanich interview by the author, November 30, 2016.

45. Files, Los Angeles County District Attorney's Office.

46. Files, Los Angeles County District Attorney's Office. This story had a major flaw, since Sarajevo at the time of Kurbegovic's birth in 1943 was still controlled by the fascist Croat Ustasha regime.

47. Files, Los Angeles County District Attorney's Office. This story also was flawed, since Kurbegovic would have been less than two years old when the Germans and the Croat Ustasha regime were in control of Sarajevo.

48. 1980 RT at 14,738.

49. Bozanich interview by the author, November 30, 2016.

50. Files, Los Angeles County District Attorney's Office; 1980 RT at 14,739.

51. Files, Los Angeles County District Attorney's Office. Kurbegovic's aversion to noise and those making it was also evident in the workplace. One day, while working at Wintec Corporation, a few female employees were listening to a radio playing loud rock-and-roll music. Kurbegovic walked over to them, turned the radio down, and pinched one of the women on the ear. He then wrote a note to the effect that he didn't like that type of music.

52. Files, Los Angeles County District Attorney's Office; 1980 RT at 14,739.

53. Files, Los Angeles County District Attorney's Office.

54. Cressey, *The Taxi-Dance Hall*, 3, 11; Dorothy Townsend, "10 Cents a Dance? Not Any More—It's $9 an Hour!" *Los Angeles Times*, November 24, 1969. The taxi dance halls evolved from the Barbary Coast dance halls of San Francisco, also known as the '49 dance halls ('49 being a name derived from the 1849 California gold rush), which were closed in 1913 due to public protests. In these dance halls, women dancers earned their income not from dancing but by a commission from the drinks they could entice men to buy. Cressey, *The Taxi-Dance Hall*, 179–80.

55. The song was inducted into the Grammy Hall of Fame in 1999 and the National Recording Registry of the Library of Congress in 2011, which preserves recordings that are "culturally, historically or aesthetically important, and/or inform or reflect life in the United States." National Recording Preservation Board, Library of Congress, https://www.loc.gov/programs/national-recording-preservation -board/recording-registry/nominate/; Charles O. Lloyd, "Ten Cents a Dance— Ruth Etting (1930)," Library of Congress; "New Additions Added to National Recording Registry," CBS News, www.cbsnews.com; Grammy Hall of Fame, www.grammy.org.

56. Cressey, *The Taxi-Dance Hall*.

57. Cressey, *The Taxi-Dance Hall*, 12, 81–82, 109.

58. Cressey, *The Taxi-Dance Hall*, 283.

59. Cressey, *The Taxi-Dance Hall*, 240.

60. 1980 RT at 4,379.

61. Files, Los Angeles County District Attorney's Office.

62. Hong and Duff, "Gentlemen's Social Club," 827.

63. Townsend, "10 Cents a Dance?"

64. Hong and Duff, "Gentlemen's Social Club," 827.

65. Files, Los Angeles County District Attorney's Office.

66. Files, Los Angeles County District Attorney's Office.

67. Files, Los Angeles County District Attorney's Office.

68. 1980 RT at 4,371, 14,742; files, Los Angeles County District Attorney's Office.

69. Files, Los Angeles County District Attorney's Office.

70. 1980 RT at 19,287–88, 14,742–43, 4,178.

71. 1971 RT at 84, 87–88.

72. 1971 RT at 140–44.

73. 1971 RT at 51.

74. 1971 RT at 3–4.

75. Files, Los Angeles County District Attorney's Office.

76. Kurbegovic claimed that he wasn't even on the toilet seat when the vice officer came into the restroom. The policeman had testified that he only saw Kurbegovic on the toilet seat for two seconds. In addressing the jury, Kurbegovic said, "Now who will justify if you were a police officer and you see someone shaking his penis up and down for two seconds, could you rightfully assume that such a person has been masturbating?" 1971 RT at 109, 141, 199.

77. 1971 RT at 89.

78. 1971 RT at 190.

79. 1971 RT at 194.

80. 1971 RT at 89, 148–60. The judge allowed Kurbegovic to drop his trousers provided he was "properly clothed" underneath, which he was. He was wearing white shorts with printed red geometric figures under his trousers.

81. 1971 RT at 194.

82. 1980 RT at 19,816–18. Kraft later said he knew Judge Campbell wanted to issue a contempt of court to Kurbegovic because he, Kraft, had previous experience in Campbell's courtroom. 1980 RT at 19,832.

83. 1980 RT at 4,202.

84. 1971 RT at 205.

85. 1971 RT at 205–6. Regarding the policeman, Campbell was probably referring to Kurbegovic's argument to the jury after the policeman had already been excused from the courtroom.

86. 1980 RT at 19,836.

87. 1971 RT at 210–11.

88. 1980 RT at 19,281–83.

89. 1980 RT at 19,285.

90. Kurbegovic was hired by RPM Industries in October 1972. Files, Los Angeles County District Attorney's Office.

91. 1980 RT at 4,177.

92. 1980 RT at 4,185.

93. Chaleff interview by the author, February 10, 1998.

94. 1980 RT at 4,177.

95. Files, Los Angeles County District Attorney's Office.

96. 1980 RT at 19,290. Kurbegovic also said, "I . . . put all my faith into this business. And then Milemore denies it." 1980 RT at 4,179.

97. Files, Los Angeles County District Attorney's Office.

98. Cressey, *The Taxi-Dance Hall*, 283.

99. Files, Los Angeles County District Attorney's Office.

100. Files, Los Angeles County District Attorney's Office; 1980 RT at 4,360.

101. 1980 RT at 19,306.

102. However, Kurbegovic reportedly told the commission that the taxi dance hall he wanted to open would be a place where a customer "could pay a fee and get anything you want [from a woman]." *People v. Kurbegovic*, 138 Cal.App.3d 731 (1982) at 736n1. Kurbegovic, though, claimed he was referring to the nonsexual benefits he believed a taxi dance hall provides, such as psychological and emotional satisfaction. In his testimony before the hearing examiner, he said, regarding taxi dance halls, "Younger customer does occasionally come in. He feels some shortage [in] sexual experience. This place may be a place to find a cheap way of engaging in sexual activities with someone. The moment he finds out that he's wrong, he never comes back." Files, Los Angeles County District Attorney's Office; see also 1980 RT at 4,383.

103. Files, Los Angeles County District Attorney's Office.

104. 1980 RT at 19,304.

105. 1980 RT at 19,312.

106. 1980 RT at 19,314–15.

107. 1980 RT at 19,316–20.

108. Bozanich interview by the author, November 30, 2016. Kurbegovic also claimed he went to the U.S. Senate to assassinate several senators. 1980 RT at 19,320–29.

109. 1980 RT at 19,329.

2. UNTIL OUR NAME HAS BEEN WRITTEN

1. Evan Andrews, "How London Bridge Ended Up in Arizona," *History in the Headlines*, October 7, 2016, http://www.history.com/news/how-london-bridge-ended-up-in-arizona; David P. Billington, "Old London Bridge," *Encyclopaedia Britannica*, October 25, 2002, https://www.britannica.com/topic/Old-London-Bridge. The nursery rhyme "London Bridge Is Falling Down," whose opening stanza is "London Bridge is falling down, Falling down, Falling down, London Bridge is falling down, My fair lady," was first published in the mid-eighteenth century. However, it was composed in the thirteenth century, when Queen Eleanor was given the tolls from the bridge, which had been built in 1209, as a present from her husband, King Henry III, in 1269. She used the toll money for her personal use instead of spending it on upgrades for the bridge, which soon fell into disrepair. That is the reference to "My fair lady" in the nursery rhyme. The bridge, however, still lasted for more than six hundred years until a new one was built in 1831. The first London Bridge had been built by the Romans in 43 AD. "The Peter de Colechurch's Bridge: Early Mediaeval," The London Bridge Museum & Educational Trust, http://oldlondonbridge.com/earlymediaeval.shtml; "London Bridge History," Lake Havasu Area Chamber of Commerce, http://www.havasuchamber.com/our-community/london_bridge_history.aspx.

2. Andrews, "How London Bridge Ended Up in Arizona."

3. Andrews, "How London Bridge Ended Up in Arizona."

4. Glib Savchenko, "Why Did an Oil Magnate Need London Bridge," *Bird in Flight Magazine*, June 8, 2016, https://birdinflight.com/inspiration/sources/20160603 -london-bridge-in-arizona.html.

5. 1980 RT at 8,807.

6. Andrews, "How London Bridge Ended Up in Arizona."

7. Andrews, "How London Bridge Ended Up in Arizona." The U.S. Customs Service (as it was known in those days) declared the London Bridge to be an "antique" and therefore duty-free, which saved McCulloch $270,600 in import taxes. The bridge was then entered into *The Guinness Book of World Records* as the largest antique ever sold. "Did You Know . . . U.S. Customs Declaration Made London Bridge the World's Largest Antique Ever Sold?" US Customs and Border Protection, March 8, 2014, https://www.cbp.gov/about/history/did -you-know/london-bridge.

8. Elborough, *London Bridge in America*, 187. The correct year is in fact 1885.

9. Andrews, "How London Bridge Ended Up in Arizona."

10. Andrews, "How London Bridge Ended Up in Arizona."

11. Bobbi Holmes, "The History of Lake Havasu City Arizona," http://www.oocities .org/havasumagazine/.

12. Files, Los Angeles County District Attorney's Office.

13. 1980 RT at 8,811, 8,815; files, Los Angeles County District Attorney's Office.

14. 1980 RT at 8,815–16, 8,825.

15. 1980 RT at 8,818, 8,821–22.

16. 1980 RT at 19,331.

17. Files, Los Angeles County District Attorney's Office.

18. Files, Los Angeles County District Attorney's Office.

19. Files, Los Angeles County District Attorney's Office.

20. 1980 RT at 19,346–52.

21. 1980 RT at 4,106, 19,351–52; 1974 RT at 126–39.

22. 1980 RT at 19,351; 1974 RT at 58–62, 129–30.

23. 1974 RT at 65–66; 1980 RT at 5,750–52, 5,764–65.

24. 1980 RT at 4,226–27, 4,230, 4,240, 4,271.

25. 1980 RT at 4,294–95, 4,325–26, 4,329, 4,399.

26. 1974 RT at 449.

27. "Famous Cases & Criminals: Patty Hearst," FBI, https://www.fbi.gov/history /famous-cases/patty-hearst.

28. Toobin, *American Heiress*, 36, 41.

29. Bozanich interview by the author, November 30, 2016.

30. Files, Los Angeles County District Attorney's Office.

31. Files, Los Angeles County District Attorney's Office.

32. Files, Los Angeles County District Attorney's Office.

33. Files, Los Angeles County District Attorney's Office.

34. Files, Los Angeles County District Attorney's Office.

35. Files, Los Angeles County District Attorney's Office.

36. "Good Moral Character," US Citizenship and Immigration Services (USCIS) Policy Manual, vol. 12, https://www.uscis.gov/policymanual/Print/PolicyManual -Volume12-PartF.html.

37. "Good Moral Character."

38. Files, Los Angeles County District Attorney's Office.

39. Files, Los Angeles County District Attorney's Office.

40. 1974 RT at 68–73, 483–88; 1980 RT at 5,719–22, 5,769–70, 5,781.

41. 1980 RT at 9,882, 9,891.

42. 1974 RT at 483–88, 1980 RT at 9,883–84, 9,891–92.

43. 1974 RT at 75.

44. Toobin, *American Heiress*, 38.

45. Toobin, *American Heiress*, 36, 42.

46. Chris Suellentrop, "What Is the Symbionese Liberation Army?" *Slate*, January 24, 2002, http://www.slate.com/articles/news_and_politics/explainer/2002/01 /what_is_the_symbionese_liberation_army.html; Douglas O. Linder, "Patty Hearst Trial (1976)," University of Missouri–Kansas City School of Law, http:// law2.umkc.edu/faculty/projects/ftrials/hearst/hearstdolaccount.html; Toobin, *American Heiress*, 58–59.

47. "Famous Cases & Criminals: Patty Hearst"; Suellentrop, "What Is the Symbionese Liberation Army?"

48. *People v. Kurbegovic*, 138 Cal.App.3d 731 (1982) at 736n3. It would not be until Patty Hearst's capture that it was learned that the SLA was a very small group, with most of its members killed in the May shoot-out.

49. 1974 RT at 119–22; 1980 RT at 4,120–21; *People v. Kurbegovic*, 138 Cal.App.3d (1982) at 736–37.

50. Bozanich interview by the author, November 30, 2016.

51. 1974 RT at 158. Kurbegovic's purpose for leaving the tape at the *Los Angeles Times* building was to ensure he would get media exposure for his comments and threats. He was most likely not aware, however, that the *Times* building had been the site of the worst terrorist attack in Los Angeles history. On October 1, 1910, a dynamite bomb exploded at the *Times* building, killing twenty-one non-union workers. John J. McNamara, the secretary-treasurer of the International Association of Bridge and Structural Iron Workers, and

his younger brother James were arrested and confessed to the crime in order to escape the death penalty. James was sentenced to life imprisonment, while John was sentenced to fifteen years. For a discussion of this case, see Simon, *The Terrorist Trap*, 40–42.

52. Transcript of tape recovered on July 5, 1974, at L.A. Times (Los Angeles Police Department Item No. 1339, files, Los Angeles County District Attorney's Office). The discussion of this first tape left by Kurbegovic is drawn from Simon, "The Alphabet Bomber," 75–77; and from files, Los Angeles County District Attorney's Office.

53. *People v. Kurbegovic*, 138 Cal.App.3d (1982) at 748; Simon, "The Alphabet Bomber," 75–76.

54. Transcript of tape recovered on July 5, 1974; Simon, "The Alphabet Bomber," 76.

55. Transcript of tape recovered on July 5, 1974; Simon, "The Alphabet Bomber," 76.

56. 1974 RT at 168–69, 172; Simon, "The Alphabet Bomber," 76–77.

57. Altman interview by the author, March 19, 1998; Simon, "The Alphabet Bomber," 77.

58. Transcript of tape recovered on August 16, 1974, at Eleventh and Los Angeles Streets (Los Angeles Police Department Item No. 1345, files, Los Angeles County District Attorney's Office); Simon, "The Alphabet Bomber," 77.

59. *Troy (NY) Times Record*, November 15, 1951; *Harrisburg (IL) Daily Register*, November 15, 1951; *The Billboard*, November 24, 1951, 57, and December 1, 1951, 93.

60. *The Billboard*, August 20, 1952, 53.

61. "Cookie! the Wonder Boy," *LOOK*, December 3, 1963, 116–22.

62. 1980 RT at 11,343–45.

63. 1974 RT at 203–8.

64. 1974 RT at 208–9; *San Bernardino County Sun*, August 13, 1974.

65. 1974 RT at 209. Dinko Bozanich, the prosecutor in the Alphabet Bomber's 1974 grand jury proceedings and 1974–80 competency and criminal trials, recalled Trostl's grand jury testimony with awe: "Trostl is the most impactful testimony, eyewitness testimony, that I think I've ever encountered. He was a circus aerialist. He was one of the people that were injured. If you go to Central Casting and you say, 'I want to have a bomb blast occur in a controlled [area like an airport]. . . . I want to have an individual who can not only survive the blast, but when tossed up into the air, can describe for you what he is seeing in terms of, first, the locker bank falling apart and then how people in the way of the locker bank are being destroyed by the shrapnel. I want you to give me someone that can do that,' Central Casting [would say], 'There is no such person. [But] wait a minute. What about a high wire guy who is just not only up there but has got to have the type of nerves of steel, if he's way up in the air like that, that he may be able to, if he's looking, describe for you [what

occurred] and still not get killed by this bomb blast?' 'Cause he did fall. He had a bad leg, but he was able to rehab himself back." Bozanich interview by the author, November 30, 2016.

66. 1980 RT at 11,348, 11,363–64.

67. 1974 RT at 210–12; 1980 RT at 11,350.

68. 1980 RT at 11,352.

69. "Pat's Story," Standing Firm Ministries, http://www.standingfm.com/pats-story; Richard West, "Injured Pastor Lives—but Loses Right Leg," *Los Angeles Times*, August 7, 1974; *Arizona Republic*, August 7, 1974; 1974 RT at 196, 200; 1980 RT at 6,553, 6,558.

70. 1980 RT at 6,562, 6,567, 6,579.

71. Toobin, *American Heiress*, 185.

72. 1980 RT at 6,401.

73. Toobin, *American Heiress*, 219.

74. Simon, *The Terrorist Trap*, 97–106.

75. There had been one major midair plane bombing in the United States prior to this, and it occurred in November 1955. The motivation for that attack, however, was financial and not political. Twenty-three-year-old John Gilbert Graham, not exactly a loving son, put several sticks of dynamite and a timer in his mother's luggage before she boarded a United Airlines flight out of Denver. Graham was hoping to collect a $37,500 insurance policy on her life. Forty-four people, including Graham's mother, were killed in the bombing. Simon, *Lone Wolf Terrorism*, 68–72.

76. *Arizona Republic*, August 7, 1974.

77. *Arizona Republic*, August 7, 1974.

78. 1980 RT at 6,439–45.

79. Ed Meagher, "Effort to Make Bomb Debris 'Talk' Pushed," *Los Angeles Times*, August 9, 1974; 1980 RT at 7,856–62.

80. Al Martinez, "Two Killed, 36 Hurt as Bomb Rips L.A. Airport Waiting Area," *Los Angeles Times*, August 7, 1974; files, Los Angeles County District Attorney's Office.

81. Mike Goodman, "Hospital's Drills Pay Off in Skill," *Los Angeles Times*, August 7, 1974.

82. Files, Los Angeles County District Attorney's Office.

83. 1980 RT at 7,850–51; 1974 RT at 258, 348. The smaller pieces of debris were where there had been a bank of lockers, indicating the impact of the explosion was greatest there. The larger pieces were scattered further out in the lobby.

84. It would also serve as a training exercise for investigators in reconstructing a bomb site in case there were future similar incidents. Bozanich interview by the author, September 27, 2017.

85. Files, Los Angeles County District Attorney's Office.

86. 1980 RT at 7,575–80; files, Los Angeles County District Attorney's Office.

87. Files, Los Angeles County District Attorney's Office.

88. See note 51 above for a discussion of the bombing of the *Times* building.

89. 1980 RT at 6,183–84.

90. Dave McNary, "Memories of L.A. Herald-Examiner Fading," UPI, October 31, 1990, https://www.upi.com/Archives/1990/10/31/Memories-of-la-Herald-Examiner -fading/4859657349200/.

91. McNary, "Memories of L.A. Herald-Examiner Fading"; "The Last Los Angeles Herald-Examiner Strike," CSU Northridge Oviatt Library, February 3, 2014, http:// library.csun.edu/sca/Peek-in-the-Stacks/Examiner. The paper folded in 1989. Its circulation that year was only 230,000, less than a quarter of that of the *Los Angeles Times*.

92. Steve Plesa, "Herald-Examiner Memories," *Orange County Register*, February 10, 2008, updated August 21, 2013, http://www.ocregister.com/articles/hearst-9669 -herald-editor.html.

93. 1980 RT at 6,402, 7,797.

94. Casler believed the spelling of the first name was "Isak." LAPD transcribers spelled the first name "Esak" when listening to a previous audiotape as well as subsequent taped messages and phone calls. The appellate court, in its ruling on Kurbegovic's appeal of his criminal conviction, spelled the first name "Isaiak." *People v. Kurbegovic*, 138 Cal.App.3d (1982) at 737.

95. 1980 RT at 6,187–89; *People v. Kurbegovic*, 138 Cal.App.3d (1982) at 737; 1974 RT at 228, 286–87; files, Los Angeles County District Attorney's Office.

96. 1980 RT at 6,184–85, 6,223, 4,127–29; files, Los Angeles County District Attorney's Office.

97. 1980 RT at 6,186, 6,193, 6,218; files, Los Angeles County District Attorney's Office.

98. 1980 RT at 6,191.

99. Transcript of tape recovered on August 9, 1974, in Maywood, California, following call to CBS (Los Angeles Police Department Item No. 1340, files, Los Angeles County District Attorney's Office); Simon, "The Alphabet Bomber," 78; files, Los Angeles County District Attorney's Office.

100. Transcript of tape recovered on August 9, 1974.

101. Transcript of tape recovered on August 9, 1974.

102. Transcript of tape recovered on August 9, 1974. The correct spelling of Shaughessy's first name is "Rhett."

103. Jim Malone, "Nixon Resignation Still Resonates 40 Years after Watergate," VOA News, August 7, 2014, http://www.voanews.com/a/nixon-resignation-still-resonates -40-years-after-watergate-scandal/2405644.html.

3. A CITY IN FEAR

1. "Airport Takes 3 Steps to Boost Security," *Los Angeles Herald Examiner*, August 8, 1974.

2. Price and Forrest, *Practical Aviation Security*, 115.

3. "Airport Explosion Pushed by FBI," *Los Angeles Times*, August 8, 1974. In order to demonstrate what he believed to be poor security at the nation's airports and to promote his anti-hijacking bill, Murphy once borrowed twenty-five pistols that had been seized in hijackings and put them in his carry-on luggage on a flight from Washington to New York. He was able to get all the weapons onboard with no questions asked. Jack Anderson, "Hughes Probe Touches White House," *Washington Post*, January 18, 1973.

4. Ed Meagher and Bill Hazlett, "Leads in Airport Bomb Reported by FBI," *Los Angeles Times*, August 8, 1974; "Tape Clue in Airport Bombing," *Los Angeles Herald Examiner*, August 10, 1974; Conrad Casler, "L.A. Bomber Pledges Gas Attack: Strike at Congress Vowed in Tape," *Los Angeles Herald Examiner*, August 15, 1974.

5. Deposition of Arleigh McCree, *Bessie Hsu, et al. vs. City of Los Angeles, et al.*, No. C 132143 (Los Angeles Superior Court, December 1975) at 9–12; 29; files, Los Angeles County District Attorney's Office; 1974 RT at 282; "Ammonium Nitrate," *Encyclopaedia Britannica*, https://www.britannica.com/science/ammonium-nitrate.

6. 1980 RT at 6,776–78.

7. Deposition of McCree at 13–14; files, Los Angeles County District Attorney's Office.

8. Deposition of McCree at 14; files, Los Angeles County District Attorney's Office.

9. Simon, "The Alphabet Bomber," 90–91; Chaleff interview by the author, February 10, 1998.

10. Deposition of Stephen Hagar Smith, *Bessie Hsu, et al. vs. City of Los Angeles, et al.*, No. C 132143 (Los Angeles Superior Court, December 1975) at 50–51; 1980 RT at 8,883.

11. Files, Los Angeles County District Attorney's Office.

12. George Lardner, "Terrorist Reportedly Sent a Justice Toxic Chemicals," *Washington Post*, December 20, 1983; 1980 RT at 7,820, 20,610; files, Los Angeles County District Attorney's Office.

13. "Airport Takes 3 Steps."

14. Transcript of tape recovered on August 9, 1974, in Maywood, California, following call to CBS (Los Angeles Police Department Item No. 1340, files, Los Angeles County District Attorney's Office).

15. 1974 RT at 305–13.

16. Transcript of tape recovered by FBI on August 12, 1974, from Glenn Evans after initial recovery by Evans in late July–early August 1974 in area of radio station

KPFK (Los Angeles Police Department Item No. 1341, files, Los Angeles County District Attorney's Office).

17. *Progress Bulletin* (Pomona CA), February 24, 1971.

18. Harry Kreisler, *Democracy, Disarmament, and Public Education*, Institute of International Studies, April 17, 2000, 2.

19. Joan Sweeney, "Man Who Claims He Bombed Airport Makes New Threat," *Los Angeles Times*, August 17, 1974.

20. Conrad Casler, "A Reprieve from 3rd Alphabet Bomb?" *Los Angeles Herald Examiner*, August 18, 1974.

21. Toobin, *American Heiress*, 121.

22. Steve Plesa, "Herald-Examiner Memories," *Orange County Register*, February 10, 2008, updated August 21, 2013, http://www.ocregister.com/articles/hearst-9669 -herald-editor.html.

23. 1974 RT at 323–26.

24. 1974 RT at 326–28; 1980 RT at 6,243.

25. Transcript of tape recovered on August 14, 1974, at 1355 South Olive Street (Los Angeles Police Department Item No. 1343, files, Los Angeles County District Attorney's Office).

26. Transcript of tape recovered on August 14, 1974.

27. Casler, "L.A. Bomber Pledges Gas Attack."

28. Transcript of tape recovered by FBI on August 12, 1974.

29. Simon, "The Alphabet Bomber," 82; Bozanich interview by the author, December 23, 1997.

30. Files, Los Angeles County District Attorney's Office.

31. Files, Los Angeles County District Attorney's Office.

32. Transcript of August 13, 1974, telephone call to Conrad Casler (*Herald Examiner*) (Los Angeles Police Department Item No. 1342, files, Los Angeles County District Attorney's Office). The correct spelling is "Milemore."

33. Doug Shuit, "Caller Links Airport Blast to 1970 Police 'Mistake' Shootings," *Los Angeles Times*, August 15, 1974.

34. Lanceley interview by the author, October 29, 2015; 1980 RT at 7,626–27; 1974 RT at 336.

35. Transcript of August 16, 1974, telephone call to Frederick Lanceley (FBI agent stationed at the *Herald Examiner*) (Los Angeles Police Department Item No. 1344, files, Los Angeles County District Attorney's Office).

36. Transcript of tape recovered on August 16, 1974, at Eleventh and Los Angeles Streets (Los Angeles Police Department Item No. 1345, files, Los Angeles County District Attorney's Office).

37. 1980 RT at 10,207–8. Ammonium chlorate "is an unstable salt that is mainly used to manufacture explosives." It is "capable of detonation or explosive decomposition under ambient temperature and pressure without any external initiating source," and "it can violently explodes [*sic*] in concentrated solutions when exposed to light or heat." No wonder McCree was worried. See "Ammonium Chlorate Formula," SoftSchools.com, http://www.softschools.com/formulas/chemistry/ammonium_chlorate_formula/394/; and "Reactive Chemicals," University of Iowa, https://ehs.research.uiowa.edu/108-reactive-chemicals.

38. 1980 RT at 7,865; Al Martinez and Bill Hazlett, "Threat of Bombing Called Off but Police Aren't Taking Any Chances," *Los Angeles Times*, August 18, 1974; Conrad Casler, "Race against Time to Find Third Bomb," *Los Angeles Herald Examiner*, August 17, 1974.

39. 1980 RT at 7,828, 7,870–71.

40. 1980 RT at 7,873–74; Bozanich interview by the author, November 30, 2016.

41. 1980 RT at 7,872–73; Susan Banashek, "LAPD Bomb Squad: They Make a Living Walking on Eggs," *Los Angeles Times*, August 21, 1974.

42. 1980 RT at 7,871–79.

43. 1980 RT at 7,882–84.

44. 1980 RT at 7,884–86, 7,891.

45. 1980 RT at 7,893–94, 7,899.

46. 1980 RT at 7,897.

47. 1980 RT at 7,895–97.

48. 1980 RT at 7,899–900, 7,905.

49. 1980 RT at 7,901, 7,915. Bozanich was impressed with Wells's rushing up and grabbing the bomb. He recalled asking him once, "How can you do that?" Wells replied, "Hey look. You got to get it from point A to point B. Once I grabbed it, if it's gonna go off, it's over. If I grab it, now I got to finish it by taking it there [into the bomb trailer]." Bozanich interview by the author, November 30, 2016.

50. 1980 RT at 7,901–2.

51. 1980 RT at 7,910–11, 7,915–16.

52. 1980 RT at 7,916–17, 10,204.

53. 1980 RT at 7,924–31.

54. 1980 RT at 7,932–34, 7,937.

55. Banashek, "LAPD Bomb Squad."

56. 1980 RT at 7,934, 7,937, 7,940–45.

57. 1980 RT at 7,945–47, 10,210.

58. 1980 RT at 7,946–51, 7,955–64, 10,389, 10,532–33. McCree also believed that "if the nitrobenzene dissolved the fuse, that would have interrupted the intended . . . function." 1980 RT at 10,533.

59. Conrad Casler, "Bomb at Bus Station, Another One Planted, Tape Warns," *Los Angeles Herald Examiner*, August 17, 1974; files, Los Angeles County District Attorney's Office; Simon, "The Alphabet Bomber," 84.

60. Martinez and Hazlett, "Threat of Bombing Called Off"; Simon, "The Alphabet Bomber," 84.

61. *Los Angeles Herald Examiner*, August 17, 1974.

62. Transcript of August 17, 1974, telephone call to Leo Batt (*Herald Examiner*) (Los Angeles Police Department Item No. 1346, files, Los Angeles County District Attorney's Office).

63. Transcript of August 17, 1974, telephone call to Leo Batt (*Herald Examiner*).

64. Martinez and Hazlett, "Threat of Bombing Called Off."

65. "Huge Chemical Blast Rocks City: Warehouse Leveled; No Link to Bomber," *Los Angeles Herald Examiner*, August 18, 1974; "Bomber Ties Self to Blast Downtown," *Los Angeles Herald Examiner*, August 19, 1974.

66. "Huge Chemical Blast Rocks City."

67. Transcript of August 18, 1974, telephone call to Jack Brown (*Herald Examiner*) (Los Angeles Police Department Item No. 1347, files, Los Angeles County District Attorney's Office).

68. "Bomber Ties Self to Blast Downtown."

69. Tyler, "Rise and Decline," 62, 74.

70. Dick Main, "Hoax Bomb Calls Plague Police Seeking Possible Third Device," *Los Angeles Times*, August 19, 1974.

71. Files, Los Angeles County District Attorney's Office.

72. Files, Los Angeles County District Attorney's Office.

73. Sweeney, "Man Who Claims He Bombed Airport."

74. Watson interview by the author, April 2, 1998.

75. Files, Los Angeles County District Attorney's Office.

76. 1974 RT at 426.

77. This discussion of the Mad Bomber is drawn from Simon, *Lone Wolf Terrorism*, 219–22. See also Greenburg, *The Mad Bomber of New York*; Cannell, *Incendiary*; Spaaij, *Understanding Lone Wolf Terrorism*, 23–24; Melissa Ann Madden, "George Metesky: New York's Mad Bomber (City Under Siege)," TruTV Crime Library; Melissa Ann Madden, "George Metesky (Small Beginnings)," TruTV Crime Library; Melissa Ann Madden, "George Metesky (The Game Begins)," TruTV Crime Library; Melissa Ann Madden, "George Metesky (Revelations)," TruTV Crime Library; Melissa Ann Madden, "George Metesky (Aftermath)," TruTV Crime Library; DeNevi and Campbell, *Into the Minds of Madmen*, 60–65; Lyn Bixby, "'Mad Bomber' of Waterbury Terrorized New York for 17 Years," *Hartford Courant*, July 2, 1995; Alexander Feinberg, "Edison Clerk Finds Case in File;

Bomber's Words Alerted Her," *New York Times*, January 23, 1957, 18; "The Bomber's Grievances Came to Light in a Series of Letters," *New York Times*, January 23, 1957, 19; Malcolm Gladwell, "Dangerous Minds: Criminal Profiling Made Easy," *New Yorker*, November 12, 2007, https://www.newyorker.com/magazine/2007/11/12/dangerous-minds; and Michael T. Kaufman, "'Mad Bomber,' Now 70, Goes Free Today," *New York Times*, December 13, 1973.

78. Jack Jones, "Bombing Suspect 'Trapped Himself,'" *Los Angeles Times*, August 21, 1974.

79. This discussion of "Rasim's" ideological beliefs and motivations is drawn from Simon, "The Alphabet Bomber," 88–90.

80. Transcript of tape recovered by FBI on August 12, 1974.

81. Transcript of tape recovered on August 9, 1974.

82. Transcript of tape recovered on August 20, 1974, at Sunset and Western (scene of arrest) (Los Angeles Police Department Item No. 1338, files, Los Angeles County District Attorney's Office).

83. Transcript of tape recovered on August 16, 1974. Excerpts from this tape were given in the Introduction.

84. Transcript of tape recovered on August 16, 1974.

85. Transcript of tape recovered on August 16, 1974.

86. Mary A. Barberis, "The Arab-Israeli Battle on Capitol Hill," *Virginia Quarterly Review* 51, no. 1 (Spring 1976), http://www.vqronline.org/essay/arab-israeli-battle-capitol-hill.

87. Transcript of tape recovered on July 5, 1974, at L.A. Times (Los Angeles Police Department Item No. 1339, files, Los Angeles County District Attorney's Office).

88. "Isaac Rasim: A Collage of Hate," *Los Angeles Herald Examiner*, August 17, 1974.

89. Transcript of tape recovered by FBI on August 12, 1974.

90. Transcript of tape recovered by FBI on August 12, 1974.

91. Files, Los Angeles County District Attorney's Office.

92. Files, Los Angeles County District Attorney's Office.

93. Files, Los Angeles County District Attorney's Office.

94. Transcript of tape recovered on August 16, 1974.

95. Sweeney, "Man Who Claims He Bombed Airport." The *Los Angeles Times* article spelled the name "Isa Krasim." It is not clear whether the LAPD searched police, FBI, and INS records for that spelling or for the spelling "Isaiak Rasim." It wouldn't have mattered, though, since Kurbegovic's name would not have shown up under those searches.

96. Ronald Koziol, "Without Telling L.A. Cops, FBI Pushes Hearst Hunt," *Chicago Tribune*, September 1, 1974.

97. Koziol, "Without Telling L.A. Cops."

98. Hurlbut email correspondence with the author, October 23, 2015; Samuel L. Williams, "Commendation on Search for the 'Alphabet Bomber,'" LAPD intradepartmental correspondence to Lieutenant II Max K. Hurlbut, August 22, 1974.

99. Hurlbut email correspondence with the author, October 23, 2015; Williams, "Commendation on Search."

100. Hurlbut email correspondence with the author, October 23, 2015; files, Los Angeles County District Attorney's Office.

101. Williams, "Commendation on Search."

102. 1974 RT at 298, 424.

103. 1974 RT at 424–26, 428; files, Los Angeles County District Attorney's Office.

104. John Fasano, "Agency Spotlight: LAPD's Elite Stakeout Squad," *Tactical-Life*, February 18, 2015, http://www.tactical-life.com/military-and-police/agency-spotlight-lapd-stakeout-squad/#lapd-tw-feb-2015-officer.

4. THE HOMEMADE EXPLOSIVES FACTORY

1. David Freed, "Special Investigations Section: Watching Crime Happen: LAPD's Secret SIS Unit: Citizens Terrorized as Police Look On," *Los Angeles Times*, September 25, 1988, http://articles.latimes.com/1988-09-25/news/mn-3844_1_special-investigations; The *Times* mistakenly used the plural "Investigations" in SIS's name. They continued to use the incorrect spelling in subsequent stories about the SIS.

2. Freed, "Special Investigations Section."

3. David Freed and William Overend, "Bradley Orders Probe of SIS Unit," *Los Angeles Times*, September 28, 1988, http://articles.latimes.com/1988-09-28/news/mn-2558_1_police-department.

4. Jerry Belcher and David Johnston, "Tragedy Ends a Celebrated LAPD Career: Accidental Shooting by Fellow Detective Saddens Elite Squad," *Los Angeles Times*, March 12, 1980.

5. Freed and Overend, "Bradley Orders Probe of SIS Unit."

6. Freed, "Special Investigations Section."

7. Sacks, *Extreme Justice*, 18–23; Ann W. O'Neill, "No Perjury Indictments Due in Probe of Sunland Shootings," *Los Angeles Times*, August 4, 1995, http://articles.latimes.com/1995-08-04/local/me-31304_1_robbery-suspects; Leslie Berger, "Feds Won't Pursue Case on Officers," *Los Angeles Times*, February 14, 1995, http://articles.latimes.com/1995-02-14/local/me-31841_1_federal-civil-rights.

8. Sacks, *Extreme Justice*, 18–23; Matt Lait and Julie Tamaki, "Pros and Cons of Police Squad Debated," *Los Angeles Times*, February 2, 1997, http://articles.latimes.com/1997-02-27/local/me-32874_1_sis-officer; O'Neill, "No Perjury Indictments."

9. Berger, "Feds Won't Pursue Case on Officers"; O'Neill, "No Perjury Indictments"; Josh Meyer, "LAPD Unit on Trial for Allowing Sunland Robbery," *Los Angeles Times*, January 5, 1994, http://articles.latimes.com/1994-01-05/news/mn-8692_1 _court-documents. The SIS members also faced perjury charges stemming from their testimony in a civil trial regarding the McDonald's incident, but federal authorities concluded that there was insufficient evidence to indict them. O'Neill, "No Perjury Indictments."

10. Richard Winton, "Pistol for Police Marketed to Public," *Los Angeles Times*, January 12, 2008, http://articles.latimes.com/2008/jan/12/local/me-sis12.

11. Files, Los Angeles County District Attorney's Office; 1974 RT at 401, 428. Kurbegovic, as noted in chapter 1, had also been described as weighing 175 pounds. Files, Los Angeles County District Attorney's Office.

12. Files, Los Angeles County District Attorney's Office; 1974 RT at 382, 395; 1980 RT at 9,148, 9,150, 9,153, 9,159.

13. Files, Los Angeles County District Attorney's Office.

14. Files, Los Angeles County District Attorney's Office.

15. Files, Los Angeles County District Attorney's Office.

16. Files, Los Angeles County District Attorney's Office.

17. Files, Los Angeles County District Attorney's Office; 1974 RT at 432; 1980 RT at 10,858–59.

18. Files, Los Angeles County District Attorney's Office.

19. Files, Los Angeles County District Attorney's Office.

20. 1980 RT at 9,153, 9,156, 9,158–59.

21. Files, Los Angeles County District Attorney's Office; 1980 RT at 9,160, 9,234.

22. Files, Los Angeles County District Attorney's Office; 1980 RT at 10,919.

23. Files, Los Angeles County District Attorney's Office.

24. Files, Los Angeles County District Attorney's Office.

25. Files, Los Angeles County District Attorney's Office; 1980 RT at 10,862–64.

26. Files, Los Angeles County District Attorney's Office; 1974 RT at 395–96; Bozanich interview by the author, December 23, 1997.

27. Files, Los Angeles County District Attorney's Office; 1974 RT at 396; 1980 RT at 10,864–65.

28. Files, Los Angeles County District Attorney's Office.

29. Files, Los Angeles County District Attorney's Office; 1980 RT at 10,866–67, 10,872, 9,168; 1974 RT at 404; *People v. Kurbegovic*, 138 Cal.App.3d 731 (1982) at 739.

30. 1980 RT at 10,867–69; 1974 RT at 403–7.

31. 1974 RT at 407–9.

32. 1974 RT at 409–10.

33. Files, Los Angeles County District Attorney's Office.

34. 1974 RT at 411–12; 1980 RT at 9,239.

35. 1974 RT at 413; 1980 RT at 9,224, 9,228; files, Los Angeles County District Attorney's Office. The arrest of the Alphabet Bomber was a boon for Hagele's career, earning him respect and admiration throughout the LAPD. While others were of course involved, he was the one who held the gun to the head of the infamous terrorist and could be considered the principal arresting officer. But Hagele's life ended tragically in March 1980 when, on another SIS surveillance, he was accidentally shot and fatally wounded by a fellow officer in a shoot-out with a bank robber. At his memorial service, Assistant Police Chief Robert Vernon surprised everyone by reading portions of a letter praising Hagele that came from an unlikely source: Muharem Kurbegovic! "Some lawmen are admired by their peers, others by their families," Kurbegovic wrote from his jail cell. "Hagele is that lawman who is admired by his prisoner." Kurbegovic also described his arrest by Hagele in the Carl's Jr. restroom: "You rushed in, flashed your 'business card' under my nose and said, 'Move (and) your head will fall off.' I didn't move, but you didn't press the trigger either. In a way, you saved my life, even though I am not grateful." See George Ramos, "LAPD Superiors, Prisoner Praise Slain Detective," *Los Angeles Times*, March 15, 1980. Hagele was the SIS officer for whom Mayor Tom Bradley ordered all flags at Los Angeles city buildings be flown at half staff, though Bradley would claim in 1988 that he wasn't aware that the SIS existed until he read about it in the exposé published in the *Los Angeles Times*.

36. Transcript of tape recording of August 22, 1974, at Parker Center (Cassette Tape No. 74-1620, files, Los Angeles County District Attorney's Office).

37. Transcript of tape recording of August 22, 1974, at Parker Center.

38. Transcript of tape recording of August 22, 1974, at Parker Center.

39. Transcript of tape recording of August 22, 1974, at Parker Center.

40. Bozanich interview by the author, November 30, 2016.

41. 1980 RT at 9,210–17, 9,233, 9,287. One inmate, however, who was in the same section of the Los Angeles County jail with Kurbegovic later claimed that Kurbegovic did make verbal and written statements to him on several occasions, including telling him, "There is no way they can tie me in with the airport bombing." Bozanich had little use for such "jailhouse informants" who wanted to cut deals for testifying for the prosecution. "Can you imagine how many guys, during the first couple of months, came out of the woodwork saying, 'I was in the cell with Kurbegovic and he talked'?" said Bozanich. "There's no way [Kurbegovic talked]. It didn't happen. This guy is good. He's not going to talk. He's not going to make a mistake." Files, Los Angeles County District Attorney's Office; Bozanich interview by the author, November 30, 2016.

42. 1974 RT at 437–40.

43. 1974 RT at 444.

44. 1980 RT at 10,424–26.

45. 1974 RT at 474.

46. Files, Los Angeles County District Attorney's Office.

47. Files, Los Angeles County District Attorney's Office.

48. Transcript of tape recovered by FBI on August 12, 1974, from Glenn Evans after initial recovery by Evans in late July–early August 1974 in area of radio station KPFK (Los Angeles Police Department Item No. 1341, files, Los Angeles County District Attorney's Office).

49. Files, Los Angeles County District Attorney's Office; Simon, "The Alphabet Bomber," 85; 1980 RT at 9,910–29.

50. 1980 RT at 9,929–39; files, Los Angeles County District Attorney's Office.

51. Dale Omenson, "Suspect Captured: Arrested for Blast at L.A. Airport," *Los Angeles Herald Examiner*, August 21, 1974.

52. 1980 RT at 10,126–27.

53. 1976 RT at 66–67. Kurbegovic knew what the police had found in the first search from either their mentioning it in previous court appearances or from his defense lawyer through discovery.

54. Bozanich interview by the author, November 30, 2016.

55. Bozanich interview by the author, November 30, 2016.

56. 1980 RT at 9,628, 10,577.

57. 1980 RT at 10,578–80.

58. Files, Los Angeles County District Attorney's Office; Bozanich interview by the author, November 30, 2016.

59. 1980 RT at 10,669.

60. Simon, "The Alphabet Bomber," 86–87; George Lardner, "Terrorist Reportedly Sent a Justice Toxic Chemicals," *Washington Post*, December 20, 1983.

61. Simon, "The Alphabet Bomber," 86–87; U.S. Congress, Office of Technology Assessment, *Technologies Underlying Weapons of Mass Destruction*, 18.

62. Simon, "The Alphabet Bomber," 87; U.S. Congress, Office of Technology Assessment, *Technologies Underlying Weapons of Mass Destruction*, 24.

63. Transcript of tape recovered by FBI on August 12, 1974.

64. *Global Proliferation of Weapons of Mass Destruction*, Hearings before the Permanent Subcommittee on Investigations of the Committee on Governmental Affairs, United States Senate, 104th Cong., 2nd sess., part 3, March 27, 1996 (Washington DC: U.S. Government Printing Office, 1996), 23.

65. Simon, "The Alphabet Bomber," 87; *Global Proliferation of Weapons of Mass Destruction*, Hearings, part 1, October 31 and November 1, 1995 (Washington DC: U.S. Government Printing Office, 1996), 613; "Carbon Tetrachloride," http://scorecard

.goodguide.com/chemical-profiles/html/carbontetrachloride.html; Eric Turk, "Phosgene from Chloroform," *Chemical & Engineering News* 76, no. 9 (March 1998): 6, http://pubs.acs.org/cen/safety/19980302.html.

66. Files, Los Angeles County District Attorney's Office.

67. Transcript of tape recovered on August 20, 1974, at Sunset and Western (scene of arrest) (Los Angeles Police Department Item No. 1338, files, Los Angeles County District Attorney's Office).

5. I SHALL RETURN!

1. Files, Los Angeles County District Attorney's Office.

2. Files, Los Angeles County District Attorney's Office.

3. Files, Los Angeles County District Attorney's Office.

4. Files, Los Angeles County District Attorney's Office.

5. Files, Los Angeles County District Attorney's Office.

6. "Dr. F. J. Hacker, 75, A Psychiatric Expert on Violence in Man," *New York Times*, June 30, 1989, http://www.nytimes.com/1989/06/30/obituaries/dr-f-j-hacker-75-a -psychiatric-expert-on-violence-in-man.html.

7. Files, Los Angeles County District Attorney's Office.

8. Bozanich interview by the author, November 30, 2016.

9. "The 'Insanity Defense' and Diminished Capacity," Cornell Law School, Legal Information Institute, https://www.law.cornell.edu/background/insane/insanity.html.

10. Simon, *Lone Wolf Terrorism*, 161–62, 290n58; Clarke, *American Assassins*, 10–11; Millard, *Destiny of the Republic*, 236–37.

11. Simon, *Lone Wolf Terrorism*, 290n58; Millard, *Destiny of the Republic*, 236–37; John Martin, "The Insanity Defense: A Closer Look," *Washington Post*, February 27, 1998, http://www.washingtonpost.com/wp-srv/local/longterm/aron/qa227 .htm; "From Daniel M'Naughten [*sic*] to John Hinckley: A Brief History of the Insanity Defense," Frontline, PBS, http://www.pbs.org/wgbh/pages/frontline /shows/crime/trial/history.html.

12. "Diminished Capacity," Cornell Law School, Legal Information Institute, https:// www.law.cornell.edu/wex/diminished_capacity.

13. "Diminished Capacity," Law.com, http://dictionary.law.com/Default.aspx?selected =516. One of the most infamous cases of diminished capacity occurred when Dan White admitted to killing San Francisco mayor George Moscone and Supervisor Harvey Milk in 1978 but only received a manslaughter conviction "on the basis that his capacity was diminished by the sugar content of his blood due to eating 'Twinkies'" ("Diminished Capacity," Law.com).

14. Bozanich interview by the author, November 30, 2016. The book was *"R.F.K. Must Die!"* by Robert Blair Kaiser.

15. Bozanich interview by the author, November 30, 2016.

16. Jerry Cohen, "Airport Bomb Suspect Pens Denial, Seeks Aid," *Los Angeles Times*, October 2, 1974.

17. *Los Angeles Magazine*, February 1998, 79–80. Johnny Cochran was the lead defense attorney for O. J. Simpson during his 1995 trial for murdering his ex-wife, Nicole Brown Simpson, and her friend Ron Goldman in 1994. Simpson was acquitted by the jury.

18. *People v. Kurbegovic*, 138 Cal.App.3d 731 (1982) at 741.

19. Files, Los Angeles County District Attorney's Office.

20. Roger M. Grace, "William B. Keene: Judge on 'Divorce Court,' in the 1980s," Metropolitan News-Enterprise, July 17, 2003, http://www.metnews.com/articles /reminiscing071703.htm; Bugliosi, *Helter Skelter*, 394.

21. Bozanich interview by the author, November 30, 2016.

22. Files, Los Angeles County District Attorney's Office.

23. Files, Los Angeles County District Attorney's Office; John Dreyfuss, "Suspect in Bombing Ruled Incompetent," *Los Angeles Times*, January 21, 1975; 1980 RT at 12,383–85, 12,392–99.

24. *People v. Kurbegovic*, 138 Cal.App.3d (1982) at 741. A judgment notwithstanding the verdict is a "reversal of a jury's verdict by the trial judge when the judge believes there was no factual basis for the verdict or it was contrary to law." See Law.com, http://dictionary.law.com/Default.aspx?selected=1061.

25. Files, Los Angeles County District Attorney's Office.

26. Files, Los Angeles County District Attorney's Office; "Asylum: 'Alphabet Bomber' Is a Dangerous Psychotic," *Pacific Stars and Stripes*, UPI, April 20, 1975.

27. 1976 RT at 3, 6; *People v. Kurbegovic*, 138 Cal.App.3d (1982) at 741.

28. 1976 RT at 19, 32, 45; *People v. Kurbegovic*, 138 Cal.App.3d (1982) at 741.

29. *People v. Kurbegovic*, 138 Cal.App.3d (1982) at 741–46.

30. Bozanich interview by the author, November 30, 2016.

31. 1978–79 RT at 7–10.

32. 1978–79 RT at 78–79; Bozanich interview by the author, November 30, 2016.

33. *People v. Kurbegovic*, 138 Cal.App.3d (1982) at 742, 755, 757; Bozanich interview by the author, November 30, 2016.

34. 1978–79 RT at 3,037.

35. Charles Maher, "'Alphabet Bomber' Case: Long Trial Stirs Controversy," *Los Angeles Times*, April 28, 1980.

36. Maher, "'Alphabet Bomber' Case."

37. Maher, "'Alphabet Bomber' Case."

38. Bozanich interview by the author, November 8, 2017.

39. "Nancy Watson, 77; Judge Presided Over Trial of Alphabet Bomber," *Los Angeles Times*, February 12, 2004, http://articles.latimes.com/2004/feb/12/local/me-watson12; Harvey Goodman email correspondence with the author, July 14, 2017.

40. Goodman, *So Too My Love*, 28.

41. Goodman, *So Too My Love*, 28.

42. Brian Goodman interview by the author, July 18, 2017.

43. Brian Goodman interview by the author, July 18, 2017; Goodman, *So Too My Love*, 29.

44. Marcia Goodman interview by the author, July 19, 2017.

45. "Nancy Watson, 77; Judge Presided Over Trial of Alphabet Bomber."

46. Bozanich interview by the author, November 30, 2016.

47. Bozanich interview by the author, November 30, 2016.

48. Simon, "The Alphabet Bomber," 92.

49. Bozanich interview by the author, November 30, 2016.

50. "The History of Capital Punishment in California," California Department of Corrections and Rehabilitation, http://www.cdcr.ca.gov/Capital_Punishment /history_of_capital_punishment.html.

51. Timothy Carlson, "Accused Alphabet Bomber: Really Insane or Just Crafty?" *Los Angeles Herald Examiner*, July 10, 1980. The Criminal Courts Building was renamed the Clara Shortridge Foltz Criminal Justice Center in 2002.

52. Watson interview by the author, April 2, 1998.

53. "Accused Bomber's 'Messiah' Plea Fails," *Los Angeles Times*, June 19, 1980; Carlson, "Accused Alphabet Bomber."

54. Watson interview by the author, April 2, 1998.

55. Bozanich interview by the author, November 30, 2016.

56. Frank Candid, "Alphabet Bomber Gets Life Sentence in LAX Deaths," *Los Angeles Herald Examiner*, November 25, 1980; "Accused Bomber's 'Messiah' Plea Fails."

57. Files, Los Angeles County District Attorney's Office.

58. 1980 RT at 14,834, 15,077, 15,084; files, Los Angeles County District Attorney's Office.

59. Janet Rae-Dupree and David Freed, "2 LAPD Officers Killed in Attempt to Defuse Bomb," *Los Angeles Times*, February 9, 1986. McCree and another member of the bomb squad were killed in 1986 when a booby-trapped pipe bomb they were trying to defuse exploded in the garage of a home in North Hollywood, California.

60. Bozanich interview by the author, November 30, 2016.

61. 1980 RT at 10,181.

62. 1980 RT at 10,471–72.

63. 1980 RT at 4,280.

64. Watson interview by the author, April 2, 1998.

65. 1980 RT at 6,579–80.

66. Bozanich interview by the author, November 30, 2016.

67. *People v. Kurbegovic*, 138 Cal.App.3d (1982) at 758–61.

68. *People v. Kurbegovic*, 138 Cal.App.3d (1982) at 759–60.

69. 1980 RT at 5,474–75.

70. 1980 RT at 4,284, 10,156–57, 10,317, 10,525.

71. Bozanich interview by the author, November 30, 2016.

72. Watson interview by the author, April 2, 1998.

73. Lewis, *The Criminal Justice Club*, 257.

74. Lewis interview by the author, June 27, 2017.

75. D'Agostino interview by the author, August 2, 2017.

76. Bozanich interview by the author, November 30, 2016.

77. D'Agostino interview by the author, August 2, 2017.

78. 1980 RT at 8,869, 13,380–82.

79. 1980 RT at 6,478.

80. Scott Harris, "Local Elections: 'Dragon Lady' D'Agostino Covets Publicity, D.A.'s Job," *Los Angeles Times*, June 4, 1988, http://articles.latimes.com/1988-06-04/local/me-3959_1_dragon-lady. D'Agostino was the lead prosecutor for the *Twilight Zone: The Movie* trial (1987–88), which resulted in the acquittal of director John Landis and four associates on manslaughter charges. Actor Vic Morrow and two child actors were killed in 1982 during the filming of a helicopter scene for the movie.

81. He also said in both voir dire and his opening statement that he would be presenting a "sewer-man" defense, in that he had been flushed down the toilet and into the sewer beginning with his arrest for lewd conduct in the taxi dance hall restroom in 1971. He stated that he had been crawling through the sewer since that time, symbolized by all the bad things that had happened to him, such as the denial of his taxi dance hall permit, obstacles to becoming an American citizen, and so forth. He drew diagrams to depict this journey. "Talk about bizarre," reflected Judge Watson years later. Watson interview by the author, April 2, 1998; 1980 RT at 4,177–93.

82. 1980 RT at 4,170–75; Richard O'Reilly, "Accused Bomber Outlines Defense on Murder Counts," *Los Angeles Times*, April 15, 1980.

83. 1980 RT at 19,378.

84. 1980 RT at 8,854, 8,874–89, 8,987–88, 9,005–6.

85. Bozanich interview by the author, December 23, 1997; *People v. Kurbegovic*, 138 Cal.App.3d (1982) at 739.

86. Bozanich interview by the author, November 30, 2016.

87. Bozanich interview by the author, December 23, 2016 (this date is correct, as I interviewed Bozanich again nineteen years after the first interview).

88. Watson interview by the author, April 2, 1998.

89. Simon, "The Alphabet Bomber," 90.

90. 1980 RT at 13,562–63, 13,851.

91. Watson interview by the author, April 2, 1998; Lewis, *The Criminal Justice Club*, 256–57. The person holding the spear in the California state seal is not a man but rather the Roman goddess of wisdom, Minerva. At her feet is a grizzly bear. "State Symbols," California State Library, http://www.library.ca.gov/history /symbols.html.

92. Harvey Goodman email correspondence with the author, July 14, 2017.

93. Marcia Goodman interview by the author, July 19, 2017.

94. 1980 RT at 21,168. "Malice aforethought" basically means "to kill either deliberately and intentionally or recklessly with extreme disregard for human life." "8.107 Murder—First Degree," United States Courts for the Ninth Circuit, http:// www3.ce9.uscourts.gov/jury-instructions/node/565.

95. 1980 RT at 21,232–34, 21,247; Robert Welkos, "Life Term Given in Alphabet Bomber Case," *Los Angeles Times*, November 25, 1980; Frank Candida, "Alphabet Bomber Gets Life for '74 Blast Killing Three," *Los Angeles Herald Examiner*, November 24, 1980; "A Yugoslov Immigrant Who Was Twice Declared Mentally Incompetent . . . ," UPI Archives, October 16, 1980, http://www.upi.com/Archives /1980/10/16/A-Yugoslov-immigrant-who-was-twice-declared-mentally-incompetent /7031340516800/.

96. 1980 RT at 21,231, 21,246.

97. Terry Pristin, "1st Parole Bid Denied for 'Alphabet Bomber,'" *Los Angeles Times*, August 26, 1987.

98. Pristin, "1st Parole Bid Denied."

99. Pristin, "1st Parole Bid Denied."

100. "A writ of habeas corpus (which literally means to 'produce the body') is a court order to a person or agency holding someone in custody (such as a warden) to deliver the imprisoned individual to the court issuing the order and to show a valid reason for that person's detention." "Writ of Habeas Corpus," FindLaw, http://criminal.findlaw.com/criminal-procedure/writ-of-habeas-corpus.html.

101. *Kurbegovic v. Unknown Policians* [*sic*], no. CV 14-6036 (Federal Central District Court, Los Angeles, Sept. 11, 2014), https://www.leagle.com/decision/infdco20140915313.

102. Pristin, "1st Parole Bid Denied."

103. *People v. Kurbegovic*, 138 Cal.App.3d (1982) at 742–47.

6. CRAZY LIKE A FOX?

1. Files, Los Angeles County District Attorney's Office.

2. Simon, *The Terrorist Trap*, 337–38; Gill, *Lone-Actor Terrorists*, 105; Post, *The Mind of the Terrorist*, 8.

3. Hamm and Spaaij, *The Age of Lone Wolf Terrorism*, 53. The authors studied thirty-nine American lone wolves active from 1940 to 2000. For their documentation of mental illness they relied "on court documents, psychiatric evaluations, and news coverage" (282n49). They also found that 42 percent of the sixty-nine post-9/11 American lone wolves they studied suffered from a diagnosed mental illness, including schizophrenia, bipolar disorder, and delusions (53–54).

4. Clarke, *American Assassins*, 13–17; Meloy, *Violence Risk and Threat Assessment*, 198–201. Among the more famous assassins who suffered from mental illness was Lee Harvey Oswald, who shot and killed President John F. Kennedy in Dallas on November 22, 1963. Oswald was diagnosed as "mentally unstable" by Russian psychiatrists who examined him after he had attempted suicide when he was in Russia in 1959. Posner, *Case Closed*, 50, 83–84.

5. Bozanich interview by the author, November 30, 2016.

6. *People v. Kurbegovic*, 138 Cal.App.3d 731 (1982) at 742–47.

7. Petition for appellate review, *People v. Kurbegovic*, 2d Civ. No. 45989 (March 25, 1975) at 4, 13.

8. 1976 RT at 192.

9. Meloy interview by the author, July 25, 2017.

10. Petition for appellate review at Appendix E, F-820–21.

11. Petition for appellate review at Appendix E, F-820–21.

12. Petition for appellate review at Appendix E, 8–9.

13. This discussion of Bruce Ivins and the anthrax letter attacks is drawn from Simon, *Lone Wolf Terrorism*, 95–103; Willman, *The Mirage Man*; United States Department of Justice, Amerithrax Investigative Summary, February 19, 2010; Noah Shachtman, "Anthrax Redux: Did the Feds Nab the Wrong Guy?" *WIRED*, April 2011, https://www.wired.com/2011/03/ff_anthrax_fbi/; Scott Shane, "Panel on Anthrax Inquiry Finds Case against Ivins Persuasive," *New York Times*, March 23, 2011, http://www.nytimes.com/2011/03/24/us/24anthrax.html.

14. Watson interview by the author, April 2, 1998.

15. Meloy, "Clinical Threat Assessment," 649–52.

16. Meloy interview by the author, July 25, 2017.

17. Meloy, "Clinical Threat Assessment," 651, 658; Romeo Vitelli, "TRAPing the Lone Terrorist, Part 1," *Psychology Today*, https://www.psychologytoday.com/blog/media-spotlight/201608/traping-the-lone-terrorist-part-1; Romeo Vitelli, "TRAPing the

Lone Terrorist, Part 2, *Psychology Today*, https://www.psychologytoday.com/blog/media-spotlight/201609/traping-the-lone-terrorist-part-2.

18. Meloy, "Clinical Threat Assessment," 658–59.

19. *Countering Violent Extremism: Actions Needed to Define Strategy and Assess Progress of Federal Efforts*, Report to Congressional Requesters, Government Accountability Office, GAO-17-300, April 2017, https://www.gao.gov/assets/690/683984.pdf.

20. *Countering Violent Extremism*.

21. *Countering Violent Extremism*.

22. Erroll Southers, "The U.S. Government's Program to Counter Violent Extremism Needs an Overhaul," *Los Angeles Times*, March 21, 2017, https://www.google.com/amp/www.latimes.com/opinion/la-fg-global-erroll-southers-oped-20170321-story,amp.html.

23. Julia Edwards Ainsley, "White House Budget Slashes 'Countering Violent Extremism' Grants," Reuters, May 23, 2017, http://www.reuters.com/article/us-usa-budget-extremism-iduskbn18j2hj.

24. Southers, "The U.S. Government's Program."

25. Nafees Hamid, "What Makes a Terrorist?" *New York Review of Books*, August 23, 2017, http://www.nybooks.com/daily/2017/08/23/what-makes-a-terrorist/.

26. Sterling, *The Terror Network*; Simon, *The Terrorist Trap*, 167–70; Simon, *Lone Wolf Terrorism*, 232.

27. This discussion of Roshonara Choudhry is drawn from Simon, *Lone Wolf Terrorism*, 139–43.

28. "From Typical Teen to Jihadist: How Martin Couture-Rouleau Became Radicalized after Converting to Islam," *National Post*, November 9, 2014; Angelica Montgomery, "Quebec Psychiatrists to Review What to Do When Mentally Ill Patients Are Radicalized," CBC News, May 12, 2017, https://www.google.com/amp/www.cbc.ca/amp/1.4110285.

29. Laura Stone, "Gen. Lawson Knew Zehaf-Bibeau Was Mentally Ill on Day of Ottawa Shooting," Global News, March 5, 2015, http://globalnews.ca/news/1866596/gen-lawson-knew-zehaf-bibeau-was-mentally-ill-on-day-of-ottawa-shooting-documents/; Anne Speckhard, "The Canadian Parliament Attacks, ISIS, and Echoes of the Toronto 18," HuffPost United Kingdom, http://www.huffingtonpost.co.uk/anne-speckhard/the-canadian-parliament-a_1_b_6062174.html.

30. Manny Fernandez, Alan Blinder, Eric Schmitt, and Richard Pérez-Peña, "In Chattanooga, a Young Man in a Downward Spiral," *New York Times*, July 20, 2015.

31. Laura Backes, Jurgen Dahlkamp, Hubert Gude, Martin Knobe, Roman Lehberger, Andrew Moussa, and Wolf Wiedmann-Schmidt, "Terrorism or Insanity? Attack Underscores Need to Address Refugees' Mental Health," Spiegel Online, http://

www.spiegel.de/international/germany/what-led-ahmed-a-to-go-on-a-stabbing
-spree-in-hamburg-a-1161442.html.

32. Ingrid Melle, "The Breivik Case and What Psychiatrists Can Learn from It," *World Psychiatry* 12, no. 1 (February 2013): 16–21, https://www.ncbi.nlm.nih.gov/pmc /articles/pmc3619172/; Simon, *Lone Wolf Terrorism*, 49–53; Hamm and Spaaij, *The Age of Lone Wolf Terrorism*, 189.

33. Simon, *Lone Wolf Terrorism* (2016 ed.), ix; Kevin Sack, "Trial Documents Show Dylann Roof Had Mental Disorders," *New York Times*, February 2, 2017, https:// www.nytimes.com/2017/02/02/us/dylann-roof-charleston-killing-mental.html?_r=0.

34. Simon, *Lone Wolf Terrorism*, 75–79. There is some debate, however, as to whether Kaczynski was mentally ill. The court-appointed psychiatrist, Dr. Sally Johnson, diagnosed Kaczynski as a provisional paranoid schizophrenic but qualified her diagnosis due to the limited number of sessions she had with him. Kaczynski was furious with this finding and pled guilty "to avoid being characterized as 'a sickie' during the trial." Turchie and Puckett, *Hunting the American Terrorist*, 157–58.

35. Romina McGuinness, "Islamic Radicals to Be Treated by Mental Illness Specialists," *Express*, August 21, 2017, http://www.express.co.uk/news/world/843944 /Islamic-radicals-treated-mental-illness-terror-attack-Barcelona.

36. Jessica Kidd, "New NSW Police Specialist Unit Hopes to Intervene before Lone-Wolf-Style Attacks," ABC News (Australia), April 25, 2017, http://www.abc .net.au/news/2017-04-26/police-strike-force-to-target-people-who-make-violent -threats/8472280.

37. Julia Edwards, "White House Plans Community-Based Prevention of Violent Ideologies," Reuters, October 19, 2016, https://www.reuters.com/article/us-usa -justice-counterterrorism/white-house-plans-community-based-prevention-of -violent-ideologies-idUSKCN12J15A.

38. Alice LoCicero and J. Wesley Boyd, "The Dangers of Countering Violent Extremism (CVE) Programs," *Psychology Today*, July 19, 2016, https://www.psychologytoday .com/blog/almost-addicted/201607/the-dangers-countering-violent-extremism -cve-programs.

39. "Five Revelations from Rolling Stone's Boston Bomber Cover Story," *Rolling Stone*, July 16, 2013, http://www.rollingstone.com/culture/news/five-revelations -from-rolling-stones-boston-bomber-cover-story-20130716.

40. "Five Revelations"; Janet Reitman, "Jahar's World," *Rolling Stone*, July 17, 2013, http://www.rollingstone.com/culture/news/jahars-world-20130717.

41. Hamid, "What Makes a Terrorist?"

42. Simon, *The Terrorist Trap* (2001 ed.), xii; Turchie and Puckett, *Hunting the American Terrorist*, 115.

7. WHAT THE STORY CAN TEACH US

1. Chris Strohm, "Lone-Wolf Terrorism," Bloomberg View, June 5, 2017, https://www.bloomberg.com/quicktake/lone-wolf-terrorism. The "lone wolf" concept evolved from the "leaderless resistance" concept, which was introduced by another white supremacist, Louis Beam. In an article ("Leaderless Resistance," *The Seditionist*, February 1992) that was written in 1983 but not published until 1992, Beam called for the creation of small, autonomous underground groups driven by ideology and shared beliefs rather than the direction of leaders and members of organizations. For Beam, the advantage of leaderless resistance over other strategies was that only those participating in an attack or any other type of action would know of the plans, therefore reducing the chance of leaks or infiltration. In the article, Beam credited the origins of the concept of "leaderless resistance" to a retired U.S. Air Force colonel, Ulius Amoss, who several decades earlier had proposed the strategy as a defense against a communist takeover of the United States. Simon, *Lone Wolf Terrorism*, 34.

2. Miriam Valverde, "A Look at the Data on Domestic Terrorism and Who's Behind It," PolitiFact, August 16, 2017, http://www.politifact.com/truth-o-meter/article/2017/aug/16/look-data-domestic-terrorism-and-whos-behind-it/.

3. Roof killed nine African American churchgoers in Charleston, South Carolina, in June 2015; Breivik set off a bomb in Oslo, Norway, and massacred scores of youths on a Norwegian island in July 2011; Bowers killed eleven people at a synagogue in Pittsburgh, Pennsylvania, in October 2018; Hodgkinson opened fire on a Republican congressional baseball practice in Alexandria, Virginia, in June 2017, injuring five people; Hasan killed thirteen people at Fort Hood in Texas in November 2009; the Tsarnaev brothers set off pressure-cooker bombs at the finish line of the April 2013 Boston Marathon, killing three people; Farook and his wife, Tashfeen Malik, killed fourteen people in a shooting spree at a disability center in San Bernardino, California, in December 2015; Mateen massacred forty-nine people at a gay nightclub in Orlando, Florida, in June 2016; Goldstein killed twenty-nine Palestinians at a mosque in the West Bank city of Hebron in February 1994; Amir assassinated Israeli prime minister Yitzhak Rabin in Tel Aviv in November 1995; Rudolph set off a bomb at the 1996 Summer Olympic Games in Atlanta, Georgia, in July 1996, killing one person, and also bombed abortion clinics and a gay nightclub in subsequent years; Stack flew a plane into a building containing offices of the Internal Revenue Service in Austin, Texas, in February 2010, killing himself and one other person; Kaczynski sent package bombs throughout the country over a seventeen-year period beginning in 1978, killing three people; and, of course,

Kurbegovic killed three people with a bombing at Los Angeles International Airport in August 1974.

4. Finn, "Media Coverage of Political Terrorism," 54.

5. Simon, *The Terrorist Trap*, 279.

6. Simon, *Lone Wolf Terrorism*, 30, 50–51.

7. Watson interview by the author, April 2, 1998.

8. Simon, *Lone Wolf Terrorism*, 15–19, 21, 68, 86, 241–42; Simon, *The Terrorist Trap*, 79, 334. Mario Buda, an anarchist, is believed to be responsible for the first vehicle bombing in the United States, which occurred in September 1920, when a horse-drawn wagon filled with one hundred pounds of dynamite and five hundred pounds of fragmented steel window sashes (which were heavy cast-iron slugs) exploded on Wall Street, killing thirty-eight people and injuring more than two hundred others. John Gilbert Graham, a criminal lone wolf, was responsible for the first major midair plane bombing in the United States, which occurred in November 1955, killing all forty-four people onboard, including his mother, in whose luggage he had put twenty-five sticks of dynamite, a timer, two dynamite caps, and a dry-cell battery, all in order to collect a $37,500 insurance policy on her life that he'd bought from an airport vending machine shortly before she boarded the plane. (He was also in line to share in his mother's $150,000 estate.) Antulio Ramirez Ortiz, a Puerto Rican lone wolf extremist, was the first person to hijack a plane in the United States when he seized a National Airlines plane en route to Key West from Marathon, Florida, in May 1961, diverting the plane to Cuba, claiming he wanted to assassinate Cuban president Fidel Castro. Kurbegovic was the first person to bomb an airport in the United States, in 1974. A mentally ill lone wolf who was never caught is believed responsible for the first product-tampering case in the United States when, in September and October 1982, he laced Tylenol capsules with cyanide, causing the deaths of seven people. And in September and October 2001, Bruce Ivins was the first person to send anthrax spores through the mail that could be deadly when opened, killing five people.

9. Files, Los Angeles County District Attorney's Office.

10. Transcript of tape recovered on August 20, 1974, at Sunset and Western (scene of arrest) (Los Angeles Police Department Item No. 1338, files, Los Angeles County District Attorney's Office).

11. *Norma Moncur, et al. v. City of Los Angeles, et al.*, 68 Cal.App.3d. 118 (1977).

12. The issue of foreseeability was at the center of a famous case in tort law, *Palsgraf v. Long Island Railroad Co.*, 162 N.E. 99 (N.Y. 1928). In August 1924, Helen Palsgraf was standing on a platform of the Long Island Railroad. A train stopped at the station, but it was not the train she needed for her destination. As the train

began to pull away, a man carrying a package jumped aboard but was unsteady and appeared about to fall. A guard on the train, who had held the door open, reached forward to help the man into the train while another guard on the platform pushed him from behind. The package, which was about fifteen inches long and wrapped in a newspaper, fell and hit the rails. The package contained fireworks, and when it hit the rails it exploded. The shock of the explosion caused some scales at the other end of the platform, where Palsgraf was standing, to fall and injure Palsgraf.

Palsgraf sued the railroad company, and a jury awarded her damages. The railroad appealed the verdict, but the Supreme Court of New York, which is not the highest court in the state, affirmed the verdict. The New York Court of Appeals, though, which is the highest court in New York, reversed the judgment for Palsgraf. Chief Judge Benjamin Cardozo, who later would become an associate justice on the U.S. Supreme Court, wrote the majority opinion, stating that "there was nothing in the situation to suggest to the most cautious mind that the parcel wrapped in newspaper would spread wreckage through the station." As the legal scholar Benjamin Zipursky observed, "The famous discussion of foreseeability in Palsgraf must be understood in connection with Chief Judge Cardozo's view that Mrs. Palsgraf failed to establish negligence relative to herself. That is because a duty of care toward someone requires vigilance of foreseeable hazards to that person, but does not require vigilance of hazards that only a person with extraordinary powers of foresight could anticipate. Chief Judge Cardozo meant just that when he said 'the orbit of the danger as disclosed to the eye of reasonable vigilance would be the orbit of the duty.' And he thought that the risk of injury to Mrs. Palsgraf from the guard's push was unforeseeable and extraordinarily low. A fortiori, the LIRR [Long Island Rail Road] guard did not fail to take precautions against foreseeable injury to Mrs. Palsgraf and did not breach his duty of care to her. Indeed, the case against foreseeability of any injury to Mrs. Palsgraf was so strong that Chief Judge Cardozo believed there was no negligence relative to the plaintiff as a matter of law." Zipursky, "Palsgraf, Punitive Damages, and Preemption," 1765–66.

13. *Moncur*, 68 Cal.App.3d. 118 (1977).

14. Urbanetti and Newmark, "Clinical Aspects of Large-Scale Chemical Events," 434.

15. *Commission on the Prevention of Weapons of Mass Destruction Proliferation and Terrorism*, Washington DC, January 26, 2010, https://fas.org/programs/bio/resource /documents/report-card.pdf.

16. "Testimony of Former Senator Jim Talent, Co-Chair with Former Senator Bob Graham of the Commission on the Prevention of Weapons of Mass Destruction Proliferation and Terrorism, 2008–2010," House Committee on Homeland Security,

Subcommittee on Emergency Preparedness, Response, and Communications, U.S. Congress, April 22, 2015, http://docs.house.gov/meetings/hm/hm12/20150422/103332/hhrg-114-hm12-Wstate-TalentJ-20150422.pdf.

17. Simon, "Nuclear, Biological, and Chemical Terrorism," 84; Simon, *Lone Wolf Terrorism*, 92.

18. David A. Relman, "Bioterrorism—Preparing to Fight the Next War," *New England Journal of Medicine* 354, no. 2 (2006): 113–15, cited in Richard J. Danzig, "A Policymaker's Guide to Bioterrorism and What to Do about It," Center for Technology and National Security, National Defense University, December 2009, 9, http://ctnsp.dodlive.mil/files/2014/10/A-Policymakers-Guide.pdf; also quoted in Simon, *Lone Wolf Terrorism*, 110.

19. As noted in chapter 2, the postcards that Kurbegovic sent featured a picture of Bob Hope's Palm Springs home on one side and on the other side a message in which Kurbegovic praised the work of the Supreme Court justices. He signed the cards, "Bob Hope." They never made it out of the Palm Springs post office and did not contain toxic materials, but there may have been other times that he was successful in sending toxic chemical agents through the mail. Arleigh McCree, the LAPD's top bomb expert, told a reporter in 1983 that Kurbegovic "threatened a lot of people and sent toxic chemicals through the mails to Supreme Court justices. I've got a picture of the one he sent to Thurgood Marshall—in late 1973 or early 1974." However, no evidence was ever publicly revealed to substantiate McCree's claim. George Lardner, "Terrorist Reportedly Sent a Justice Toxic Chemicals," *Washington Post*, December 20, 1983. Hoaxes, whether they involve weapons of mass destruction or conventional weapons, can raise fears throughout the country. There was initial speculation that a wave of package bombs that were sent to critics of President Donald Trump in October 2018 was a hoax since none of the devices exploded. However, the FBI said after the arrest of a suspect, Cesar Sayoc, that under certain conditions, the devices were capable of exploding. See Richard Winton, "Bomb Suspect Had List of 15 Targets in L.A., Sources Say," *Los Angeles Times*, October 30, 2018.

20. "Las Vegas Shooting: Trump Dubs Killer 'Sick and Demented,'" BBC News, October 3, 2017, http://www.bbc.com/news/world-us-canada-41487593.

21. Joseph Frankel, "Why Trump Was Wrong to 'Guess' the Las Vegas Shooter Was a 'Sick' Man," *Newsweek*, October 3, 2017, http://www.newsweek.com/why-trump-was-wrong-guess-las-vegas-shooter-was-sick-man-676601.

22. Watson interview by the author, April 2, 1998. Watson also said, "I never saw the slightest hint of remorse on his part that he had killed people or that he had injured people."

8. IT'S A HORRIBLE SHAME

1. Tyler Harman, "South Park," August 27, 2014, http://www.tylerharman.com/south
   -park/.

2. I wrote a letter to Kurbegovic in April 2016 when he was at Corcoran State
   Prison, asking him questions regarding his background, motivations, and so
   forth, but I did not receive a response.

3. Bozanich interview by the author, December 23, 1997.

4. Bozanich interview by the author, December 23, 1997.

5. D'Agostino interview by the author, August 2, 2017.

6. San Fernando City Council Regular Meeting Notice and Agenda, July 20, 2015,
   260. In one of his petitions for a writ of habeas corpus, Kurbegovic stated that
   "he has been a member of the Al-Qaeda terrorist organization since 1963."
   The terrorist group was not formed until 1988. Christopher Dickey, "Shadow-
   land: T Is for Terror," *Newsweek*, February 26, 2003, http://www.newsweek.com
   /shadowland-t-terror-140385. Kurbegovic has also changed the spelling of his
   name to "Kurbegovich," which was how it has always been pronounced.

7. "'God Will Take Care of Me'—Pastor Recalls Bomb That Cost Him His Leg,"
   Desert Sun, June 29, 1977; "Pat's Story," Standing Firm Ministries, http://www
   .standingfm.com/pats-story.

8. "Finding His Feet after Falling from the High Wire," Australian Red Cross,
   https://www.redcross.org.au/getmedia/ff456213-9ad3-401e-b6bd-e5a5cb24765e
   /20140804-Homelessness-Brochure.pdf.aspx.

9. "Finding His Feet."

10. Marcia Goodman interview by the author, July 19, 2017. Judge Watson's experi-
    ence dealing with Kurbegovic, who acted as his own lawyer, led her to consider
    sending a letter to the judge in the trial of Theodore Kaczynski, the Unabomber,
    when Kaczynski also requested to act as his own lawyer for his criminal trial
    in 1998. "Don't let him do it!" she intended to write. "You will be sorry!" She
    didn't need to send the letter, as Kaczynski pleaded guilty. Watson interview by
    the author, April 2, 1998.

11. Bozanich interview by the author, July 28, 2017.

12. Bozanich interview by the author, July 28, 2017.

13. Bozanich interview by the author, July 28, 2017.

14. Bozanich interview by the author, July 28, 2017. Bozanich would also like to ask
    Kurbegovic if he was responsible for the Stratford Apartments fire in downtown
    Los Angeles, which killed twenty-five people and took place on November 15,
    1973, just six days after Kurbegovic had set fire to the homes of the two police
    commission members who denied his permit to open a taxi dance hall and of

the judge who presided over his lewd conduct trial. Kurbegovic claimed credit for the Stratford Apartments fire, which began in a sofa in the lobby of the apartment building, in one of his taped messages. But Bozanich did not bring the setting of that fire as one of the charges against Kurbegovic in his criminal trial. "Could I prove it beyond a reasonable doubt? No."

15. Bozanich interview by the author, July 28, 2017.

16. D'Agostino interview by the author, August 2, 2017.

17. Kurbegovic admitted to being the Alphabet Bomber at a parole board hearing in July 2018. He claimed that he was "idealistically deranged" when he launched his reign of terror upon Los Angeles in 1974. He also acknowledged that the group, Aliens of America, never existed. When asked by the presiding commissioner, Brian Roberts, why he placed a bomb at LAX that killed innocent people, Kurbegovic said, "I just wanted to see if my bomb would explode because I didn't even know whether I possessed the necessary knowing—I was simply training myself to become a soldier." Roberts then asked him why he didn't test the bomb in the mountains where there would not be any victims. Kurbegovic replied, "I don't know." The parole board denied his request for parole, stating: "We find that he continues to pose an unreasonable risk of danger to society and threat to public safety and is therefore not suitable for parole today." See Initial Parole Consideration Hearing, State of California, Board of Parole Hearings, In the Matter of the Life Term Parole Consideration Hearing of: Muharem Kurbegovic, CDC Number: C-23700, California State Prison in Los Angeles County, Lancaster, California, July 24, 2018, 52, 54, 71, 88.

BIBLIOGRAPHY

INTERVIEWS BY THE AUTHOR

Altman, Robert T. Los Angeles County Deputy District Attorney (Retired), judge of the Superior Court (Retired), and prosecutor in Kurbegovic's 1974 grand jury proceedings

    March 19, 1998, telephone

Bozanich, Dinko. Los Angeles County Deputy District Attorney (Retired) and prosecutor in Kurbegovic's 1974 grand jury proceedings and 1974–80 competency and criminal trials

    December 23, 1997, Norwalk, California

    November 30, 2016, Long Beach, California

    December 23, 2016, Long Beach, California

    July 28, 2017, Long Beach, California

    September 27, 2017, telephone

    November 8, 2017, Long Beach, California

Chaleff, Gerald L. Public defender for Kurbegovic from 1974 to 1977

    February 10, 1998, Los Angeles, California

D'Agostino, Lea Purwin. Los Angeles County Deputy District Attorney (Retired), assisted in the prosecution of Kurbegovic for his criminal trial in 1980

    August 2, 2017, Los Angeles, California

Dedmon, Rick. Lieutenant (Retired) Los Angeles Police Department

    November 10, 2015, telephone

Goodman, Brian. Son of Nancy B. Watson, judge for Kurbegovic's criminal trial in 1980
    July 18, 2017, telephone

Goodman, Harvey. Son of Nancy B. Watson, judge for Kurbegovic's criminal trial
    in 1980
       July 14, 2017, email correspondence

Goodman, Marcia. Daughter of Nancy B. Watson, judge for Kurbegovic's criminal
    trial in 1980
       July 19, 2017, Long Beach, California

Hurlbut, Max K. Lieutenant. LAPD officer (Retired) who worked on the Alphabet
    Bomber case in 1974
       October 23, 2015, email correspondence

Lanceley, Frederick J. FBI agent (Retired) who worked on the Alphabet Bomber
    case in 1974
       October 29, 2015, telephone

Lewis, Walt. Los Angeles County Deputy District Attorney (Retired), calendar deputy
    district attorney in Judge Watson's courtroom during the Alphabet Bomber case
    June 27, 2017, telephone

Meloy, J. Reid. Forensic psychologist
    July 25, 2017, La Jolla, California

Watson, Nancy B. Judge for Kurbegovic's criminal trial in 1980
    April 2, 1998, Rancho Mirage, California

PUBLISHED SOURCES

Bugliosi, Vincent. *Helter Skelter: The True Story of the Manson Murders*. With Curt
    Gentry. New York: Bantam Books, 1975.

Cannell, Michael. *Incendiary: The Psychiatrist, the Mad Bomber, and the Invention of
    Criminal Profiling*. New York: St. Martin's, 2017.

Clarke, James W. *American Assassins: The Darker Side of Politics*. Princeton NJ: Prince-
    ton University Press, 1982.

Crenshaw, Margaret. "The Causes of Terrorism." In *International Terrorism: Charac-
    teristics, Causes, Controls*, edited by Charles W. Kegley Jr., 113–26. New York: St.
    Martin's Press, 1990.

Cressey, Paul Goalby. *The Taxi-Dance Hall: A Sociological Study in Commercialized
    Recreation and City Life*. Chicago: University of Chicago Press, 1932.

DeNevi, Don, and John H. Campbell. *Into the Minds of Madmen: How the FBI's Behav-
    ioral Science Unit Revolutionized Crime Investigation*. Amherst NY: Prometheus
    Books, 2004.

Elborough, Travis. *London Bridge in America: The Tall Story of a Transatlantic Crossing*.
    London: Vintage Books, 2014.

Finn, John E. "Media Coverage of Political Terrorism and the First Amendment: Reconciling the Public's Right to Know with Public Order." In *Terrorism and the Media*, edited by Yonah Alexander and Richard Latter, 47–56. McLean VA: Brassey's U.S., 1990.

Gill, Paul. *Lone-Actor Terrorists: A Behavioural Analysis.* London: Routledge, 2015.

Goodman, Harvey. *So Too My Love.* Westcliffe CO: Jupiter Sky Publishing, 2013.

Greble, Emily. *Sarajevo, 1941–1945: Muslims, Christians, and Jews in Hitler's Europe.* Ithaca NY: Cornell University Press, 2011.

Greenburg, Michael M. *The Mad Bomber of New York: The Extraordinary True Story of the Manhunt That Paralyzed a City.* New York: Union Square Press, 2012.

Hacker, Frederick J. *Crusaders, Criminals, Crazies: Terror and Terrorism in Our Time.* New York: W. W. Norton, 1976.

Hamm, Mark S., and Ramon Spaaij. *The Age of Lone Wolf Terrorism.* New York: Columbia University Press, 2017.

Hoare, Marko Attila. *The Bosnian Muslims in the Second World War: A History.* New York: Oxford University Press, 2013.

Hong, Lawrence K., and Robert W. Duff. "Gentlemen's Social Club: Revival of Taxi-Dancing in Los Angeles." *Journal of Popular Culture* 9 (1976): 827–32.

Kaiser, Robert Blair. *"R.F.K. Must Die!" A History of the Robert Kennedy Assassination and Its Aftermath.* New York: Grove Press, 1970.

Lewis, Walt. *The Criminal Justice Club: A Career Prosecutor Takes on the Media—and More.* Montrose CA: Walbar Books, 2008.

Mackay, Charles. *Memoirs of Extraordinary Popular Delusions and the Madness of Crowds.* Vol. 1. London: Richard Bentley, New Burlington Street, Publisher in Ordinary to Her Majesty, 1841.

Meloy, J. Reid. "The Clinical Threat Assessment of the Lone-Actor Terrorist." *Psychiatric Clinics of North America* 39, no. 4 (August 27, 2016): 649–62.

———. *Violence Risk and Threat Assessment: A Practical Guide for Mental Health and Criminal Justice Professionals.* San Diego: Specialized Training Services, 2000.

Millard, Candice. *Destiny of the Republic: A Tale of Madness, Medicine, and the Murder of a President.* New York: Doubleday, 2011.

Posner, Gerald. *Case Closed: Lee Harvey Oswald and the Assassination of JFK.* New York: Anchor Books, 2003.

Post, Jerold M. *The Mind of the Terrorist: The Psychology of Terrorism from the IRA to al-Qaeda.* New York: St. Martin's, 2007.

Price, Jeffrey C., and Jeffrey S. Forrest. *Practical Aviation Security: Predicting and Preventing Future Threats.* 3rd ed. Oxford, UK: Butterworth-Heinemann, 2016.

Rapoport, David C. "Fear and Trembling: Terrorism in Three Religious Traditions." *American Political Science Review* 78, no. 3 (September 1984): 658–77.

Sacks, Frank. *Extreme Justice: The Secret Squad of the L.A.P.D. That Fights Violence with Violence*. New York: S.P.I. Books, 1993.

Simon, Jeffrey D. "The Alphabet Bomber." In *Toxic Terror: Assessing Terrorist Use of Chemical and Biological Weapons*, edited by Jonathan B. Tucker, 71–94. Cambridge MA: MIT Press, 2000.

———. *Lone Wolf Terrorism: Understanding the Growing Threat*. Amherst NY: Prometheus Books, 2013.

———. *Lone Wolf Terrorism: Understanding the Growing Threat*. Paperback edition. Amherst NY: Prometheus Books, 2016.

———. "Nuclear, Biological, and Chemical Terrorism: Understanding the Threat and Designing Responses." *International Journal of Emergency Mental Health* 1, no. 2 (Spring 1999): 81–89.

———. *The Terrorist Trap: America's Experience with Terrorism*. Bloomington: Indiana University Press, 1994.

———. *The Terrorist Trap: America's Experience with Terrorism*. 2nd ed. Bloomington: Indiana University Press, 2001.

Spaaij, Ramon. *Understanding Lone Wolf Terrorism: Global Patterns, Motivations and Prevention*. New York: Springer, 2012.

Sterling, Claire. *The Terror Network*. New York: Henry Holt, 1981.

Toobin, Jeffrey. *American Heiress: The Wild Saga of the Kidnapping, Crimes and Trial of Patty Hearst*. New York: Doubleday, 2016.

Turchie, Terry D., and Kathleen M. Puckett. *Hunting the American Terrorist: The FBI's War on Homegrown Terror*. Palisades NY: History Publishing, 2007.

Tyler, Bruce M. "The Rise and Decline of the Watts Summer Festival, 1965 to 1986." *American Studies* 31, no. 2 (Fall 1990): 61–81.

Urbanetti, John S., and Jonathan Newmark. "Clinical Aspects of Large-Scale Chemical Events." In *Disaster Medicine: Comprehensive Principles and Practices*, edited by Kristi L. Koenig and Carl H. Schultz, 430–53. New York: Cambridge University Press, 2010.

U.S. Congress, Office of Technology Assessment. *Technologies Underlying Weapons of Mass Destruction*. OTA-BP-ISC-115. Washington DC: U.S. Government Printing Office, December 1993.

Willman, David. *The Mirage Man: Bruce Ivins, the Anthrax Attacks, and America's Rush to War*. New York: Bantam Books, 2011.

Zipursky, Benjamin C. "Palsgraf, Punitive Damages, and Preemption." *Harvard Law Review* 123 (2012): 1765–97.

INDEX